£45.00

The Political Thought of Sun Yat-sen

Also by Audrey Wells and published by Palgrave

BRITAIN AND SOVIET COMMUNISM (*with F. S. Northedge*)

The Political Thought of Sun Yat-sen

Development and Impact

Audrey Wells
Professor of Politics
Regent's College London

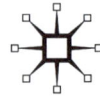

© Audrey Wells 2001

All rights reserved. No reproduction, copy or transmission of this publication may be made without written permission.

No paragraph of this publication may be reproduced, copied or transmitted save with written permission or in accordance with the provisions of the Copyright, Designs and Patents Act 1988, or under the terms of any licence permitting limited copying issued by the Copyright Licensing Agency, 90 Tottenham Court Road, London W1T 4LP.

Any person who does any unauthorised act in relation to this publication may be liable to criminal prosecution and civil claims for damages.

The author has asserted her right to be identified as the author of this work in accordance with the Copyright, Designs and Patents Act 1988.

First published 2001 by
PALGRAVE
Houndmills, Basingstoke, Hampshire RG21 6XS and
175 Fifth Avenue, New York, N. Y. 10010
Companies and representatives throughout the world

PALGRAVE is the new global academic imprint of
St. Martin's Press LLC Scholarly and Reference Division and
Palgrave Publishers Ltd (formerly Macmillan Press Ltd).

ISBN 0–333–77787–5

This book is printed on paper suitable for recycling and made from fully managed and sustained forest sources.

A catalogue record for this book is available from the British Library.

Library of Congress Cataloging-in-Publication Data
Wells, Audrey.
    The political thought of Sun Yat-sen : development and impact / Audrey Wells.
     p. cm.
    Includes bibliographical references and index.
    ISBN 0–333–77787–5
    1. Sun, Yat-sen, 1866–1925—Views on political science. I. Title.
DS777 .W45 2001
951.04'092—dc21

2001032717

To the Memory of my Parents

Contents

Preface		x
Acknowledgements		xii
Introduction		xiii

1 The Early Evolution of Sun Yat-sen's Political Thought — 1
- Sun's petition to Li Hung-chang in 1894 — 4
- The founding of the Hsing Chung Hui in 1894 in Hawaii — 5
- The Hong Kong Manifesto of the Hsing Chung Hui — 7

2 The Development of Sun Yat-sen's Political Ideas in England, 1896–97 — 10
- Sun's 'two-year' stay in 'Europe' meeting 'leading politicians' — 11
- Sun's social circle — 13
- Sun's reading — 15
- Sun Yat-sen's publications — 16
- The Three Principles of the People — 22
- Henry George and Sun Yat-sen — 27

3 Sun's Western Influences in the Japanese Crucible — 29
- The influence of Johan Kaspar Bluntschli — 31
- Sun's political ideas in 1906 — 34

4 Sun's Thought between 1905/6 and 1919: Populism and Elitism — 39
- Direct democracy and local self-government — 40
- 1917 — 43
- *The International Development of China* — 44
- *The Psychological Reconstruction of China* — 46

5 Sun's Thought between 1919 and 1924: National Reconstruction — 54
- Introduction — 54
- *The Fundamentals of National Reconstruction* — 55

6	**Sun's Three Principles of the People: The Principle of Nationalism**	**61**
	Introduction	61
	Lecture 1	62
	Lecture 2	63
	Lecture 3	64
	Lecture 4	65
	Lecture 5	66
	Lecture 6	67
	A comparison between Sun's Principle of Nationalism as expressed in 1905/6 and in 1924	68
	A critique of Sun's Theory of Nationalism	70
7	**Sun's Three Principles of the People: The Principle of Democracy**	**73**
	Lecture 1	73
	Lecture 2	74
	Lecture 3	75
	Lecture 4	77
	Lecture 5	78
	Lecture 6	79
	A comparison of Sun's Principle of Democracy as expressed in 1905/6 and in 1924	81
	A critique of Sun's Theory of Democracy	82
8	**Sun's Three Principles of the People: The Principle of Livelihood**	**91**
	Lecture 1	91
	Lecture 2	92
	Lecture 3	93
	Lecture 4	93
	The development of Sun's Principle of Livelihood, 1905–24	94
	A critique of Sun's Principle of Livelihood	95
	The influence of Maurice William	97
9	**The Influence of Christianity on Sun Yat-sen**	**102**
	Sun's Taiping Christianity	106
	Sun's sincerity	109
10	**The Influence of Confucianism on Sun Yat-sen**	**113**
	Sun's classical learning	113
	The Confucian revolutionary	118

11	**The Development of Sun Yat-sen's Political Thought by Chiang Kai-shek**	122
	Chiang's anti-Communism	122
	Chiang's repression	126
12	**The Development of Sun Yat-sen's Ideas by Wang Ching-wei, Hu Han-min and Tai Chi-t'ao**	130
	Wang Ching-wei	131
	Tai Chi-t'ao	135
	Hu Han-min	138
13	**Sun Yat-sen's Three Principles and the Chinese Communist Party**	141
	The United Front	141
	The Communist state	146
	Democracy	150
14	**The Implementation of Sun Yat-sen's Three Principles in Taiwan**	153
	The implementation of Sun's Principle of Livelihood in land reform	153
	The implementation of Sun's Principle of Livelihood in the industrial sector of Taiwan's economy	156
	The implementation of Sun's political ideas in Taiwan	164
15	**Sun Yat-sen and Other Third World Countries: Indonesia, Vietnam and the Philippines**	171
	Indonesia	171
	Vietnam	180
	Sun Yat-sen and the Philippines	182
16	**Sun Yat-sen's Influence on Muammar Gaddafi**	188
	Democracy	191
	Socialism	195
	Nationalism	197
Conclusion		199
Notes		204
Bibliography		221
Index		228

Preface

My purpose in writing this book is to examine the development of Sun Yat-sen's political thought and its impact. First I trace Sun's revolutionary ideas from the nineteenth to the twentieth century. I begin by looking at the early development of Sun's thought when he was in China until 1895. In the second chapter I study Sun's experiences in England during 1896–97 in much detail since he later claimed his Three Principles were formulated during that period. I argue that his claim is substantiated. My third chapter deals with Sun's stay in Japan and summarises his Three Principles as he expressed them in 1906.

I then examine the development of Sun's thought between 1906 and 1919. I claim that Sun came to believe in the importance of direct democracy earlier than the time suggested by current scholarship. Sun's *The International Development of China*, which anticipated Teng Hsiao-p'ing's opening China to foreign capital, is also discussed in this chapter.

I next consider Sun's other major works between 1919 and 1924: *The Fundamentals of National Reconstruction* and *The Three Principles of the People*. I argue that Sun's ideas are not only still relevant to China but that some of them are pertinent to Western liberal democratic thought. His ideas on socialism can be used in the Third World. In the two subsequent chapters I discuss Sun's unconventional Christianity and his unorthodox Confucianism. I then consider the later impact of Sun's thought on Chinese revolutionary leaders as well as on Third World countries. These include not only China and Taiwan but also Indonesia, Vietnam, the Philippines and Gaddafi's Libya. This last study is my original contribution to an appreciation of the impact of Sun's thought.

It might be appropriate here to mention how I discovered a link between Sun Yat-sen and Muammar Gaddafi. While teaching a course on Arab politics I read Gaddafi's *The Green Book*. I was struck by the similarity between his ideas and Sun's Three Principles. I thought, however, that there could be no evidential connection and forgot about the matter. Then I read, surprisingly in the *Evening Standard*, on 27 January 1989, a quotation from Gaddafi in which he mentioned Sun Yat-sen. I was therefore encouraged to search Gaddafi's writings and interviews for his referring to Sun Yat-sen. I found two references: in Mirella Bianco's *Gaddafi: Voice from the Desert* and in Musa M. Kousa's M.A. thesis *Muamar*

Qadafi: The Libyan Leader. I then returned to study the similarities between Gaddafi's and Sun's political thought.

It is difficult to sum up this book, but basically I am suggesting that Sun's political thought was and still is significant not only to China but also to the rest of the world. The Western powers were short-sighted in treating him and his ideas dismissively.

On a technical note: I have endeavoured to use the Wade–Giles system of romanisation throughout.

I hope this book will be a modest contribution to the debate on the significance of Sun Yat-sen's political ideas.

AUDREY WELLS

Acknowledgements

I am deeply indebted to my supervisor at the LSE, Dr John Morall, for his patience, encouragement and stimulus in supervising my PhD thesis. I am also grateful to Jack Gray and David Steeds for their comments on its script. My use of them is of course my responsibility.

I owe much to the late Graham Bevan (who unusually for a retired biochemist enjoyed typing scripts) not only for his efficient word-processing but also for his perceptive comments. To his son Jason, who gallantly took over the typing of the book, I equally owe many thanks.

AUDREY WELLS

Introduction

Sun Yat-sen's political thought is relevant to China today. The debate over whether Chinese society is suited to some form of democracy has yet to be resolved. In 1919, when Sun was writing, students demonstrated in Peking for Western liberties. Sun commented on their slogan:

> 'Give me liberty or give me death'... Chinese students, in translating Western theories, have introduced these words into China... But the mass of the people in China do not understand what liberty means...[1]

Eighty years later students in T'ien-an-men Square echoed the cries of their predecessors. However, the Chinese Communist Party does not believe that Western democracy is appropriate to China; a strong government is needed to keep China united and stable. This belief was also held by Sun Yat-sen, but he devised a unique synthesis of Western and Chinese political ideas which, he argued, would give China a strong government and the people democratic control. It would be superior to any Western form of democracy.

Sun Yat-sen's revolution toppled the Manchu dynasty in 1911, and he is still regarded as the Father of Modern China on the mainland and in Taiwan. His impact was not merely in his revolutionary actions; the political leaders of the Chinese Communist Party and of Taiwan have claimed to have developed his *The Three Principles of the People* which he fully expounded in 1924. His political thought has been dramatically and variously assessed. His *Three Principles* and other works (the original manuscripts of which were destroyed by enemy gunfire in 1922) have been ridiculed for their inchoate state. His idealism has been seen to indicate a lack of realism. In *The West in Russia and China*, for example, Donald W. Treadgold speaks dismissively of Sun's 'hodge-podge of slogans derived from the West'.[2] In contrast, Richard Wilhelm referred to his thought thus:

> The greatness of Sun Yat-sen rests, therefore, upon the fact that he has found a living synthesis between the fundamental principles of Confucianism and the demands of modern times, a synthesis which, beyond the borders of China, can again become significant...[3]

W. Franke in *A Century of Chinese Revolution* does view Sun's work with admiration. However, for this he has been severely criticised:

> Franke views Sun as 'idealistic and unselfish' and the leader of the Chinese Revolution in the early decades of the century... Nor are Sun's 'Three People's Principles' worth the emphasis given them.[4]

President Sukarno of Indonesia, on the other hand, viewed Sun's political thought with great respect:

> In his work San Min Chu I, or 'The Three People's Principles', I found a lesson... Therefore, if the whole Chinese people consider Dr. Sun Yat-sen their preceptor, be sure that Bung Karno also, an Indonesian, with the uttermost respect will feel grateful to Dr. Sun Yat-sen until he lies in his grave.[5]

In 1977, Simon Leys in *The Chairman's New Clothes* saw fit to remark:

> It is symptomatic, where Sun Yat-sen is concerned, that since Sharman's competent but rudimentary and dated (1934) study, no serious work has been published or undertaken in the West.[6]

At the time of Ley's writing, H. Z. Schiffrin's study of *Sun Yat-sen and the Origins of the Chinese Revolution*, which is perhaps the most balanced assessment, went only as far as 1905. Since then, in 1980, Schiffrin extended his study of Sun Yat-sen until 1925, and C. Martin Wilbur's work on *Sun Yat-sen: Frustrated Patriot* (1976) has been a valuable contribution to illuminating Sun's career.

J. Y. Wong (1986) has exerted 'strange vigour', heroic standards of research and stout boots in attempting to show Sun's heroic image was a myth originating in London during 1896–97. More recently Sidney H. Chang and Leonard H. D. Gordon have written an admirable account of Sun Yat-sen and his revolutionary thought in *All Under Heaven* (1991). However, as Marie-Claire Bergère in her scholarly and highly readable biography *Sun Yat-sen* (1994) has pointed out, 'in the West, Sun's *Three Principles of the People* has never been rated as one of the great works of contemporary Chinese thought.'[7]

Indeed, it could still be argued that Sun Yat-sen's theories have been treated with contempt by most Western academics. This is partly due to the fact that some, although certainly not all, of his ideas were unsound and they were not presented in an academically impressive way as he was too ill in 1924 to rewrite the destroyed original manuscripts. Sun's courageous originality was received unsympathetically. Above all, Sun's ideas were never implemented. His revolution appeared to have failed. His ideas might, therefore, seem not to merit serious study. Nevertheless, some of the greatest revolutionary leaders, including Mao Tse-tung, Chou En-lai, as well as Sukarno, respected him. It is argued in this book that Gaddafi was influenced by his ideas.

Indeed it is likely that Sun's ideas have significance even now and not just for China.

1
The Early Evolution of Sun Yat-sen's Political Thought

Sun Yat-sen was born on 12 November 1866 in the village of Ts'ui-heng (Choyhung) in the Hsiang-shan county of Kwangtung province. His father was a farmer who, because of the poor soil in his village and exorbitant taxes, had to supplement his earnings by labouring in nearby Macao. Sun had a traditional Chinese upbringing and is depicted in photographs of his youth wearing a skull cap, queue and a long gown. He had an early education in the classics. He learned about the Taiping Rebellion and its leader Hung Hsiu-ch'üan became his hero. When he was 13 Sun went to join his eldest brother, Sun Mei, who had become a successful businessman in Hawaii. There Sun received a Western education and learned English.[1]

These four aspects of Sun's early life: his experiences of the problems of peasant farming, his Chinese and Western education and admiration for the Taiping Rebellion were to have a profound influence on his political thought. One further point which seems never to have been mentioned before is that in a speech in 1916 Sun recalled:

> In my boyhood I was full of curiosity, and once spent several months in teaching five or six thousand people in my birthplace to understand that the earth is round.[2]

While Sun might have exaggerated the size of his audience, this statement indicates that early in life Sun probably had a magisterial-like obligation to educate his compatriots in new truths which had a scientific basis and a belief that the masses would want to be enlightened. Until his death Sun showed this faith and obligation to preach.

In Hawaii Sun enrolled in the Anglican Iolani school and in 1883 transferred to Oahu College, an American Congregationalist school. However, at this time his brother reported Sun's involvement with Western Christianity to his father who ordered Sun home. There, with a friend, Lu Hao-tung, he damaged three idols in the village temple, including the one his mother had dedicated for him. The consequent anger of the village caused him to depart, at the age of 17, for Hong Kong. Sun's hero Hung Hsiu-ch'üan had also mutilated his village's idols. It is possible that by his extreme action Sun was revealing the mainspring of his revolutionary personality: a Christian faith based on rebellion.

It is reasonable to assume that Sun was acquainted with the ideas of the Taiping Rebellion since his childhood was spent in its aftermath and Sun showed such admiration for the Taiping leader, Hung Hsiu-ch'üan. The Taiping influence on Sun's Christianity will be considered in the chapter on that subject. However, it is arguable that Sun's anti-Manchu feelings expressed later in 1894 were partly influenced by the ideas of the Taiping Rebellion. Moreover, the latter's leaders proclaimed their ideal was a kingdom in which 'nowhere will inequality exist and no one not be well fed and clothed'.[3] Sun never expressed a desire for complete equality, neither did he seem ever openly to acknowledge the influence of the Taiping Rebellion, on his thought. He would have been foolish had he done so in Manchu China which had crushed the Taiping Rebellion, or in England which had aided the Manchu to do so. There would appear to exist no documentary evidence of the direct ideational influence of the Taiping Rebellion on him. Nevertheless, because Sun admired its leaders so much it is rational to assume Sun's thinking was affected by it. In order to understand the development of Sun's thought it is important to remember that unlike most political theorists Sun was also a politician who had to be careful to keep the support of certain social classes or foreign powers for his cause. Even when founding the Hsing Chung Hui in 1894, Sun needed to tailor his ideas to suit the overseas Chinese businessmen who supported it. Therefore had Sun entertained any ideas of the extreme Taiping socialist variety it would have been impolitic of him to express them. Later in the West, Sun wanted to gain the support of foreign governments to aid his cause. Sun may have needed to cut and trim his ideas to suit his political needs, but unlike most political theorists he also aimed at achieving power to implement them on a large proportion of the world's population which still respect him. For that reason his ideas and their development are of particular interest.

Therefore Sun's early life in Hong Kong to where he had to flee to escape the wrath of his village over his iconoclasm, will now be considered.

In Hong Kong in 1883 Sun entered a Church of England school but while receiving a Western education he was tutored in the classics by Ch'ü Feng-ch'ih, a Christian minister connected with the London Missionary Society. He gave Sun (who was given the name Ti-hsiang at birth but was known as 'Sun Wen') the name 'Yat-sen'. In a letter to the sinologist Herbert Giles (who was compiling a Chinese biographical dictionary in 1896), Sun said that he liked the 'Three Dynasties and the classics of the two Hans'.[4] By that time he was greatly attracted to Darwinism. In 1884, Sun transferred to Queen's College in Hong Kong. Then, following an association with an American missionary, Charles Hager, Sun was baptised. Yet Sun also agreed to the marriage his parents had arranged for him. His wife remained in their household while he pursued his career which in 1886, at the age of 20, he had decided would be medicine. He entered the Canton Medical School which was under the direction of an American, Dr John Kerr. In 1887 Sun transferred to the new College of Medicine for Chinese in Hong Kong. Its founder, Dr Ho Ch'i (Ho Kai) probably impressed Sun with some of his ideas but its second Dean, Dr James Cantlie, was to have an even greater influence on him and become a lifelong friend. It says much for Sun's personality that these men befriended him and held him in high esteem. Sun graduated from the school with distinction in 1892. The previous year he wrote an essay on 'Agricultural Skills' which argued for the Westernisation of agricultural methods. It is possible, however, that in its final form it owed much to Cheng Kuan-ying who was an official from Sun's home district with whom Sun communicated.[5]

Sun's qualification in medicine was not recognised by the British Medical Council since his college had been established for only five years. Therefore Sun opened a pharmacy in Macao in 1892 for both Chinese and Western medicine, treating the poor without charging and practising surgery at a hospital in Macao. As the Macao authorities would not recognise his qualifications either, Sun transferred his pharmacy in 1893 to Canton. While he again treated the poor free of charge he made sufficient funds from services to the better-off to amass funds for his developing revolutionary activities.[6]

In his autobiography Sun claimed that from 1885, the year of China's defeat in the war with France over Annam, he was determined to overthrow the Manchu dynasty and establish a Chinese Republic on its ruins. Medical science was to be the 'kindly aunt' who would bring him out on the high road of politics.[7] His higher education and medical career offered opportunities for revolutionary propaganda. While studying in Hong Kong he and his friends had carried out research on the history of revolutions with regard to effecting the Chinese revolution.

Sun's petition to Li Hung-chang in 1894

Nevertheless, despite the revolutionary undertones to Sun's life at this time, Sun did not initially in 1894 openly express a revolutionary aim. Instead he wrote a deferential petition to the Grand Secretary in Tientsin, Li Hung-chang. Sun travelled north to present his petition with his childhood friend Lu Hao-tung. In Shanghai they discussed it with two influential reformers, Cheng Kuan-ying and Wang T'ao.[8] However, unfortunately for Sun, Li was preoccupied with the developing hostilities between Japan and China, and possibly for that reason he refused to see Sun. Had he done so Sun might never have become a revolutionary. Sun's petition was not a grandiose scheme that he expected the high-ranking official to accept. He humbly asked Li to consider employing him and also for his help in obtaining a passport for Sun to travel to France to study sericulture and then agriculture in other countries. Sun stated that he had admired the Grand Secretary as one who considered the recruiting of talented men as an urgent matter. A person like himself might also be drilled and listed among Li's employees. Therefore he disregarded the modest dimension of his own ability in order to seek Li's recognition. Sun stated that after deep reflection he had realised that the roots of wealth and power in Europe did not lie in solid ships, efficient guns, strong forts and crack troops, but also in the fact that men's talents and natural resources could be used fully. China needed rational employment and educational policies which would enable men to use their talents fully in governmental service and involve the training of personnel in schools to be established throughout the Empire. Even more importantly the resources of the land should be fully exploited by a government department directing agriculture, adopting Western agricultural methods, machinery and electricity. Mines should be opened and rivers dredged with modern machinery whch should likewise be employed in the weaving of cloth. The circulation of commercial goods should be facilitated by the removal of the numerous transit taxes, the building of steamships and railways. Part of China's weakness lay in her shortage of able people. Therefore foreign experts should be recruited to help China.[9]

It is perhaps worth noting here that when he was dying in 1924 Sun still called for an end to the 'likin', transit taxes, and the adoption of

Westernised methods of agriculture. He showed then the interest in the silk industry that had occupied his mind 30 years earlier. However, in 1924 he did not emphasise the need for an educational policy that would result in men of talent leading the country. This is probably because China had modernised her educational system by that time (beginning with the abolition of the Confucian examinations in 1905). However, in 1924 Sun did stress the need for an Examination Yuan to ensure the highly educated govern the country.

In his petition Sun wrote nothing revolutionary or anti-Manchu, probably because he did not want to alienate Li Hung-chang. Sun's demands were moderate. He did not ask for the radical reorganisation of society but suggested that Li Hung-chang or other officials of the Manchu government should employ individuals such as himself with modern training to assist the Manchu government in reforming China. This document does not, however, necessarily show Sun's political ideas in their entirety at the time since of necessity he would have concealed some in order to appeal as a suitable candidate for employment by the Manchu government. It is perhaps noteworthy that in his petition Sun used the term 'min-sheng',[10] an ancient phrase which was used by some Chinese reformers at the time and which was later to become his third slogan.

Although Li did not meet Sun he did receive his mailed petition.[11] This was also widely published in such journals as the *Wan Kuo Kung Pao* (in September and October 1894).[12]

The founding of the Hsing Chung Hui in 1894 in Hawaii

After Li Hung-chang had refused to grant Sun an interview, Sun gave up his medical career and went to Honolulu where he set up a political organisation, the Hsing Chung Hui or Revive China Society, with about 20 of his mainly Chinese friends from Hawaii and Canton, including his brother, Sun Mei. China was being defeated in the war with Japan: Sun no doubt had decided that the incompetent Manchu government had to be removed by revolutionary methods. He demonstrated this the next year. However, the Hsing Chung Hui's Inaugural Manifesto of 24 November 1894 did not express this.

The Manifesto stated that China had long been a weak nation; her high officials were inefficient and arrogant, while the lower ranking ones were usually uneducated. They lacked vision. China, once a great nation was regarded with contempt by foreigners. With four hundred million people and a vast, rich land China could become impregnable in the world if the Chinese were determined to make her strong. However, misgovernment had enfeebled her.

China was surrounded by foreign powers who were like greedy tigers coveting her rich mineral resources and products. They had been annexing parts of China which was consequently in danger of dismemberment. Those who cared for China's interests would want to protest and save China from collapse. For this reason the Hsing Chung Hui had been founded. It was hoped that the wise and courageous would join in the common cause of regenerating China.

The Society's constitution stated that it had been established for the purpose of rebuilding China and maintaining her national existence. It had been necessitated by the fact that China had long been subjected to foreign oppression for many reasons. She had been isolated in foreign relations and had remained backward in domestic administration; the nation had been unaware of the damage done to its stature; while the people had been deprived of all chances to air their grievances. This sorry state of affairs had been aggravated day by day. Therefore the Society, composed of Chinese at home and abroad, would be an organ to express the popular will and buttress the national tradition.

The members of the Society were to pay a membership fee of five dollars and make voluntary financial contributions according to their ability; they should elect a President together with other officers and meet every Thursday evening. The revenues should be used to help the country.[13] The members also swore an oath with their right hand raised and their left hand on the Bible.[14] There is a problem about this oath: Schiffrin argued in 1968 that there was no extant record of it;[15] Chang and Gordon (whose book was published in 1991) also claim this;[16] as does Marie-Claire Bergère.[17] It is true that in the Taipei collection of Sun's works published in 1957/8 there is no record of such an oath. However in the Beijing edition of the *Complete Collected Works of Sun Yat-sen* (*Sun Chung-shan ch'üan chi*), published in 1981, there is a record of a pledge taken by the members of the Hsing Chung Hui. It is based on documents not only of the historian Feng Tzu-yu, but also on a *Brief History of the Moyi Branch of the Chinese Republican Party*. The members of the Hsing Chung Hui vowed 'to throw out the Tartars, restore China and establish a united government' (ho-chung cheng-fu).[18]

The Chinese historian Wu Yü-chang has commented:

> In 1894 Hsing Chung Hui (the Society for the Revival of China) included in its programme a call for the establishment of a 'united government'. What was meant by this 'united government'? It may

have been derived from the term 'the United States of America'. If so, it would mean a federal government...After the founding of the Revolutionary League the demand for the establishment of a republic soon became widespread and the old slogan calling for a Han empire was dropped.[19]

Thus although Sun first used the term 'min-kuo' for 'republic' in 1903, by 1894 he was not thinking in terms of the Ming dynasty or Han empire but of establishing a form of republic. Schiffrin has noted in fact that in July 1894 Hawaii became a republic and the effect would not have been lost on Sun.[20]

The Hsing Chung Hui Manifesto contained some of the key concerns of the petition to Li Hung-chang: the lack of educated competent officials with vision who could make China strong with her vast potential of people and land resources. However, unlike the petition it did not mention the need for an agricultural policy using Western methods, probably because it was concerned with broader political aims. Of course Sun did not in his petition to Li Hung-chang express the Hsing Chung Hui's pledge that the Tartars should be overthrown and a united government be established. Obviously Sun had not wanted to offend Li whom he hoped would find him a post in his administration. It is also possible that China's defeat in the Sino-Japanese war made Sun more aware of the foreign danger and that the Manchus should be removed. Moreover, as Li had not received him, Sun probably saw his way to reforming China peacefully from inside Chinese officialdom blocked.

The historian Leonard Hsu is correct in arguing that the purpose of the Hsing Chung Hui was to organise mass movement for reform but quite wrong in arguing that 'there was not one anti-Manchu or revolutionary expression'.[21] The Hsing Chung Hui's oath demonstrates that there was. Moreover, the revenues to be collected by the Hsing Chung Hui were to be used, it is reasonable to surmise, for the purchase of explosives and arms for revolutionary activity. This would not have been expressly written down since it would provide clear incriminating evidence.

The Hong Kong Manifesto of the Hsing Chung Hui

In January 1895 Sun left Hawaii for Hong Kong where he established another headquarters for the Hsing Chung Hui. There he was joined by the Western-educated, Hong Kong born Yang Ch'ü-yün, who brought his revolutionary organisation, the Furen Literary Society, to join up with Sun's. The Manifesto of the Hsing Chung Hui in Hong Kong of 21 February 1895 was almost the same as the original one drawn up in Hawaii. There was expressed, however, additional concern about corruption and bribery among officials, the exploitation of the people, banditry and widespread starvation.[22] There was consideration for the future generations of Chinese who would be subjected to foreign slavery if timely action were not taken. There was more specification as to the activities of the Hsing Chung Hui: the publication of newspapers to enlighten the people, the establishment of schools to train the younger generation, the planning and implementation of construction projects to improve the people's livelihood (here Sun used the term 'min sheng' as he had earlier in his petition to Li Hung-chang), and the eradication of age-long abuses to revitalise the national spirit and to promote the peace and prosperity of the country. There was also an expressed goal of achieving a decent standard of living for the four hundred million Chinese which was absent from the Manifesto in Hawaii.

The Hong Kong Manifesto stated that a fund society would be established with the double purpose of raising revenue for public use and generating profits for the shareholders. It may be assumed that the real dividend would be paid when a successful revolution was carried out, although this was not expressly stated. The Manifesto also provided that other branches of the Hsing Chung Hui could adapt to local conditions.

In October 1895 Sun was elected president of the Hsing Chung Hui but, because this election had been controversial, for the sake of a united organisation Sun allowed Yang Ch'ü-yün to occupy the office.[23] Nevertheless, Sun remained its effective leader. The Hsing Chung Hui finally in October 1895 planned to realise its revolutionary intent. The Manchu dynasty's inability to stop Japan's invasion of Manchuria had given rise to a level of unpopularity that made an anti-Manchu uprising seem opportune. The day when the Chinese would visit their family graves, 26 October 1895, was decided on as the date for the operation. A society called the Agricultural Studies Society was set up in October 1895 under Sun's leadership as a front to conceal the revolutionary activities of the Hsing Chung Hui in Canton. However, Yang Ch'ü-yün in Hong Kong warned Sun that there would be a delay in the shipment of explosives. The uprising had therefore to be postponed. Unfortunately, informers in Hong Kong discovered the plot and told the local police. The plotters attempted to disappear but some, including Sun's childhood friend Lu Hao-tung (with whom he had smashed his village's idols), were caught and executed. Sun escaped to Macao, then Hong Kong and finally arrived in Kobe, Japan. In Japan he cut off his queue, put on Western clothes and grew a moustache. This disguised him as a Japanese. His removal of his queue was, of course, an anti-Manchu symbolic act, but the alteration of his appearance might also have indicated an increasingly Western outlook. In order to rally support for his cause and to raise financial contributions from the overseas Chinese, Sun went to the Philippines and then the United States where his reputation as a revolutionary leader became established among his 'hua ch'iao'. Sun's exact relationships with the Triads and other secret Chinese societies in Hawaii and the United States cannot be established because of the lack of evidential material for such secret organisations. However, he certainly had links with them, and needed their foreign finance and insurrectional organisation. Nevertheless, although the Triads had wanted the restoration of the Ming dynasty, Sun's thinking had moved on to the goal of a republic. The precise nature of this government was probably not clear in Sun's mind; certainly there are no details available about it.

Sun, it seems, accepted himself as a revolutionary leader when in 1895 he saw himself described as such in a Kobe newspaper he read in Japan. At that time the Japanese were using the term 'ko-ming' for the Western idea of revolution. This phrase was entering the Chinese language with its modern meaning although it had previously meant an imperial changing of the heavenly mandate:

> We saw the characters 'Chung-kuo ko-ming tang Sun Yat-sen'... Hitherto our cast of mind had been such as to consider 'ko-ming' something applying to the will to act as emperor, with our movement only to be considered as rebelling against this. From the time we saw this newspaper, we had the picture of the three characters 'ko-ming tang' imprinted on our minds.[25]

However, Sun himself asserted that his idea of a complete social revolution for China, comprising the recovery of China for the Chinese as a nationalist goal, the implementation of democracy and a form of socialism that Sun called 'livelihood' did not begin to take shape in his mind until he visited England in October 1896, invited by his old friend Dr James Cantlie. There he stayed near Gray's Inn in lodgings found by the Cantlies who lived nearby. It is this sojourn in England that will now be considered.

2
The Development of Sun Yat-sen's Political Ideas in England, 1896–97

Sun Yat-sen reached London on 1 October 1896. He spent his first few days visiting the British Museum and other tourist attractions. The Chinese Legation, alerted to his presence by Chinese diplomats in the USA where Sun had spent three months fund-raising before coming to England, employed Slater's Detective Agency to follow him as he posed a threat to the Manchu dynasty.

Sun would often visit his friends, the Cantlies, who lived in Devonshire Street, near Portland Place where the Chinese Legation was situated. On 11 October 1896, as he was passing it on his way to visit Dr James Cantlie, some Chinese officials kidnapped him. Accounts of how this took place vary, but it is clear that they forced him into a locked, guarded room on the third floor of the Chinese Legation. Its Secretary was, surprisingly, a Scottish military surgeon, Sir Halliday Macartney, who had fought against the Taipings. When Sun had arrived in London, Macartney had tried in vain to get the British Foreign Office to agree to Sun's being extradited to China. Now that Macartney held Sun captive he informed the Manchu government of his prize prisoner and awaited instructions.

As the week passed, Sun records in his book *Kidnapped in London* that only prayer gave him solace. He faced the prospect of being shipped back to China where he would be executed by having his eyelids cut off and then his body chopped into small fragments.

On 16 October 1896, Sun Yat-sen arose from praying in his guarded room at the Legation. He later wrote that he felt a calmness and hope that made him realise that his prayer was answered.[1] He renewed his attempts to persuade an English porter, Cole, who brought his food, to take a message to his friend Dr Cantlie, and this time the porter agreed to do so. On receiving the news Dr Cantlie informed Scotland Yard and the Foreign Office, which took no relevant action. He then alerted *The Times* which waited to see what the Foreign Office would do. Aware of this, the Foreign Office began to pressure Macartney, warning that *The Times* was holding the story. Cantlie finally applied to an Old Bailey judge for a writ of 'habeas corpus' against the Legation. The newspaper *The Globe* heard of this and broke the news of Sun's kidnapping on 22 October 1896. The next day all the London newspapers published the story. Soon angry Londoners and journalists surrounded the Chinese Legation clamouring for Sun's release. In the afternoon of 23 October Sun was freed. The following day he wrote a letter to *The Times* thanking its readers for their support, public spiritedness and love of justice.

Sun's kidnapping made him famous and later facilitated his fundraising activities around the world.

Sun's 'two-year' stay in 'Europe' meeting 'leading politicians'

While Sun Yat-sen was in London during 1896 to 1897 he began formulating his famous Three Principles of the People: Nationalism, Democracy and Livelihood (Socialism). From his experiences in England he realised that European governments, despite their power and wealth could not give their people 'complete happiness'. The goal of Sun's Three Principles was to give happiness to the Chinese people. He observed the unhappiness of the impoverished masses in London, and, writing after he left that city, he expressed sympathy with the socialist movement. He did not do so while in England, however, probably for fear of alienating those social circles who were supporting him. Sun wanted to achieve in China a nationalist, democratic and socialist revolution in one blow. Sun described his experiences thus:

> After escaping from danger in London, I stayed in Europe to carry out studies of its political practices and make the acquaintance of its leading politicians. During these two years [*sic*] what I saw and heard made a tremendous impression upon me. For the first time I understood that though the European powers achieved national wealth and power, they were not able to give their peoples full happiness. For this reason, European men of determination were still striving for a social revolution. I now wanted to create a single-effort, eternal plan which would simultaneously solve the problems of socialism, nationalism and democracy. The Three Principles of the People which I advocated were perfected from this [idea].[2]

There is much debate over this passage. Sun arrived at Liverpool on 30 September 1896 and left around 2 July 1897. He did not stay a full two years in England. Some scholars have criticised him for a 'lapse of memory'[3] in saying he stayed for two years. However, the operative phrase in Chinese is 'liang nian zhi zhong' which can mean 'within' or 'in the midst of' the two years. Thus Sun's meaning could be that in the middle of the period stretching over two calendar years 1896–97 (specifically not from 1 January 1896 to 31 December 1897) he stayed in Europe, which is precisely what he did.

Did Sun visit other countries in Europe in 1896–97? There is much evidence of his intention to visit France but no concrete evidence that he actually did. In *My Reminiscences* published in *The Strand Magazine* in 1912 Sun wrote: 'After some time spent in travel and study in London and Paris, I felt that the time had come to return to China.'[4] It is unlikely that Sun would have written in *My Reminiscences* that he had visited Paris when he had not, since he knew the Cantlies would read it (which they did[5]) and be alienated by a lie that could easily be exposed.

T'ang Liang Li, who later became a leading member of the Kuomintang, stated that in this period Sun came into contact with the leading French socialists Charles Longuet and Paul Lafargue (both sons-in-law of Karl Marx).[6] However, there seems to be no evidence of any meeting between Sun and Longuet or Lafargue. It is possible that he met them during 1896–97 when they visited their relatives in England and was invited back for a short stay in Paris. Because Sun was not then the political luminary he became later, and because Longuet and Lafargue were used to mixing with such people as Marx, Engels and leaders of the Socialist International, they probably did not think their conversations with Sun at that time were worth recording.

Surprisingly, a reading of Jean Longuet's work on international socialism has highlighted not Sun's meetings with Longuet's father, but with another socialist leader with whom the Longuets had much contact and with whom Sun Yat-sen seems never before to have been associated; the English Independent Labour Party leader, Keir Hardie. In 'Le Mouvement Socialiste International', Jean Longuet wrote: 'Sun-Yat-Sen depuis longtemps s'est proclamé socialiste et pendant son long séjour en Angleterre il fut fréquemment en rapport avec Keir Hardie'.[7]

When Sun was kidnapped by the Chinese Legation, according to the porter Cole, Sun had told him that he might be compared to the leader of the Socialist party in London. Sun later denied Cole's statement at the Treasury and compared himself to the persecuted Armenian Christians. It is possible that Sun may have tried both approaches to Cole but later felt it would be prudent to conceal his socialist sympathies from the British establishment and even from the comfortably well-off Dr Cantlie. If Cole's statement is true, then Sun might have been so interested in Keir Hardie that he made a point of meeting him. However, because he was uncertain as to whether his socialist sympathies might alienate his influential British friends he possibly did not even tell the Cantlies he was meeting Keir Hardie, yet alone the Marxists Lafargue and Longuet. Thus the Cantlies would have no record of this aspect of Sun's life. Unfortunately, in the *Labour Leader* which Keir Hardie edited, the latter made no reference to any personal meeting with Sun. This, however, may well be because he did not consider Sun significant enough at the time, or possibly Sun may have asked him not to mention any socialist conversations in his newspaper for the reasons given above. It is of interest to note in this context that in the Working Class Movement Library at Salford there is a plaque commemorating the Jubilee of the Independent Labour Party in 1943. On it are featured prominent socialists building an edifice on which stands the Socialist Man. Sun Yat-sen's name appears near the top, near to Keir Hardie's and Jean Jaurès'.

The point of this discussion has not been to evidence that Sun undoubtedly did meet leading European politicians, but to argue that Sun's assertion that he did may have been true. It is incorrect to argue that his statement was necessarily misleading. If Sun did meet prominent European socialists they would have strengthened his socialist awareness.

Sun's social circle

Sun Yat-sen was naturally influenced by the individuals (other than the socialist leaders) whom he met during his sojourn in England. Some academics are very dismissive of Sun's circle of contacts at this time, but it might well be argued that to Sun's credit he established, in a comparatively short period of time, relationships with an international range of scholars and persons of outstanding qualities who had a considerable influence on him.

It has been established that Sun met up with a group of Russian exiles who frequented the British Museum and whose leading figure was Felix Volkhovsky to whom Sun presented a copy of his *Kidnapped in London*.[8] Volkhovsky edited *Free Russia*, a monthly publication of the English 'Society of Friends of Russian Freedom', and had escaped from Siberia to where he had been exiled after seven years of solitary confinement in St Petersburg's Schusselburg fortress for his liberal views. Sun must have been influenced by this man's courageous struggle against despotism and by the strength of his liberal views. Sun also met an Irish nationalist and soldier, Rowland J. Mulkern, who later participated in the Waichow campaign of 1900 and who probably reinforced Sun's determination to fight for national freedom.[9]

At the British Museum, Sun also sometimes visited Professor R. K. Douglas who held the Chair of Chinese studies at King's College, London University, and was head of the department of Oriental printed books in the British Museum. Douglas would have guided Sun in his Oriental reading. Through Douglas, Sun met a Japanese botanist Minakata Kumagusu, with whom he had frequent talks. Minakata's Pan-Asianism and anti-Western views most probably influenced Sun.[10] Minakata was a scholar who later merited a biography[11] and who could be regarded as a memorable intellectual with whom Sun could proudly claim friendship and who no doubt reinforced, if not initiated, Sun's Pan-Asianism.

Sun also met the distinguished missionary, Timothy Richard, soon after his escape from the Chinese Embassy.[12] The latter did not support Sun's anti-Manchuism but he might have been the mysterious writer 'L' whose article in the *Fortnightly Review* in August 1896 provoked a profound response in Sun. This will be discussed later.

A scholar and British Israelite, Edwin Collins, influenced Sun Yat-sen both in the writing of his two articles 'China's Present and Future' and 'Judicial Reform in China' (published in the *Fortnightly Review* and *East Asia* respectively), and in his ideas of racial purity. However, Collins was more than a British Israelite. His academic worth merited the title of Hollier Hebrew Scholar at University College, London in 1876 and he published several books.[13] Collins' influence on Sun will be examined in fuller detail later. Suffice it to say here that the influence was probably in a two-way form. Collins in his preface to Marie Trevelyan's *Britain's Greatness Foretold* refers to the 'noble revolt of the Taiping'[14] which probably reflects the strength of Sun's political influence on Collins just as the latter influenced Sun with regard to ideas on race.

Sun's friendship with Dr and Mrs Cantlie would have enlightened him about British liberal democracy, if not about the rising tide of socialism. Cantlie would also have helped Sun get a sense of perspective on Chinese society. (Cantlie was later knighted for his services to first aid, writing the standard manual for the British Red Cross and St John's Ambulance as well as organising an ambulance service.)

Thus Sun, despite his critics' denial, did attract to himself during his short sojourn in London people of distinct qualities, intellectual and personal, who influenced him and who reflected creditably on him.

Sun's reading

During his sojourn in England, Sun Yat-sen spent many hours in the British Museum.[15] His reading, it may be assumed, included the writers to whom he referred in his Three Principles as well as others: Rousseau, Montesquieu, Marx, Mill and Henry George. Thus Sun would have had an opportunity to study Western political systems, as he claimed. Moreover Sun would have been given guidance with his Oriental reading by the Keeper of the Department of Oriental Books, Professor R. K. Douglas. Cantlie remarked:

> When residing with us in London, Sun wasted no moments in gaieties; he was for ever at work, reading books on all subjects which appertained to political, diplomatic, legal, military and naval matters, mines and mining, agriculture, cattle-rearing, engineering, political economy, etc., occupied his attention and were studied closely and persistently. The range of his opportunities for acquiring knowledge has been such as few men have ever had, and the result is known to us.[16]

Cantlie's description of Sun's voracious reading habits is supported by the description given later by Yoshihiro Yamakawa in his article 'On the First President of China' published in *The Independent* in 1912 and quoted here to show that Cantlie was not overstating the case for his close friend's wide reading, Yamakawa stated of Sun:

> He is very fond of books. It is said that he cannot live even one day without a book. The scope of his reading extends from diplomacy, international law, history, etc even to astronomy, which to the ordinary mind would seem to be of no practical benefit to a man of affairs. While in Japan, it is said, he astounded his friends by his deep knowledge of astronomy.[17]

It can therefore be assumed that Sun did not waste his time at the British Museum nor indeed when he had the opportunity to use other libraries. The precise extent to which he was influenced by his reading is impossible to gauge, not least because the British Museum has no record of readers' request slips.

Further evidence that Sun was widely read comes from an unlikely source: Wu Chih-hui (an anti-Manchu intellectual) who had declined to meet Sun in 1901 as he had the idea that Sun was a 'rough-mannered, militant outlaw'. However, when Wu was in England in 1905 Sun called upon him, and Wu was quite surprised at his 'good appearance and gentle manners':

> At first I did not like Sun Yat-sen', Wu recalled, 'because he was not a member of the literati, nor did he hold any degree under the old civil examination system. I even suspected him of being illiterate. It was only after I met him that I began to realise that he was an avid reader.[18]

It is now relevant to consider what Sun published during his stay in London.

Sun Yat-sen's publications

While in London Sun wrote (with the aid of Dr Cantlie) his account of his kidnapping which was published as *Kidnapped in London* in January 1897. Current scholarship holds that, apart from his book, Sun wrote two more articles only. However, it will be argued here that Sun also wrote a third article.

The first, which appeared in the *Fortnightly Review* on 1 March 1897 was entitled 'China's Present and Future'.[19] Its discovery by Professor H. Z. Schiffrin in 1968 was regarded as an important contribution to studies on Sun Yat-sen. The second article was found by Professor Nakamura Tadashi in 1982. It had been published in the journal *East Asia* in July 1897 and was entitled 'Judicial Reform in China'.[20]

The distinguished contemporary scholar on Sun Yat-sen, Professor J. Y. Wong, has found in Mrs Cantlie's diary evidence that Sun gave lectures in January and March 1897. He assumes that Sun read the draft of the first article when he gave a lecture in Oxford in January 1897 (there seems to be no extant record of this lecture). Wong also assumes that Sun read the same for his March lecture:

> On 11 March 1897, Mrs. Cantlie again wrote, 'The lecture on "Things Chinese" at St Martin's Town Hall came off tonight for the benefit of Charing Cross Hospital. Dr Sun read an *article* (my italics)[21] on the Government of China and Hamish talked about different things. It was attended by 260 people'. Those who had the leisure to go to St. Martin's Town Hall, the money to donate to Charing Cross, and the interest to listen to 'Things Chinese', were most probably middle and upper class Londoners. Here again Sun Yat-sen would have had the satisfaction of addressing a relatively distinguished gathering.

Mrs. Cantlie referred to *an article* which he read on this occasion and to the fact that this article was on the Government of China. His first London article had been published on 1 March 1897, and was in substance about the government of China, while the second was not published until July 1897. It is likely, therefore, that Sun Yat-sen would have read the first, rather than the second, piece of work.[22]

However it will be here argued that the article read by Sun Yat-sen at St Martin's Town Hall on 11 March 1897 was neither the first nor the second of the articles hitherto discovered but a third that is still missing in its complete form. A report of the lecture was published in the *London and China Express* (this source seems to have been neglected by scholars of this period which seems a pity as the newspaper carried reviews of the aforementioned two articles by Sun which could have been discovered much earlier than they finally were).[23] With regard to Sun's talk on 11 March 1897, the *London and China Express* published the following day this information:

> Dr. Sun Yat-Sen lectured last night with the assistance of Mr. James Cantlie in St. Martin's Town Hall, on 'Things Chinese'. Dr. Watt Bleich occupied the chair. Dr. Sen sketched the history of China and dilated on the abuses practised by the officials. The cruelties practised, and the impositions by which the people were robbed, called for the interposition of civilized nations; and he hoped the day was not far distant when the sympathies of Western Europe would be enlisted on behalf of China, and she would be free from misrule, and kept from falling under the power of another Tartar avalanche, which Russia threatened to pour over the country. Mr. James Cantlie gave an account of the social manners of the Chinese in Canton and related many amusing stories of his residence amongst the people. The lecture was illustrated by a number of photographs thrown upon a screen.[24]

This report gives an account of a feature that is different in content from either of the two discovered articles, neither of which mention a call for Western Europe to impose itself to save China from the Tartar horde. Furthermore, although the local newspapers most likely to report the lecture (*Westminster Gazette, Pall Mall Gazette* and the *Westminster and Pimlico News*) do not do so, there is a report in the *New York Times* of 23 March 1897 which most probably complements the *London and China Express* report of Sun's lecture on 11 March in so far as it also refers to

18 *The Political Thought of Sun Yat-sen*

the history of China, criticises official corruption and similarly ends with Sun's call for Western intervention in China against a possible Russian invasion. The subject of the lecture is also about the Government of China which Mrs Cantlie noted was the subject in her diary. (It is however possibly the report of a fourth missing article by Sun.) The report runs thus:

> Dr. Sun Yat-sen, the man whom the Chinese Minister at London caused to be seized in the streets of that city, not long ago, and who was kept a prisoner in the garret of the Embassy for some time, the intention being to send him to China and the headsman when opportunity offered, has evidently given up the idea of soon returning to his native land. This is, at all events, the conviction naturally to be drawn from the fact that he is lecturing in England and saying many harsh things about that strange system which for lack of a more exact name is called the Government of China. Originally, says Dr. Sun Yat Sen, the people had a voice in the Celestial Kingdom's public affairs, and then there is said to have been enough of prosperity and contentment to make the phrase more or less descriptive of reality. In those days the crown was not hereditary, but often passed over an incompetent Prince to eminent men not members of the royal family. Then followed several dynasties by which education was turned in fantastic and useless directions and progress was made impossible. It was not until 1640, however, when the Manchus seized the imperial power, that the present era of utter misrule began. Then the study of geography, law, history and science was forbidden, and students were confined to the acquisition of what is little more than the art of conversation. It is now high treason to criticize the powers that be, and the collection of taxes is entrusted to men who if they turn in the expected amount, can extort from the people and keep as much as they please. Dr. Sun shows his oriental ability to adapt his arguments to his hearers by pathetically appealing to Englishmen to save China from the new Tartar horde which Russia is now threatening to pour into his unhappy country by way of Siberia. That is a cry into whose sincerity at least a part of the outlawed Chinaman's hearers will not inquire too closely.[25]

This account differs from that of the *London and China Express* only in that it contains a reference to Sun's lecturing on the history of the monarchy and educational system in China. The *London and China Express* does report that Sun 'sketched the history of China', and a compilation of both these newspaper reports points to an article being read by Sun that is very different from either of the two already known articles.

Even if the *New York Times* reported a reading from a fourth missing article, the *London and China Express* report indicates that Sun did not read from either 'China's Present and Future' or 'Judicial Reform in China'. It is therefore now pertinent to summarise the contents of both known articles. The first article, 'China's Present and Future', was published in the journal the *Fortnightly Review* on 1 March 1897 and was subtitled: 'The Reform Party's Plea for British Benevolent Neutrality'. (This according to the report in the *London and China Express* is precisely what Sun Yat-sen was not asking for on 11 March 1897.)

The article was a collaborative work between Edwin Collins and Sun Yat-sen. It argued for the entire overthrow of the corrupt Manchu regime which was to be replaced by a good native Chinese government with at first European advice and European administrative assistance. It declared:

> Nothing short of the entire overthrow of the present utterly corrupt regime and the establishment of a good government and a pure administration by native Chinese with, at first, European advice, and, for some years, European administrative assistance, can effect any improvement whatever.[26]

Sun claimed that while it was common knowledge that China suffered from four major afflictions 'famine, flood, pestilence, insecurity of life and property',[27] most people were unaware that these problems were the result of official corruption which encouraged negligence of duty. The four problems are delineated in such vivid detail that any newspaper report of the article, had it been read as a lecture, would surely have referred to them.

Sun showed how officials, after passing the examinations, had to bribe their way into the system, even to the extent of bribing the gateway man in Peking for the essential audience with the Emperor. In military service promotion was also through bribery with officers fabricating the names of men in their service in order to claim more pay and to sell the promoted posts of the dummy soldiers to Chinese who had the same names.[28]

Sun argued China's defeat by Japan was due to the corrupt condition of the armies due to Manchu rule. Sun thus concluded:

> The whole people is ready for a change; there are plenty of honest men ready and willing to enter public life; the army is so corrupt, that

even were it not to a great extent leavened with sympathisers with the Reform Party, it could not be depended on by the Government. It is only from the Manchu soldiers or from short-sighted selfish interference of foreigners that the Reform Party has anything whatever to fear. Indeed one object I have in writing this article is to prove to the English people that it is in the interests of Europe generally, and of England in particular, to allow us to succeed, and that the policy often recommended (as for instance by 'L' in the August number of this review), that of protecting the present Government, is entirely mistaken.[29]

Sun ended with a call for the benevolent neutrality of Britain and the other 'Powers' which would enable the Reform Party to clean up the corruption, reform the government and develop the natural resources of China to the benefit of the whole world.

It is perhaps worth noting that *Le Temps* did report this article (before Sun's lecture on 11 March 1897) as a piece from the *Fortnightly Review* and included the salient points mentioned above as any newspaper report might do.[30] This adds weight to the argument that Sun's article 'China's Present and Future' was not the one reported in the *London and China Express* and *New York Times* of March 1897.

The identity of 'L' mentioned in the article will now be discussed. Whoever 'L' was he certainly stimulated Sun's response by writing an article entitled 'The Future of China' which was published in the *Fortnightly Review* on 1 August 1896. Like Sun, 'L' criticised the corruption and the educational system which 'emasculates the life of the people'.[31] 'L' deprecated the clannishness and lack of patriotism of the Chinese (which might well have stimulated Sun's 'Principle of Nationalism').[32] 'L' also argued that as there was no hope of China reforming herself[33] and as China might be dismembered by an advancing Russia it would be best that China: 'be put into tutelage, and there are strong reasons why the tutor should be England.'[34]

Unlike Sun, 'L' was not arguing for the overthrowing of the Manchu system but for its propping up by British tutelage. However, it is arguable that the idea of political tutelage for China did influence Sun and later bore fruit in his theory that the Kuomintang would supervise China's tutelage. Above all, 'L' referred to the possibility of protecting China and British interests from the possibility of a Russian onslaught. This argument may well have influenced Sun's call in March 1897 for Western intervention against the Russian hordes taking over China; but at the same time there was a general concern in the press as to Russia's designs on China. While Sun took up the epistolary cudgels against 'L' then, the latter's article obviously made a profound impression on his mind and it is probable some of the ideas, modified, bore fruit in his theories later on.

The identity of 'L' remains an intriguing puzzle. Professor Wu Xiangxiang has suggested that 'L' was the famous missionary Timothy Richard whom Sun visited shortly after he escaped from being kidnapped. 'L' would have stood for 'Li', Richard's Chinese name.[35] This would indeed be a felicitous solution to the identity of the mysterious author who provoked a profound response from Sun. However, there are problems with this idea since the stand taken by 'L' in 'The Future of China' seems unsympathetic to missionaries.[36]

What is perhaps puzzling is that Richard does not mention the article in *Forty Five Years in China* nor in his autobiography in *Conversion by the Million*. Nor did Sun Yat-sen, if he knew 'L' was Timothy Richard, reveal this fact while he was criticising 'L'. In *Conversion by the Million* there appears a letter written by Richard (in January 1897) which was obviously to be circulated to influential men in the United Kingdom:

> It is therefore proposed to ask some of the best statesmen, best professors in our universities, best ecclesiastical leaders, best press leaders, best business men and best labour leaders in the United Kingdom to give us each a scheme of reform for China.[37]

Richard, like 'L' was concerned with reforming tutelage for China. But while clues do point to Timothy Richard, the true identity of 'L', who may have had a profound effect on Sun Yat-sen, remains as elusive as the Tao.

The second of Sun's articles that has been discovered (by Professor Nakamura in 1982) and must be considered is that entitled 'Judicial Reform in China' which was published in the first issue of *East Asia* in July 1897. It was also written in collaboration with Edwin Collins with the express probability of it forming part of a book that they were writing together. The article was concerned with the corrupt judicial system and torture in China and ended by reminding the readers of the recent murder of a dozen missionaries in China: crimes which should bring home the fact that:

> the laws of China, as enforced with the sanction and support of England, are a blot upon Creation and a disgrace to our common humanity. If England could realise this, the Reform Party of Young China might hope for at least freedom from molestation in its

attempt to make possible the introduction of a Europeanised judicial system into our country.³⁸

The significance of the reports of Sun's speech on 11 March 1897 as reported by the *London and China Express* and the *New York Times* is that it indicates Sun Yat-sen called for the intervention of Western states to overthrow Manchu rule at a time when it is assumed that Sun Yat-sen pursued a policy requiring the benevolent neutrality of the foreign powers.

The Three Principles of the People

Sun Yat-sen's most famous work, *The Three Principles of the People*, which became the ideology of the Kuomintang and later implemented, in a distorted form, in Taiwan, were not expressly propounded by him until 1905, then more fully in 1924. Nevertheless he claimed his Three Principles of Nationalism, Democracy and Socialism were profoundly influenced by his stay in London during 1896–97. There he found European governments could not give their people full happiness; a social revolution was needed.³⁹ There is no evidence that he actually formed the three principles in his mind at this time. Indeed his nationalism probably developed earlier.

Early nationalist influences

Sun recorded that he experienced nationalist desire to free his country from Manchu rule in 1885 when France defeated Manchuria.⁴⁰ He may also have felt anti-Manchu resentment from his earlier Taiping influences (to be discussed in Chapter 9). Thus when he arrived in England he would have been well-prepared to listen to the ideas of his friend Edwin Collins who had helped him write his articles in 1897 on 'China's Present and Future' and on 'Judicial Reform in China'.

Sun's concept of the Han race as 'a single pure race'⁴¹ may have been derived from Edwin Collins influence. On the other hand racial theories, particularly those of the French writer Gobineau were well-known at this time. There is, however, a more important source for Sun's nationalism that has not been previously identified. Sun's nationalism was not only anti-Manchu, it also involved the idea that the Chinese must be welded together by a common national pride since they suffered from excessive clannishness. It has been remarked before that Sun was deeply influenced by the article on 'The Future of China' by 'L' published in the *Fortnightly Review* in August 1896. It is arguable that Sun was influenced by 'L's criticism of China's excessive clannishness and lack of patriotism.[42] Sun's comment that:

> the Chinese people have only family and clan groups there is no national spirit. Consequently, in spite of four hundred million people gathered together in one China, we are in fact but a sheet of loose sand. We are the poorest and weakest state in the world[43]

may possibly have been inspired by 'L's article.

Early democratic influences

Sun's experience of liberal democracy in England during his sojourn from 1896–97 undoubtedly sharpened his political vision. Sun could witness the political debate around him and read about controversial issues in newspapers and books, in contrast to his freedom to do so in China. As Sun observed in his *Kidnapped in London*: 'books on politics are not allowed; daily newspapers are prohibited in China; the world around, its people and politics, are shut out.'[44]

According to Slater's detective, Sun regularly visited the British Museum (where he no doubt would have read about Western constitutional systems) and he visited the Houses of Parliament (Wong points out that the date given is probably incorrect as it does not tally with Sun's own account of his activities that day).[45] It is, however, probable that Sun did visit the Houses of Parliament during his stay in London. If the visit was around the time given by Slater's then the Houses of Commons and Lords would have been in recess and there is no record of what Sun might have been doing there. According to Slater's, Sun also visited the Constitutional Club in Northumberland Avenue on 18 January.[46] There seems to be no record of any proceedings there.

Wong is possibly right in his interesting suggestion that a law student, Horniman, instructed Sun in constitutional law.[47] Obviously, however, Sun could also have derived his ideas on constitutional government by talking to any informed Briton, such as his friend Dr Cantlie or his circle of exiled revolutionary friends, like Felix Volkhovsky, who edited the magazine *Free Russia* and who was passionately concerned with constitutional guarantees against tyranny. The issue of *Free Russia* on 1 May 1897, for example, began its editorial thus 'Yes, clear the way for Liberty and the Rights of Man.'[48]

Above all Sun was obviously greatly impressed with the British sense of justice which had been outraged by his kidnapping. On 24 October

1896 Sun sent a letter to the newspapers thanking the Government and the Press for their support. He concluded:

> Knowing and feeling more keenly than ever what a Constitutional Government and an enlightened people mean, I am prompted still more actively to pursue the cause of advancement, education and civilisation in my own well-beloved but oppressed country.[49]

Sun's experience of liberal democracy in the West obviously involved an understanding of the rule of law. That in China there was no such thing and that the judicial system was but a facade for corruption and tyranny expressed itself in Sun's article, written with Edwin Collins, on 'Judicial Reform in China' and published in *East Asia* magazine in July 1897.

One of Sun's key ideas was that the Chinese people needed tutoring in democracy. In his article on 'China's Present and Future' (which Sun also wrote with Edwin Collins) Sun argued:

> Nothing short of the entire overthrow of the present utterly corrupt 'regime' and the establishment of good government and a pure administration by native Chinese with, at first, European advice, and for some years, European administrative assistance, can effect any improvement whatever.[50]

This notion of tutelage could well have been echoing the idea expressed in the article by 'L' in the *Fortnightly Review* of August 1896, to which Sun was replying and in which 'L' had argued for political tutelage by England.[51] 'L' later concluded:

> The sceptre of the Manchus may fall into our hands without any effort on our part, and China may be the last and greatest of our foster children. Posterity may see a Parliament on the banks of the Yangtse, and the man whom Macaulay predicted would one day survey the ruins of London from Westminster Bridge may come not from New Zealand but from Pekin.[52]

Sun was probably influenced by 'L's idea of tutelage for China's democratic developments. However, because of nationalist and anti-imperialist feelings, Sun later dropped the idea of European political assistance and developed the idea of his party's tutelage for the Chinese people instead.

Sun stated in 1906 that he had studied various constitutions and believed that the best unwritten constitution was the British. However, as it has evolved over seven or eight hundred years by convention it could not be copied. Moreover, the three powers of the executive, legislature and judiciary were not clearly separated. Therefore Britain did not provide a constitutional blueprint for China.[53]

In his lecture reported in the *New York Times* of 12 March 1897, Sun did speak approvingly of a certain type of monarchical system in the felicitous stage of the Celestial Kingdom when the crown was not hereditary, but often passed over an incompetent Prince to men who were not members of the royal family. Here can be seen an early example of Sun Yat-sen's interest in the competence of the ruler above all else. However, by the time Sun came to London in 1896 he had given up any idea of reforming the Chinese imperial system which he intended to overthrow. Nevertheless, in his articles published in London he portrayed himself as a reformist, no doubt to avoid upsetting the establishment whose support he needed.

In his lecture as reported in the *New York Times* of 23 March 1897, Sun said that originally the people had a voice in the Celestial Kingdom's public affairs, and then there was said to have been enough of prosperity and contentment to make the phrase more or less descriptive of reality. This passage, redolent of Sun's idea of returning to the Great Harmony which he expressed in his lectures on the Three Principles in 1924, is significant in that it links two ideas of the 'people's voice in public affairs' and 'prosperity and contentment'. To Sun the first idea was insufficient without the second. It is interesting to note that it is in his lectures on Democracy, not on Livelihood in 1924 that Sun spoke of organised labour.[54]

It is possible that this idea germinated when Sun was in London during 1896–97 and witnessed the strikes as an expression of liberal democratic right and socialist struggle. In contrast to the political theorists who have argued that liberal democracy and capitalism are intrinsically linked, Sun saw democracy and socialism essentially connected: 'Socialism was originally closely related to democracy and the two should have developed simultaneously.'[55]

Sun possibly derived certain negative lessons from witnessing Western democracies, either directly or reading about them while he was in England during 1896–97. It is not usually stressed that while Sun experienced parliamentary democracy in England at the end of the nineteenth century, this consisted of the Conservatives competing against the Liberals; the Socialist presence was only a sporadic handful of MPs. The Labour

Party had not yet organised itself with the financial power of the trade unions and emerged effectively on to the English parliamentary scene. If Sun did have conversations with socialist leaders he would have had his beliefs even more reinforced that liberal democracy in Europe had its limitations. Sun's expressed conclusion that the European powers could not give their peoples 'full happiness' no doubt impelled him to the belief that China must advance on all three fronts of nationalism, democracy and socialism simultaneously.

Early socialist influences

Sun Yat-sen later recollected that his sojourn in England during 1896–97 was the decisive and seminal source of his socialist ideas:

> what I saw and heard made a tremendous impression upon me. For the first time I understood that though the European powers achieved national wealth and power, they were not able to give their peoples full happiness. For this reason, European men of determination were still striving for a social revolution.[56]

Obviously the visual impact of the immiserised poor and the comfortably wealthy in late nineteenth-century London must have had a great effect on Sun's mind. The slums near his lodging in Holborn, beside Gray's Inn, where the rich and privileged barristers pursued legal justice mainly for the rich and privileged classes, must have presented him with a cameo of British social injustice on his doorstep. What, however, should be noted is the fact that Sun omitted mention of this impression in his book *Kidnapped in London* which he wrote with the help of Dr Cantlie and published in January 1897:

> What impressed me, a Chinaman, most was the enormous vehicular traffic, the endless and unceasing stream of omnibuses, cabs, carriages, wagons and wheeled conveyances of humbler character which held the streets; the wonderful way in which the police controlled and directed the traffic, and the good humour of the people.[57]

Sun's favourable impression of modernised transport in London may have been the genesis for his later great concern with the subject in China. However, perhaps the significance of this passage lies in what Sun did not say. It is possible that he did not mention that he had noticed the wide disparities between rich and poor in London lest he embarrass Dr Cantlie, who was comfortably well-off, and alienate members of the upper classes who might read his book and whose help he might need later in his political struggle. Thus, while in London, Sun played down his socialist sympathies (as perhaps was seen, for example, when he denied he had compared himself with the English socialist leader to Cole, at the Chinese Embassy). For that reason Sun might not have mentioned to Dr Cantlie or generally publicised that he had met any European socialist leaders.

Sun would have appreciated, by reading newspapers, that England's social ills were replicated throughout Europe. He would have read of the plight of the poor and of their struggle to improve their conditions. When recollecting his London experience Sun spoke of 'European men of determination' who were struggling for a social revolution. These could have been socialist leaders. They could also have been the unionised workers. Sun witnessed not only the immiserisation of the poor but also the extent to which they were organising and clashing with their employers. Many strikes were reported in the British press while Sun was in London. Sun may also have attended such meetings as the Eighth Miners' International Congress in London in June 1897.

There are differences of opinion as to whether the great Engineering Lock-out of 1897 influenced Sun as it took place after he left London.[58] Nevertheless Sun would naturally continue to follow the events of a country which he had just left and in which he had taken such a close interest.

Henry George and Sun Yat-sen

Sun Yat-sen may have been acquainted with the ideas in Henry George's *Progress and Poverty* (published in 1879) before Sun came to London. However, it seems it was in England that Sun felt the full impact of George's ideas. George's slogan was 'common ownership of land'. By this he meant not land nationalisation but government appropriation for rent which would obviate the need for other forms of taxation, provide revenue to abolish poverty and render land speculation useless.

Unlike John Stuart Mill who first popularised the term 'future unearned increment' (in his *Dissertations and Discussions* published in 1874), Henry George had wanted government appropriation of all unearned increment (past as well as future). As the scholar Harold Schiffrin has pointed out, as Sun was asking only for future increments in land values, he was taking a stand closer to Mill than to George.[59] Sun was no doubt also influenced after he left London by the German introduction in

Kiaochow (after it was acquired by Germany in 1898), of a future unearned increment.

It is perhaps a curious but noteworthy fact that in reading the article by 'L' in the *Fortnightly Review* of August 1896 which Sun undoubtedly did, Sun must have read that:

> The result is that Shanghai is rapidly becoming a great manufacturing city; land in and near the city is worth what is for China a fabulous price and the Shanghai Taotaiship is one of the most prized appointments in the Chinese service. Well, if railways are constructed there is room for a dozen Shanghais in China.[60]

It is just possible, particularly because Shanghai is pluralised in the statement, that this idea, stored in Sun's mind bore fruit in his address at the farewell banquet given in his honour at Shanghai by the Revolutionary Association on 18 April 1912:

> If you compare the value of land in Shanghai today with what it was one hundred years ago, it has increased ten thousandfold. Now, industry in China is about to be developed. Commerce will advance, and in fifty years time we shall see many Shanghais in China. Let us take time by the forelock and make sure that the unearned increment of wealth shall belong to the people and not to private capitalists who happen to be the owners of the soil.[61]

Thus Sun's experiences in London deeply impressed upon him the problem of land values rapidly increasing due to industrialisation. Direct contact with the debate over Henry George's ideas were undoubtedly a prime factor in increasing his awareness of the problem; his reading of 'L's article may have been a secondary factor.

Above all Sun wanted to give the Chinese people 'full happiness' which he saw was lacking in the West. Sun did not articulate his Three Principles which he thought would largely achieve this until 1905. Partly because he expressly wanted British support he had reason to be silent about some of his impressions of London while he was there. In July 1897 he left for Japan. The question therefore arises as to what happened during his sojourn in Japan, which will be dealt with in the next chapter.

3
Sun's Western Influences in the Japanese Crucible

Japan was the crucible in which Sun's ideas were refined. Had certain ideologies such as socialism not been flourishing during Sun's stay there, it is possible that his Three Principles would have emerged with a different emphasis in 1905.

By the time of Sun's arrival in Japan in 1897, Western socialism was influential there alongside Western capitalism. Ten years earlier the views of Henry George were evidentially disseminating socialist ideas. During this decade 10 per cent of the workers had organised themselves into trade unions and Marx's *Communist Manifesto* had been translated into Japanese.[1] In 1897, J. Sen Katayama, a Christian, had founded his socialist newspaper the *Kodo Sekai*.[2] Japanese socialism originated from two sources: the Christian and the liberal;[3] the former source was primarily that of American Christian missionaries who introduced the ideas of such socialists as Richard Ely whose *Socialism and Social Reform* was published in 1894. (Later as Schiffrin and Scalapino show, both the Sun and Liang factions would argue over the true interpretation of Ely's *Outlines of Economics* published in 1904.)[4] The liberal source of Japanese socialism was dominated by Kotoku Shusio who had been much influenced by the struggle for constitutional rights in Japan during the 1880s.[5] He began writing articles in support of Western socialism which were very influential. In 1901 Japanese socialists and trade unionists formed a Social Democratic Party. However, this was immediately banned by the Meiji government.[6]

In 1902, Liang Ch'i-ch'ao and his reformists founded a publishing house in Shanghai which introduced Western socialist ideas into China.[7] Initially socialism was regarded as the Western equivalent to the Chinese ancient golden age of Ta-t'ung and the system of land tenure as Ching-t'ien (by which 900 'mou' of land was divided into the shape of the character of 'ching', a well; eight families had a hundred 'mou' and communally farmed the central common field). Indeed Liang Ch'i-ch'ao may have been the first to see the parallel between Ta-t'ung and Western socialism, an idea which Sun Yat-sen also adopted.[8] In 1906 a more liberal government came to power in Japan and allowed the establishment in that year of the Japanese Socialist Party.

There can be little doubt that Japanese socialists, especially those influenced by Henry George and Liang Ch'i-chao's own ideas on socialism, helped refine and reinforce Sun's own socialist beliefs. The precise extent is obviously difficult to gauge. Had there not been a socialist matrix for Sun's beliefs, they may well have developed differently. Sun would also have had his awareness intensified, when the Meiji government banned the Japanese Socialist Party in 1901, of how careful he had to be about publicly supporting an ideology which would provoke the wrath of a government whose support he needed.

Precisely when Sun first put forward his policy of 'equalisation of land rights' is uncertain. It was included in the oath of a branch of the Hsing Chung Hui in Hanoi which he established in 1903, and in the 'New Regulations Governing the Chih-kung-tang' which he reorganised in San Francisco in 1904.[9] In 1905 the T'ung Meng Hui proclaimed the 'equalisation of land rights'. *Min Pao* interchanged 'min-sheng chu-i' with the Japanese 'Shakai shugi' (in Chinese script 'she hui chu-i') by which it meant a single tax system and the appropriation of the unearned increase of land values.[10]

It is arguable that Sun came to the West already predisposed to accept Western socialist ideas because of his early Taiping influence (about which of course he kept quiet because of the associations of subversion). The Chinese historian Wu Yü-chang has argued precisely that Sun: 'came under the influence of the Taiping Revolution when he was only a boy. This is one of the reasons why he later advocated the principle of the equalisation of land ownership.'[11]

By 1905 Sun and his followers were calling themselves 'social revolutionaries'. This idea probably derived from the example of the Russian Revolution of that year which was seen as being a simultaneously 'political' and 'social' revolution.[12] It is likely that Sun first believed that the West would have violent social revolutions when he witnessed the social conflict there during his visit of 1896–97. Sun's belief in the importance of nationalism was probably reinforced by his experience of Japanese nationalism and by his contact with Liang Ch'i-ch'ao who was influenced by Japanese scholars such as Kato Hiroyuki[13] in emphasising the importance of the state's unity with society to increase national power.

Sun's Western ideas were mainly reinforced by his stay in Japan. Nevertheless there was one Western thinker whose ideas Sun probably first came into contact with either through Japanese scholars or Liang Ch'i-ch'ao; this was the 'Swiss scholar' whom Sun never named and has never been identified.

The influence of Johan Kaspar Bluntschli

Johan Kaspar Bluntschli was a Swiss political thinker who greatly influenced Liang Ch'i-ch'ao's tendency, after 1903, to emphasise the strength of the state as being of prime importance; a state had to be united under a strong central government in order to survive international competition.[14] While in Europe Bluntschli made little impact, in Japan he was exalted to national fame by Kato Hiroyuki who published a translation of his *Allgemaines Staatsrecht (Public Law)* in 1872.

The influence of Bluntschli on Sun Yat-sen has never been examined before. Nevertheless it is reasonable to suppose that it was he whom Sun had in mind when he curiously referred to 'a certain Swiss scholar' when he delivered his lectures on Democracy in 1924. Sun had already frequently mentioned the name of Rousseau (who was French but had lived in Switzerland) and it is unlikely that he was referring to him in this way. Bluntschli's name was less well-known and this may be why Sun did not or could not provide it. Sun said:

> A certain Swiss scholar has said that since various nations have put democracy into practice, the power of government has declined and the reason has been the fear on the part of the people that the government might secure a power which they could not control. Hence the people have always guarded their governments and have not allowed them power, lest they become all powerful... The Swiss scholar whom I mentioned saw this evil train of events and as a remedy proposed that the people should change their attitude to government.[15]

It is perhaps noteworthy that even a thesis based partly on the above quotation (Liu Yeou-hwa's *A Comparative Study of Dr Sun Yat-sen's and Montesquieu's Theory of Separation of Powers*) has not attempted to discover the identity of the 'certain Swiss scholar'.[16]

Bluntschli certainly argued that democracy weakened the authority of the government:

> The government on the other hand, has great difficulty in making its authority really strong and vigorous. The frequency of elections makes its position insecure and dependent upon the changeable opinions of the people.[17]

It is likely that Bluntschli influenced Sun by his argument that democracy weakens governmental authority. It is also possible that Bluntschli influenced Sun in two other aspects of his theory: distinction between sovereignty and ability, and the acceptance that to the usual three powers of government more could be added. Bluntschli did not expressly distinguish between sovereignty and ability, but he discussed the difficulty of obtaining the best men to govern in representative democracy:

> Its principle is that the best men of the nation govern in the name and by the commission of the nation. But the great difficulty lies in organising the election so as to secure that the best men both in intellect and character shall be chosen.[18]

With regard to the usual three powers Bluntschli points out that some states have added others, including the power of inspection.[19]

However, probably the person who influenced Sun Yat-sen most with regard to his theories of distinguishing between the sovereignty of the people and the ability of officials and of examinations for all candidates for office was probably Dr Ho Kai[20] (a former teacher of Sun in Hong Kong) whose writings between 1895 and 1900 had an influence on Sun that the latter later acknowledged.[21]

Some passages in Sun's writings also resemble those of Bluntschli. For example Sun wrote:

> What is the People's Sovereignty? In order to define this term we must first understand what a 'people' is. Any unified and organised body of men is called a 'people'. What is 'sovereignty'? It is the power and authority extended to the area of the state.[22]

Bluntschli similarly wrote:

> to whom belongs sovereignty... An opinion, widely diffused since Rousseau and the French Revolution assigns sovereignty to the

people. Yes, but who are the people? According to some, simply the sum of individuals united into the state.[23]

Like Bluntschli, Sun regarded Rousseau's ideas crucial to understanding the meaning of the people's sovereignty. Both writers believed that states throughout the world were moving to an era of democracy.

While in Japan, Sun may have formulated the idea of the provisional constitution. Schiffrin has made the interesting point that the Japanese political activist Miyazaki Torazo[24] related how when Sun met him in 1897 he mentioned the need for a hero to rise up to arouse the patriotic spirit of the Chinese to replace the Manchus with beneficial rule and 'agree upon laws'. Schiffrin argues that Miyazaki said Sun used the term 'yüeh-fa' for 'agree upon laws' which in modern Chinese means a provisional constitution. Thus at this time Sun was already thinking of his tutelary or second stage of constitution government. This second stage was renamed 'hsün-cheng' or 'tutelage' in 1914. Further, Schiffrin argues that if Miyazaki's memory served him correctly, Sun used the phrase 'Yueh fa san chang' – basic laws in three articles – which is a phrase which occurs in the history of the Han Dynasty. It might indicate that Sun had studied this history; if this be so, Sun was more of a classical scholar than is often appreciated. However, it has also been argued elsewhere in Chapter 2 that Sun might well have been influenced by the idea of tutelage as expounded by 'L's article in August 1896 in the *Fortnightly Review*. Sun might have developed the idea to suit his own purposes.

With regard to the idea of constitutional rights and personal liberty it is likely that Sun was directly influenced by his own reading of John Stuart Mill's *On Liberty* rather than by Liang Ch'i-ch'ao's interpretation of his work. Liang paraphrased Mill in terms of 'people and government' rather than the original 'individual' and 'society'. Sun, however, wrote in terms of the latter:

> therefore an English scholar named Mill said that only individual liberty which did not interfere with the liberty of others can be considered true liberty. If one's liberty is incompatible with another's sphere of liberty it is no longer liberty. Before that, Westerners had no set limits upon freedom, but when Mill proposed his theory of a limited freedom the measure of personal liberty was considerably reduced.[25]

(Because of the national impact with which Sun credits Mill's ideas, it was most unlikely that he was referring to the scholar J. S. Millar as Linebarger, quoting Paschal d'Elia has attempted to argue.)[26]

In 1904 in New York, Sun published in English his pamphlet *The True Solution to the Chinese Question*. Its message was anti-Manchu and not anti-foreigner, no doubt to avoid offending its American audience. But it had little impact.

In the spring of 1905 Sun put forward his tentative ideas on his Three People's Principles to the students in Brussels, Berlin and Paris. It is of significance that Sun described his theory as being 'sheng p'ing suo huai pao' (long-cherished).[27] How long it had been cherished is difficult to ascertain but Sun clearly regarded it as a secret guarded closely for a considerable time.

In August 1905 the T'ung Meng Hui Revolutionary Alliance was founded in Tokyo. Sun was its president who gave it his Three People's Principles as its ideology. The Alliance was formed from anti-Manchu movements with the help of Japanese mediation from such people as Miyazaki. Hundreds of Chinese students in Japan supported the T'ung Meng Hui. Sun's Three Principles were deliberately short and vague to gain maximum acceptance; Sun did not expound them fully until 1924. However he did explain them in a little more detail in 1906.

Sun's phrase 'The Three People's Principles' clearly shows the influence both of Abraham Lincoln's 'of the people, by the people, and for the people' and of the French Revolution's 'Liberty, Equality and Fraternity'.[28] Sun may well have been aware of these watchwords before he came to the West, but his experience in Europe and the USA obviously meant he would have heard these slogans re-echoed. Sun probably adopted the term 'min-sheng chu-yi' for alliteration with the terms 'min-tsu chu-yi' and 'min-chüan chu-yi'; it also made the idea seem more Chinese and be therefore possibly more acceptable. Sun had already used the term 'min-sheng' in his petition to Li Hung-chang in 1894. (Bernal suggested that Sun may have noticed the term if he had read articles by Dr Edkins on 'How to Enrich the Nation' which appeared in *The Review of the Times* during the early 1890s.)[29]

Sun's political ideas in 1906

On 2 December 1906 in Tokyo, Sun made a speech on the first anniversary of the *Min Pao*.[30] Since he seems to have made no further elaborations on his governmental theories for another five years, it is pertinent to sum up Sun's political ideas at this stage and reflect on the influences that shaped them. As this speech has never been translated before and is rarely referred to, I shall highlight its significance here.

In his talk, Sun said that the Principles of Nationalism, Democracy and Livelihood were the ideas which the *Min Pao* propagated for China's salvation. The Principle of Nationalism involved a sense of natural relationships akin to the other. However, the Han people were not like the children of the Manchus who had invaded China 260 years earlier. The Principle of Nationalism held that the Han people should have their own government; they formed the oldest and most civilised nation and were the largest in the world, yet they lacked their own country. The Transvaal, despite a small population, had resisted England for three years and America spent several years annexing the Philippines. The Han people had tried to resist the Manchus: if they united they would surely win. The Han people did not want to kill the Manchus nor take revenge, but to recover their own government.

The Principle of Democracy involved the political revolution without which the national revolution would be incomplete. An autocratic monarchy had existed in China for several thousands of years and was unbearable to people who loved freedom and equality. When the Ming emperor had reunited China and driven out the foreign invader, he had a national revolution but, as his politics were the same as the Han, T'ang and Sung dynasties, three hundred years later China was again invaded. Even if the Emperor was of Han origin it would not be satisfactory. There had to be a democratic constitutional government such as had been set up in France and was being attempted in Russia. (Sun may well have been influenced by the fact that in 1905 a constitutionally governed Japan had defeated an autocratic Russia.) It was important that the revolutionaries did not fight each other as other countries were looking at China with covetous eyes.

The Principle of Livelihood was the peaceful social revolution that would obviate the coming violent social revolution that must occur in the West. As countries made progress in civilisation, introducing electricity and machines, so the rich would get richer and the poor poorer. This was unfair to the poor. The European countries could not solve their social problems because they had not solved the land problem. As civilisation developed so too did the price of land. Whereas in the previous century England could produce enough food for her people, she now had to import wheat and use her navy to protect her transport of food. The rich had changed the arable land into grazing and hunting areas and the poor had to work in factories having lost their land. Sun stressed that China could obviate this situation by solving the land problem. Land could be priced at, for example, 1000 yuan. If its value increased ten-fold, the landlord would still receive the original

1000 yuan but the surplus would go to the government. Then there would be no need for other taxes which were high in Japan and the West. Sun referred to the fact that Germany in Kiaochow and Holland in Java had carried out policies similar to those which he had proposed. However, as the West had left the land problem too late it could not solve it as easily as could China. While England had the best unwritten constitution and America the best written, China would copy either with amendments.

China would improve on the three powers constitution by adding two further powers: that of examination and supervision. Sun pointed out that in the USA a good orator was more likely to achieve power than someone who had ability but not eloquence. Sun remarked that in the American Congress there were some stupid men. He observed that China had originated the examination system which the West had borrowed yet not made truly an independent organ of the state. China would make it so and examine all officials whether appointed or elected. On a Confucian note, Sun remarked that Chinese people were interested in seniority and qualification, and he implied that these would count in his government. Moreover, the supervisory power would be independent of the legislative unlike the system in the USA which allows 'Congress autocracy'.

Thus Sun delineated his Three Principles and Five-Power Constitution. In his Principle of Democracy in 1906 he was concerned with emphasising the need for republicanism and not with China's problem of having too much liberty as he was in 1924. In his Principle of Livelihood he was concerned with the single-tax solution and not with the best method of bringing about the Great Commonwealth as he was in 1924. In his Principle of Nationalism he emphasised anti-Manchuism and not anti-imperialism. There is, however, a problem with Sun's nationalism as he expressed it in 1906 that deserves attention, since it does not seem to have been commented on before and concerns a significant omission of any reference to a controversy in 1906. This is that Sun referred to the Transvaal without mentioning the issue of Chinese coolie labour there. In 1906 this was a scandal that was blazing across Western headlines; it was an issue that could have helped weld the Chinese together in racial indignation. Sun seems to have ignored or have been ignorant of this fact.

Sun may have first become aware of South African politics during his stay in London during 1896–97. Certainly he would have become aware of the Transvaal from press reportage of the Boer War over the period 1899–1902.

In January 1906, Lloyd George and the Liberals swept to power using a cartoon on Chinese slavery depicting Chinese manacled with chains round their necks, being driven by whips to their labour by their task-masters. This was later deemed to be a pictorial falsehood.[31] However, in 1906 it was not clear what were the facts. It seemed that the Chinese were treated cruelly. What is significant is that Sun Yat-sen seemed to have kept quiet on this issue, whereas the British Liberals profited politically from it. Sun showed more sympathy with the Boers than with his own race in South Africa. It is possible that as his references to the defeated Boers would not have alienated the vested interests in the British establishment as much as championing the cause of Chinese slavery. It is just possible that Sun was informed by his English friends such as Cantlie that there was no truth whatsoever in the rumour of British treatment of Chinese in South Africa. It is also possible that Sun was ignorant of the matter. It is more likely that Sun was concerned not to make accusations that could later be shown to be unfounded and thus alienate the vested interests of a country whose support he needed. However, as the British Liberal Party itself exploited the issue of Chinese slavery it is puzzling that Sun did not use it as a political weapon. It should, however, be remembered that Sun's nationalism did not take on an anti-imperialist colour at this time.

Sun may well still have wanted European assistance to the extent of intervention to which he referred in his lecture on 11 March 1897.

How far was Sun indebted to his experience in Europe during 1896–97 for his Three Principles which were not enunciated until 1905? To what extent was Sun more influenced by his experiences in Japan? It is possible that Sun came to the West in 1896 with a mind already sympathetic to nationalist, liberal and socialist ideas. However, direct experiences have an immediacy which is often indelible even if disappearing into the unconscious. The visual impact of what Sun saw of the immiserised poor in Europe and his probable conversations with socialists, which would have given him an overview of the social situation in Europe, undoubtedly had a lasting impact. His awareness of the increasing will of 'men of determination' to contest their lot with employers through strikes must have filled him with a desire to prevent the development of such violent clashes in China. He would also have developed an awareness of the need to keep secret his socialist sympathies which would be deemed subversive by those with the political power to give him refuge (as the British could in Hong Kong) and support for the movement. In Japan, Sun would have been reinforced in his national, democratic and socialist beliefs. Perhaps only Bluntschli's ideas were new to him there. It is impossible to set a date for his introduction to the theories of this Swiss scholar. There is then little to discredit Sun's own description of how he formulated his long cherished idea, that during 1896–97:

> What I saw and heard made a tremendous impression upon me. For the first time I understood that though the European powers achieved national wealth and power they were not able to give their people full happiness. For this reason, European men of determination were still striving for a social revolution.[32]

It was the goal of giving people 'full happiness' (rather than perhaps merely the freedom to pursue it) that Sun stressed was the aim of the Three Principles: a Celestial Republic redolent of the virtues of the ancient utopian dream that Sun had evoked when lecturing in London.

4
Sun's Thought between 1905/6 and 1919: Populism and Elitism

Sun's energies from 1906 until 1918 were largely expended on his political activities. In 1907 he fled to Annam as the Manchu government had pressured the Japanese government to expel him; and in this year there were also abortive revolutionary attempts in Chaochow, Waichow, Yamchow and Limchow. In 1908 Sun went to the United States on a financial campaign, and in 1910 he travelled to Siam and the Straits Settlements. Throughout this time he was overseeing the opening of branches of the T'ung Meng-Hui in China, Southeast Asia, the United States and Europe.

While Sun was fundraising in the USA at Denver, Colorado, the anti-Manchu uprising that eventually led to the overthrow of the Manchu dynasty began in China at Wuchang on 10 October 1911. After attempting to raise diplomatic and financial support for his revolution in the USA, Britain and France, Sun returned to China in December 1911.

In Nanking a republican government had been established. On 29 December 1911 it elected Sun as the first (provisional) president of China. However, Sun's attempts to gain international support failed; foreign powers saw General Yüan Shih-k'ai as the best person to become president of China. He had helped crush the anti-foreigner Boxer Rebellion (1900–01), and, moreover, he had a powerful army. Yüan received a favourable coverage in the British press, unlike Sun. For example, G. E. Morrison of *The Times* was an adviser to Yüan Shih-k'ai's government, and his reporting alienated sympathy from Sun Yat-sen. When he returned to Britain, Morrison expressed his regret to Sun's friend Dr Cantlie, acknowledging that he was mistaken about Sun's character and his mistake might well have changed the history of China.[1]

In order to avert civil war, Sun resigned the presidency after 45 days in favour of Yüan Shih-k'ai. The T'ung Meng Hui was transformed into the Kuomintang. However, Yüan proved to be no democrat. The parliamentary system broke down because of a power contest between Yüan Shih-k'ai and Sung Chiao-jen (the leader of the first Kuomintang's majority in parliament). Yüan arranged Sung's assassination and illegalised the Kuomintang. Sun (whom Yüan had made Director of Railways) was forced to flee to Japan.

In December 1915, Yüan issued an order to restore the monarchy and proclaimed himself 'emperor'. Sun Yat-sen issued an 'Anti-Yüan Manifesto'. In March 1916, Yüan was compelled to rescind the monarchy. Sun left Japan for China, arriving in Shanghai in May. On 6 June 1916 Yüan died of illness in Peking.

China then gradually disintegrated into warlordism; she was not to experience democracy in the twentieth century. Sun might have been able to implement it had he had Western backing. Yüan Shih-k'ai was more respected by the Western powers in 1911, but today he is not revered as is Sun Yat-sen whose charisma, idealism and unusual political vision have earned him a lasting place in Chinese history. The poor judgement of the foreign powers helped to prevent Sun from implementing his ideas.

Direct democracy and local self-government

Nevertheless, after Yüan's death Sun tried to rebuild democratic government in China. In July 1916 he delivered a speech on 'Self-Government as the Basis of Reconstruction' at a meeting of the Arcadia Forum at Chang's Garden in Shanghai. There Sun welcomed his fellow countrymen, members of Parliament and leaders of various occupations whom he had not seen during three years of exile. As the task of reconstructing the country now seemed a viable prospect, Sun wanted to influence Chinese thinking on the matter.[2]

The foundation for national reconstruction, Sun urged, should be local self-government and the model for it was to be found in Cleveland City in the USA. Sun showed his audience a chart of this latest pattern of self-government. America, Sun informed his audience, had become an independent nation through the will of the early settlers after waging a war for seven years. The settlers were by nature independent and self-governing. They were composed of Puritans and other elements who, dissatisfied with conditions in Europe, had bravely left their homelands. As a result, the foundation of their political structure was firmly laid in popular sovereignty. Sun observed, however, that talented people in America prefer to devote their lives to industrial enterprises rather than to politics. The central government was strong in personnel but the local governments were poorly manned. Consequently the system of self-government was deteriorating. Sun commented that a Dr Goodnow, who had been a political adviser to the late Yüan Shih-k'ai, had become a blind believer in monarchism because he had seen enough of the corruption of local self-government in America.

However, Sun told his audience that when, a few years earlier, an American coastal city had been swept away by a tidal wave, its inhabitants, not wishing to rebuild it themselves, had commissioned several people to do the task and had thus achieved the most successful results. This system was called the commission system and had been adopted by more than a hundred cities. There was therefore in the United States an upsurge of public confidence in the commission self-government system because able people were willing to serve in it.

Sun had discussed this phenomenon with a Chinese student who was returning from America and who happened to be Sun's fellow-passenger on his voyage home.[3] Sun asserted that just as the existence of greedy Confucian scholar-officials did not invalidate Confucian ideas, so, despite its limitations, most Americans had faith in the principle of popular sovereignty. Therefore Cleveland City in 1913 started on the system of local government and had met with remarkable success. Sun wished to introduce this model to the Chinese.

Sun explained how the people elected 26 representatives to the District Assembly that legislated for Cleveland City. The people also elected a Magistrate who directed six bureaus in accordance with the laws passed by the Assembly. The bureaus were concerned with the Judiciary, Administration, Public Welfare, Finance, Public Safety and Public Utilities. Under this local self-government system the powers of the people were considerable. In addition to the power of election they now had the power of recall. They could change the actions of the District Assembly. Sun explained to his audience that in the past its members could be bribed by capitalists to act contrary to the public interest. The people of Cleveland City themselves, if of a sufficient proportion, could make their own laws and nullify those from the District Assembly if contrary to public opinion. Sun argued that just as the citizens of Cleveland had the power of recall and initiative so should the Chinese.

According to Sun, many Chinese students returning from America knew of the commission system but not the Cleveland system which had only been in operation for three years and was not included in the college curricula. Sun believed Cleveland to be the best system for China.

Sun argued that the 'hsien' ('district' or 'county') should be the unit of popular sovereignty. China had over 2000 districts and when Mongolia and Tibet had been developed this number would be increased to over 3000. These would be like 3000 foundation stones on which a skyscraper of a nation could be constructed. Each of the 3000 districts would elect a delegate who would form the National Assembly and elect the President of the Republic. They would exercise the right of amendment with reference to the legislation of the central government. This right represented the direct power of the people in national affairs.

To this aim, training schools in local self-government should be established. When self-government had shown successful results, the people were to be given the right of exercising their direct political power. For the present, men with foresight should undertake to enlighten them and prepare them for the adoption of this new system of government. Thus Sun, by 1916, was expressly promoting the idea of local self-government on the model of Cleveland City in the USA. It is possible that he was enlightened as to the nature of Cleveland City's local self-government by the student who had been studying in the USA and whom he met on his voyage home. He certainly made a point of mentioning this. However, it is also likely that Sun's voracious appetite for news of developments in the West resulted in his reading or hearing about developments in Cleveland City while he was in Japan

Sun's ideas on local democracy are significant as Taiwan's democracy was later built upon it (however, in Taiwan the rights of recall, initiation of legislation and referendum have not been implemented although Taiwan's constitution provides for them). From the late 1970s mainland China has also been democratising at the local level beginning with village committee elections. The villagers now have right of recall.[4] China may well have been influenced by Taiwan's model of village elections (but of course would never acknowledge this expressly). Therefore Sun's theory of local self-government is important.

The above-quoted speech of Sun Yat-sen on building up democracy first from local electoral units has been ignored by commentators on Sun's thought. The scholar Corinna Hana, for example, noting how Sun's ideas on democracy as expressed in 1905 had changed by 1924 to include an emphasis on direct democracy, has suggested Sun acquired his ideas on this from a magazine, *Chien-she*.[5] This was published monthly from 1919 until 1920. Like many of the new pamphlets of that time it was inspired by the May Fourth Movement. This expressed Chinese patriotic indignation at Japan's being given concessionary rights over Shantung (formerly held by Germany) at the Paris Peace Conference in 1919. *Chien-she* was a party organ but not all contributions were from Kuomintang members and only one article (on industrial planning) was actually written by Sun Yat-sen. He did not write on democracy in *Chien-she*. However, some of his supporters did.

This magazine contained translations by the brilliant intellectual Chu Chih-hsin of William E. Rappard's *The Initiative and Referendum in Switzerland* and Jonathan Bourne's *The Function of the Initiative, Referendum and Recall*. Chu Chih-hsin argued in the *Parliament's Character of Non-Representation and the Method for Improvement* that representative democracy as practised in the West does not reflect the will of the people. Sun Fo translated Lawrence Lowell's treatise *Public Opinion and Popular Government* while Liao Chung-k'ai translated Delos F. Wilcox's *Government by all the People* and argued against Western forms of representative democracy.

Did Sun acquire the idea of representative democracy from the Western writings that appeared in *Chien-she* as Hana suggests? The answer must be that he did not. However, they may have been reinforced by *Chien-she*. As has already been shown, Sun expounded on local direct democracy in 1916: three years prior to the publication of *Chien-she*.

1917

In the summer of 1917, Sun's *The Question of China's Survival* was published. It was later translated into English, entitled *The Vital Problem of China*. It was actually written by Chu Chih-hsin but voiced some of Sun's ideas, notably his antagonism towards imperialism, particularly that of Britain. Therefore, according to Sun, she did not merit China's support in the war against Germany.

After China severed links with Germany in March 1917, Sun Yat-sen and the German government established contact as they had a mutual interest in overthrowing the Peking government. In September 1917 a military government in Canton was established. Sun was elected as its Grand Marshall and received German financial aid for his government. Whether Sun supported Germany in order to gain financial advantage, or whether he genuinely believed his argument against China's entry into the war, is impossible to ascertain.

In October 1917 the Bolshevik Revolution in Russia produced another potential ally for Sun who promptly sent Lenin a letter of congratulations.

By 1921 Lenin was making overtures to him.[6] (The British Foreign Office had noted Sun's sympathy with Bolshevism the previous year.[7]) Before Sun consolidated his support from any ally however, dramatic developments changed the course of his life and gave him breathing space to think and write.

The International Development of China

In May 1918 Sun found he was outmanoeuvred by local militants and politicians who reorganised the Canton government. Sun was no longer the Grand Marshal of Canton; he became only one member of a seven-man Military Commission, and had little power.

Sun turned his misfortune into an advantage. He left Canton and settled down in Shanghai with his wife Soong Ching-ling (whom he had married after divorcing his first wife from an arranged marriage). There, at 26 Rue Molière in the French concession, Sun wrote out his first plans for China's future. These included his *The International Development of China* which was eventually published in 1921. Sun wrote it in English as he hoped Western political leaders would read it. He argued that if the foreign powers cooperated and invested in China's modernisation they would benefit as well as China. He sent copies of his book to their various representatives. However, since his scheme would have involved an investment of millions of dollars daily in China, the foreign powers approached, including the United States, dismissed it as unrealistic.[8]

The Western powers were short-sighted. Sun's vision, like most daring designs, needed to be drawn down to practical dimensions. However, in essence, Sun's plan of foreign investment benefiting both China and the West was sound. It was not implemented due to the Western powers' lack of vision, not his own. Today they have awakened to China's enormous investment potential. Sun's *The International Development of China* could be seen as anticipating Teng Hsiao-p'ing's policy of opening up China to foreign capital (in the late 1970s).

Sun's idea was 'to make capitalism create socialism in China so that these two economic forces of human evolution will work side by side in future civilisation.'[9] Sun believed that all industry that was better developed by private enterprise should remain in private hands, encouraged by liberal tax laws, the abolition of internal taxes and improved transport.[10] However, unlike Teng, Sun believed that only industry which could not be developed privately should be developed as national undertakings for which foreign capital would have to be invited, foreign experts enlisted and 'gigantic methods' should be adopted.[11] These state-owned industries would be managed for the benefit of the whole nation by foreign experts who would employ and train Chinese. When the capital and interest of the national undertaking were paid off, the Chinese government would have the option of employing either foreigners or Chinese to manage the concern as it thought fit.

Sun argued that to attract foreign capital the most remunerative projects that met the most urgent needs of the nation should be selected. Therefore Sun advocated the building of a great northern port (on the Gulf of Bohai where it would not freeze in winter), which would be linked to the rest of China by thousands of miles of railways and canals. All transport and communication systems would be improved, including those of the telephone and telegraph. China's great rivers, under Sun's scheme, would be made more navigable. Showing foresight (with regard to the Three Gorges dam project) Sun argued:

> To improve the Upper Yangtze, the rapids should be dammed up to firm locks to enable crafts to ascend the river as well as to generate water power.[12]

China's vast resources of coal, iron, oil and copper as well as other minerals were to be exploited by national undertakings. Sun stated that China would need foreign help to develop industries which provided for personal needs, such as housing (which Sun considered in future should be more concerned with comfort than with ancestral rituals), food, clothing and the printing industry which provided man with intellectual food. Sun even envisaged China as a car-owning society (foreign experts and capital were to be used to manufacture automobiles of all types). For this a million miles of road would be laid and the oil industry exploited: 'The Chinese are a stagnant race...China, in order to catch up with modern civilization, must move!'[13]

Sun also had plans for colonising Tibet, Mongolia and Sinkiang. Sun's *The International Development of China* may have been rejected by short-sighted foreign powers, but the National Planning Commission, established in China in 1941, was directed to work out Sun's projects in detail.[14] Sun's ideas may have eventually borne fruit in the tax-free zones for international investment established in Taiwan in the 1960s and later in China in the 1980s.

At the end of *The International Development of China* Sun expressed concerns over the designs of the Japanese militarists on China. It was about this that Sun spoke to students during the May Fourth Movement. Sun was not a leading participator in the movement.[15] It is probable that the French had given him permission to stay in Shanghai on the condition that he remained politically inactive. However, by the summer of 1919 Sun realised that with the help of students and intellectuals he could regenerate his party.

In October 1919 Sun, speaking to students in Shanghai, first publicly denounced Japan's Twenty-One Demands for concessions in China (in 1915 Japan had presented these to the Peking government which would virtually have lost its sovereignty had it agreed).

In 1920 Sun was openly supporting the New Culture movement which advocated the abandonment of the traditional cultural style of Chinese writing, the spread of literacy and the politicising of the masses. In January 1920 he announced that: 'The success of the revolution... must depend on a change of thought... the new culture movement is really the most valuable thing.'[16]

Nevertheless Sun still oscillated between elitism and populism. The former is clearly evident in Sun's *The Psychological Reconstruction of China* which was published in 1919. It showed that in 1918 Sun had not supported the Chinese students' campaign to modernise the Chinese written language.[17] However, as has been shown above, by 1920 he had come to recognise the propaganda value of the vernacular.

The Psychological Reconstruction of China

Sun wrote his Programme of Psychological Reconstruction when he had a period of rest and reflection in Shanghai in 1918. Sun's problem was to change the traditional political behaviour of the Chinese but this meant introducing political activities partly alien to the Chinese tradition and which therefore could not be learned by way of gradual inheritance.

What happens when an attempt is made to graft the new political forms of society on to an alien tradition? Decades after Sun's death the distinguished English political philosopher, Michael Oakeshott describes two methods:

> When a manner of attending to arrangements is to be transplanted from the society in which it has grown up into another society (always a questionable enterprise), the simplification of an ideology may appear as an asset... There is, of course, an alternative method: the method by which what is exported is the detail and not the abridgement of the tradition and the workmen travel with the tools – the method which made the British Empire. But it is a slow and costly method.[18]

Sun was a man in a hurry. He had to choose an abridgement of a traditional manner of behaviour. Indeed he synthesised ideas from both Western and Chinese traditions and produced a political system not implemented by any society. Whether or not Sun produced an ideology is perhaps a question of semantics for a definition of an ideology is perhaps an ideological question in itself.

What seems clear, however, is that Sun's system of thought did not capture support as have the more successful ideologies of Communism and Fascism. These in their multitudinous forms have had more temporary lives but still had a more cohesive and galvanising effect than did Sun Yat-sen's thought. It could be argued that had Sun been militarily successful he could have imposed his system on the Chinese people. However, Sun himself believed that his failure lay in the rejection of his ideas:

> ...unfortunately, the Revolution was scarcely completed when the members of our party unexpectedly turned out to be of a different opinion from myself, considering my ideas too elevated and unattainable for the reconstruction of modern China.[19]

To obviate this problem, Sun wrote his *Programme of Psychological Reconstruction* which was published in 1919. However, it could be argued that Sun's approach to the problem was inappropriate. Sun Yat-sen's theory of thought and action, delivered initially in the form of lectures to the Kuomintang, appealed more to the reason than the emotions of the listeners. Sun Yat-sen did not employ, as did Communist and Fascist leaders, simplified assumed universal truths that incorporated the whole cosmic system. These truths were put over by Communists and Fascists with methods using myth and symbol, rhythm and repetition, that appealed to the imagination which resulted in galvanised action. In attempting to appeal to reason, Sun was inviting doubt and reflection: the very modes of thought he was wanting to dispel.

Sun believed that part of his problem lay in the essential passivity of the Chinese people. They had long been imbued with the paralysing ancient notion that to know is easy but to act is difficult. Contrary to popular belief, Sun pointed out that this idea was not really attributable to Confucius who had said: 'If the people are capable of action, let them proceed along its path: but if not, then make them first of all understand this truth.'[20] Sun argued that this saying showed that the Sage foreshadowed this theory.

Sun asserted also that the Ming scholar Wang Yang-ming had led the Chinese astray by teaching the unity of knowledge and action. Sun had initially attempted to inspire his comrades with Wang Yang-ming's teaching but found it did not overcome the Chinese inability to act. Sun argued that Yang, in speaking of the functional unity of action and knowledge, still mistook the difficult for the easy:

> Instead of starting with the habit of 'action without consideration, acting according to custom, without reflection, and continuing on their path, throughout the whole of life, without understanding its purpose', people became irresolute and fell under the influence of the theory of Wang Yang-ming.[21]

The key to this passage is no doubt 'acting according to custom'. Sun wanted to alter the traditional Chinese behaviour but not of course to encourage thoughtless irresponsible action. The activity with which he was concerned was political activity which, as Michael Oakeshott has demonstrated, is essentially traditional and difficult to alter. Sun Yat-sen's method of changing Chinese behaviour was to write lectures for the Kuomintang arguing that far from knowledge being easy and action difficult the reverse was true. He felt that the Japanese had achieved their reform in spite of Wang Yang-ming's influence and not because of it. In Sun's view, the Japanese were more enterprising than the Chinese:

> The majority of the reformers of Japan, probably had no conception of the problem which stood before them, but the reforming of Japan proved a brilliant success, thanks to the enterprise of the Japanese. Things are otherwise with China: when the Chinese feel the necessity of reform, they must first of all comprehend its full significance, and, if they are not able to do so during the course of their whole life, death will come before their work at the application of reforms can begin.[22]

Moreover, as Sun rightly pointed out, the teaching of Wang Yang-ming could not be applied in all circumstances. However, neither, it might be argued, could Sun Yat-sen's. The questions crucial to his argument were the nature of political activity, and how much knowledge is required by most participants of it.

Sun attempted to demonstrate in his lectures that knowledge is more difficult than action. However, it could be argued that none of the arguments he used were precisely like the political activity he wanted to encourage. Moreover, in appealing to his audience's thinking processes and not strongly to their feelings, he did not galvanise his supporters as did the Communists, who had entered his party, were later to achieve on a wide scale.

As Treadgold has noted, John Dewey may have told Sun that Westerners believe that action is easy but it: 'need not necessarily be concluded that Sun was a follower of Dewey. The liberal missionary ethos was one of eternally 'doing' and there was a strong pragmatic streak in Protestant modernism.'[23]

Sun opened his demonstration of the ease of action with a consideration of acts involved in nutrition. However, in the *Memoirs of a Chinese Revolutionary* which was a translation in 1927 of Sun's *Programme of Psychological Reconstruction* (wherein his theory of thought and action are to be found), the translator has placed the chapter on the use of money first, whereas in the original Chinese the chapter on nutrition is the initial subject (as it is in the Cult of Sun Wen, translated by Wei Yung in 1919). Treadgold suggests the translator was obviously writing with the needs of the Canton–Moscow entente in mind.[24] This may be so, particularly as the translator has rendered Sun's title of the chapter 'The Use of Money' as 'Labour and Money'. Unfortunately the translator is anonymous and the publishers of *Memoirs of a Chinese Revolutionary* (Hutchinson) have no record of his name. It would therefore be difficult to find out more about the translator (Sun did not of course provide a Marxist analysis of history in terms of class struggle and economic determinism in his chapter on finance). Whatever the political views of the translator they have not significantly altered Sun's meaning.

In the original Chinese version, then, Sun concerned himself first with the problems of cooking and nutrition. Sun believed that the action of cooking preceded the theoretical knowledge of it. He pointed out that without understanding why, the Chinese have practised culinary skills that have surpassed those of other nations. Since to Sun a nation's culinary art is an indication of its civilisation, China was indeed highly civilised. The popularity of Chinese cooking in the West showed that. Moreover, it was not only a question of the variety of textures and flavours, but also the Chinese had without consciously being aware of it, produced a culinary tradition that is essentially nutritious. The Chinese could learn from their culinary achievement and appreciate it was easier to practise it than to fully comprehend the theory behind it. Indeed Sun's nationalist pride shines throughout his lectures on thought and action.

In his chapter on nutrition, Sun also concerned himself with the instinctual knowledge of eating which every animal possessed. Moreover, the body 'knew' the mystery of how to digest food. Yet it could be argued that neither example was an appropriate analogy for showing the ease of political action. More comparable was Sun's example of the question of food production and distribution (with which he had been concerned at an early stage in his career).[25] Sun argued with reference to the example of Germany in the First World War that knowledge of the most effective methods of food distribution at a national level is difficult to obtain while it was easier to manage food at a local level. Sun implied that only a few, such as himself, could devise a plan on a national scale.

In his next chapter on finance Sun argued that it is easy to spend money but difficult to appreciate the real significance of currency, its laws and history. He then gave a version of it: that the introduction of money had played an important part in the growth of civilisation which had grown up by three stages; the production of necessities, the production of conveniences and the production of luxuries which has been made possible by the invention of machinery. Sun pointed out that when this last was possessed by only a wealthy few they could exploit the poorer majority. Yet they would also not be able to understand the system in which they were immiserised. It was the task of governments to understand how economies should be regulated. Sun was undoubtedly right in arguing that understanding economic development is extremely difficult and few people, if any, possess this knowledge. His implication that he himself did, shows the elitism of his thought.

Sun then concerned himself with another form of activity which, like cooking, is learned traditionally: that of language. Sun argued that the Chinese, when learning to write, studied the characters but not the theory of grammar. Here again, however, Sun used an example of pragmatically acquired knowledge: the action and knowledge are combined. Indeed, the theory is difficult to abstract from the practice. Certainly the theory is not worked out beforehand. This is another example of a traditionally acquired form of knowledge. However, Sun's objective was to give the Chinese an abridgement and synthesis of traditions, which was tantamount to a political grammar never before practised.

Sun's next concern was architecture which, like cooking and grammar, was, in China, a traditional activity. Sun argued that the Chinese could build houses well before the West introduced the science of architecture. However, here again, Sun was really concerned with pragmatic knowledge. Moreover, he was incorrect in arguing: 'China up to this day has no architecture. Chinese houses are not built according to the plans of architectural science.'[26]

It is true that Chinese houses were not built according to the Western methods and conformed to the laws of geomancy rather than to explicit architectural rules, since the builders handed down their knowledge orally and through demonstration. Thus Chinese houses were very similar. However, there was at least one attempt to expound the techniques of Chinese architecture. Still extant is a treatise, written in 1103, 'The Ying tsao fa shih', *The Method of Architecture*, which was printed in accordance with imperial command to supersede a handbook of the same title which was compiled by the Board of Works seven years earlier. Its author was Li Chieh. However, the existence of the treatise does not refute Sun's theory that generally house-building in China was an unreflective traditional activity, easier to practise than to understand in abstraction. Sun's problem was that he was introducing a new political architecture to China.

Sun also pointed out that China, in the past, had built huge ocean-going ships without technological knowledge later gained from the West. Likewise, the greatest architectural achievement in China, the Great Wall, was built more by the force of necessity rather than extensive reflection. An architect today would certainly have to spend a long time planning and costing such a feat. Similarly, Sun argued, canals have been built without the benefit of much knowledge of civil engineering. These examples demonstrate that action is often easier than understanding.

Sun used China's invention of the compass, while still ignorant of the nature of electromagnetism, as an example of what can be done without full comprehension. Thousands of years later, the properties of electricity are appreciated and more fully utilised. Everyone can use electricity, few can understand really what it is. Likewise the Chinese, Sun pointed out, produced porcelain before the West developed the complexity of its chemical manufacture. Also, China's achievement in devising printing, gunpowder, silk and tea could be used to show how China could achieve things through action without comprehensive knowledge. Sun rounded off his demonstration of the difficulties of knowledge by referring to Darwin's discovery of evolution and Newton's theory of gravity. These theories, concerned with time and space, were not arrived at easily.

Sun's lectures on knowledge and action were underpinned by the implicit idea that knowledge was not only very difficult but needed to be possessed by only a few people. The rest, like troops following generals, needed to have little comprehensive knowledge of the task of the army in order to function. In Sun's lectures, an elitist stance was already apparent. However, it could be argued that it was a realistic one. Sun was concerned with revolutionary action and with the reconstruction of the political and economic life of the country. To fulfil such a task, the revolutionary should follow the leaders with unhesitating obedience. However, it could be argued that elitist leadership is suitable for revolutionary activity but it is not appropriate for the construction of a democracy.

The problem with Sun's lectures, moreover, is that he did not distinguish between the different forms of knowledge: the skills pragmatically acquired, innate knowledge, theoretical knowledge, and activity that could and should be planned beforehand.

The classification of certain forms of knowledge mentioned by Sun Yat-sen as being pragmatically acquired was made by Hu Shih in his criticism of Sun's theories of thought and action. Hu Shih was a disciple of the pragmatist John Dewey and naturally identified many of Sun's examples as being of a pragmatic nature. Both Hu Shih and John Dewey visited Sun Yat-sen in Shanghai, where the latter had recently completed his writings on thought and action (the book was finally published in the spring of 1919). Hu Shih stated that Sun Yat-sen's belief that his revolution failed because his supporters were paralysed by traditional passive acceptance of the difficulty of action, which Sun aimed to transform, was a reflection of Sun's own noble and forgiving character.[27] The Revolution failed, Hu Shih argued, not because men feared to act, but because they acted only in their own selfish interests.

Hu Shih argued that much of Sun Yat-sen's evidence demonstrated how precious and useful is intelligence. However, he feared that in emphasising the difficulty of knowledge, Sun would either discourage young people from learning, or else encourage the cry of 'down with the intelligentsia'. Hu Shih accepted that the Chinese were poisoned by pessimism, but argued that, in the West, knowledge was acquired through action. He asserted that Sun was in error in splitting knowledge from action. Significantly, Sun Yat-sen had not used his own profession, medicine, as an example, since that knowledge was practically acquired. The constitutional theories for which he argued were not the 'Platonic thoughts of savants', but the result of nations' experience. This knowledge was thus experientially acquired. The danger in Sun's theory, according to Hu Shih, was that it discouraged criticism. Therefore Chiang Kai-shek had been able to use it to suppress opposition. The gist of Sun's theory was: 'Obey me, and carry out my programme of national reconstruction'.[28]

Thus Hu Shih put the pragmatist argument, yet in mentioning 'Platonic savants' he brought up a key problem never resolved in political science. Plato wrote *The Republic* after reflection, yet in response to experience. It is doubtful whether he believed it would ever be implemented. Nevertheless his work stands as a timeless reminder of important questions in political science: how to obtain the right people to govern justly. Sun Yat-sen was not unmindful of his work and rightly stated that Plato's *Republic* was still read with profit by students of political science.[29] It is true that Plato was certainly elitist in his theory, but it could be argued that he demonstrated, as Sun would argue, that few people have finely attuned, reflective minds of statesmanlike vision. Sun did not accept that his leaders would be mere salesmen to the electorate, as he saw they often were in the West. Nevertheless, his theory, like Plato's, was susceptible to abuse. It made possible not only a benevolent elitist government, but also a corrupt self-interested dictatorship.

Indeed to Sun and his supporters 'truth' was not yet to be discovered, but lay splendid in Sun's theories. Sun was propounding absolute truth, which some would regard as being inimical to liberal democracy based on scepticism and relativism. Yet in order to gain mass support for action, certain absolute stands do have to be taken. The human condition makes commitment to a stand, even the contradiction of the absolute relativist inescapable. Sun Yat-sen was doing no more than a human being could do in order to give his followers a clear lead and plan to follow. He showed before his death how far he could compromise in the interests of political expediency.

Sun divided people into three groups: the inventors and thinkers; the people who disseminated and agitated; and the performers, those who practised what had been discovered. These latter might have no knowledge. On the other hand, 'everybody can be a theoretician, everybody can be a man of action'. Nevertheless, Sun came down firmly on the elitist side and exalted himself: 'in the building up of a country it is easy to find men of action, but very difficult to find people who can work out plans of reconstruction.'[30]

Sun's political thought by 1919 had thus shown an oscillation between populism (with his concern for direct democracy) and elitism (as expressed in his *Psychological Reconstruction of China*). This was an ambiguity that was ultimately never resolved.

5
Sun's Thought between 1919 and 1924: National Reconstruction

Introduction

In November 1920, Sun Yat-sen returned to Canton from where he wanted eventually to gain control of all China. His political thought between 1919 and 1924 was expressed in works which remained his most important testimony after his death and which elevated the Kuomintang from being a regional to a national party. The May Fourth Movement helped inspire this concern with propaganda. The Bolshevik Revolution also had a major effect on Sun's thought, particularly as he later discovered only Soviet Russia would give him the aid he needed.

In Canton, Sun made overtures to the Western powers for their support. However the USA was not favourably disposed to him since in 1917 he had opposed China's entry on the side of the Allies against Germany. He had claimed that this was not in China's interests. As a result, after the war, his letters to President Wilson and, in 1921, to President Harding, were ignored.[1]

Sun fared no better with Britain. In May 1921 Sun had himself elected President of the Military Government in the South. He published *A Manifesto to the Powers* asking for recognition of his government in Canton as opposed to that in Peking. However, the British Embassy in Peking reported unfavourably to the Foreign Office in London that Sun was losing the support of the Chinese and 'the belief is growing that his acceptance of the Presidency was equivalent to political suicide'.[2] In Hong Kong the government forbade the Chinese to celebrate Sun's inauguration as President or to contribute to a fund for Sun since his government was 'in imminent danger of bankruptcy'.[3]

Britain believed that Sun's government would weaken the Chinese central government which she, the USA, France and Japan had agreed to strengthen at the Washington Conference of 1921–22. Nevertheless, the Western powers might have seen that they were driving Sun into the arms of Soviet Russia and that his plans for China's international development were in the West's interests.

Sun wanted eventually to reconquer all of China beginning with a northern expedition from Canton. However, his commander of the Canton forces, Ch'en Ch'iung-ming, opposed the policy as being too ambitious. Sun took away his command. As a result in June 1922 Ch'en turned his guns upon Kwan-yin Shan, a hill near Sun's headquarters. Sun's notes and manuscripts which represented the mental labour of years and hundreds of foreign books which he had collected for reference were all destroyed by fire.

In 1923, lacking support from the West, Sun concluded the Sun–Joffe agreement with Soviet Russia whereby Sun was to receive Russian military and financial aid in return for allowing Chinese Communist members to join the Kuomintang on an individual basis. Sun was not a Communist but, as his lectures on Nationalism and Livelihood in 1924 show, his allying with Soviet Russia did influence his thought.

Despite his scripts being destroyed Sun was determined to reorganise the Kuomintang's attack on the minds of the Chinese people. In 1923 Sun wrote an article entitled *The History of the Chinese Revolution*, in which he gave a detailed account of how his followers had failed in their revolutionary work of building a modern state according to his Three Principles. This review led him to re-examine his revolutionary programme and to set out clearly the stages of the revolution in an updated version of his *Fundamentals of National Reconstruction* which he had written in 1905. The new version of the *Fundamentals* expounded Sun's revolutionary programme in 25 articles. It is of particular interest to those who would graft a form of liberal democracy on to a previously oppressive regime in a very short time. It was made public on 12 April 1924 after the reorganisation of the Kuomintang. This chapter will consider the *Fundamentals*, and the following chapters will examine the Three Principles.

The Fundamentals of National Reconstruction

The programme of the *Fundamentals of National Reconstruction* was to consist of three stages: military government, political tutelage and then constitutional government. The military government was to be the destructive phase, involving the overthrow of the Manchu dynasty and the enforcement of martial law. The period of political tutelage was the reconstructive stage, in which the people would be educated in their civic rights and obligations.[4] The concept of tutelage may well have derived from Sun's reading an article by 'L' when he was in London in 1896. Sun published a reply to 'L' whose mysterious identity is discussed in Chapter 2.

When the provinces had well-established self-governments, periods of constitutional rule involving the Five-Power government would be introduced for the whole country.[5] Sun originally emphasised his idea of political tutelage to refute Liang Ch'i-ch'ao's argument that a period of 'enlightened despotism' would best prepare the Chinese people for constitutional monarchy. From 1905 until 1923 Sun held that the period of tutelage should involve the provisional constitution and last for only six years. This change of plan to one-party rule in 1924 will be discussed later. Sun stated that the period of political tutelage was to begin in a province as soon as the military stage came to an end. The Government was to send persons 'trained and qualified through examination' to assist the people in the preparation for self government.[6]

A district could elect representatives to legislate in order to become self-governing after the census of the district had been taken and a survey of the land completed. Training was to be given to the citizens to enable them to exercise their powers of suffrage, recall, initiative and referendum. In accordance with the Principle of Livelihood, each district government was to tax private land at the landowner's assessment, and expropriate on that basis if it wished.[7] Any unearned increment for the land was to be set aside for the people of the district. Revenue thus received, with land tax and the products of the land, forests, lakes and minerals, would belong to the local government and be used for public enterprises, the care of the young, poor, sick and relief of disasters.[8]

Every district was to elect a representative to an assembly to participate in the nation's political affairs.[9] All the officials and candidates in central and local government could only hold their positions after either passing public examinations or being judged qualified by the central government. Constitutional government would commence in the province when all its districts attained self-government.[10] The Assembly of the People's Representatives could elect a governor to supervise self-government in the province, subject to the national government's direction. There was to be, however, an equilibrium between local and central government, and no inclination to either centralisation or decentralisation.[11] The province was to link the national and district governments.

In giving direct democratic rights to the people at the local and provincial levels, Sun made it clear that he was not arguing for federalism and decentralisation which involves giving power to local bureaucrats and to the people.[12] Provided communications were good, the government of a large country like China could control it; constitutional government would prevent autocracy. It is, however, difficult to comprehend how Sun's idea of giving power to the people at the local and provincial levels would not result in a form of federalism however it may be defined.

To begin the constitutional government the central government was to establish the five 'Yuan' of the Executive, Legislative, Judiciary, Examination and Control. A draft constitution was to be prepared by the Legislative Yuan and published among the people for their comments.[13] When more than half of the provinces in the country reached the constitutional stage, the National Assembly (or 'People's Congress') was to be convened to decide on the Constitution.[14] The National Assembly was to exercise the powers of election, recall, initiative and referendum with regard to the officials and laws of the central government. In accordance with the Constitution, the citizens were to participate in a national election, three months after which the National Government was to resign and hand over its function to a government elected by the people.[15] This would mark the accomplishment of the national reconstruction.

As has been shown in the previous chapter and here, Sun Yat-sen thus placed great emphasis on the importance of local government. His views are remarkably similar to those of Sir Charles Petrie in *The History of Government*:

> Indeed, it is difficult to praise too highly the good sense of the American people in setting its faith so sternly against centralization and in this attitude has lain the political salvation of the country ... In the first place the widely extended local government has in the past prevented the line of division in national politics ever being between those who have and those who have not, and there is no reason to suppose that, in this respect, there is likely to be any great change in the future.[16]

In emphasising the value of local autonomy, Sun was surely guiding all who would create a more democratic society.

Sun may have been influenced by the late Ch'ing experiment with local elections[17] but these did not involve direct democracy. Sun's prime source of inspiration for his theory of local direct democracy was that in the USA as has been argued in Chapter 4.

The idea of local government being a form of political education was not new. This will now be discussed. As Carole Pateman points out in *Participation and Democratic Theory*, J. S. Mill stressed its educational value. However, in his model, the delegates elected under a system of plural voting based on educational attainment were denied the right of legislation which was to be given to a special commission appointed by the Crown. This would not be a situation conducive to participation: '...If a predetermined elite are to gain political power, why should the majority ever be interested in discussion?'[18]

In contrast, Sun's form of local autonomy seems to offer the people more opportunities for participation in decision-making than have ever been. But the people were not only to have the right to vote, but to recall representatives, initiate legislation and hold referenda.

Since Schumpeter in 1944 in *Capitalism, Socialism and Democracy* attacked the supposed classical doctrine of democratic theory for ascribing an empirically unrealistic participatory decision-making role to the people, theorists have hotly debated the place of participation in democratic theory. A number such as Dahl and Sartori have argued that it is not of central significance and that increased political participation by the masses is in fact a dangerous step towards totalitarianism. Dahl argues that the lower socio-economic group are those who are not now politically active and, since they are more authoritarian in their attitudes, learnt from the workplace, they should not be encouraged to participate in politics. Sartori argues that we should not accept the apathy of the lower socio-economic groups as something inexplicable (literacy and poverty will not explain it), and appreciate that the disillusion of the ordinary man with the democratic system is because classical democratic theory has unrealistically ascribed to him his role:

> the ingratitude typical of the man of our time and his disillusionment with democracy are the reaction to a promised goal that cannot possibly be reached.[19]

It could, however, also be argued that if the 'ordinary man' has increased opportunities to participate in local politics under a system such as described by Sun Yat-sen, he could not only lose his 'authoritarian attitude' but also his ingratitude and disillusionment that might otherwise be channelled into activities leading to the overthrow of the democratic state. Sun's form of local government was thus a model for civic education, encouraging participation on a scale that has never been, in modern times, practised. But, if Sun's programme for political tutelage emphasised democracy so strongly in local government, how could it have developed into the dictatorship as implemented by Chiang Kai-shek? Sun's *Fundamentals of National Reconstruction* contained a fatal flaw to be magnified by Chiang. As has earlier been stated, from 1905 until 1923 Sun held that the period of tutelage should involve a provisional constitution and last only six years. However, in 1924, probably because of the influence of Soviet Russia, Sun argued for a strong party rule for an indefinite period. In January 1924 Sun argued:

> There is one thing which we may take as our model. Russia is governed entirely by one party, which wields greater powers than parties in Great Britain, the United States and France. At present, we have no state to govern and we can only say we would use the Party to build a state and when it is built, let us govern it.[20]

However, Sun's idea of the period of tutelage under one party rule was not the same as the Communist dictatorship of the proletariat, for it would give the citizens education in their rights of suffrage, recall, initiative and referendum, as well as an understanding of the Principle of Livelihood. Indeed, after Sun's death the Kuomintang introduced a very different form of tutelage from that envisaged either by Sun or the Communists. Thus, whereas Sun's Soviet supporters hoped to swing the Kuomintang to the left, this alteration of Sun's original *Fundamentals of National Reconstruction* enabled Chiang Kai-shek to maintain a right-wing dictatorship in the name of the Three Principles for 21 years from 1927. Chiang did not provide the political education stipulated by Sun, and he was not restricted by the 1924 *Fundamentals* to a deadline for introduction to full constitutional government. In 1931 Chiang Kai-shek did propose introducing a provisional constitution while yet prolonging the period of tutelage. This constitution made provision for a Presidency of the Republic and would merely have legalised his dictatorship. The organisation that the Communists had hoped to strengthen for their benefit was thus ironically to become Chiang's weapon against them.

Sun's *Programme for Psychological Reconstruction* thus demonstrated an elitism which made the development of an authoritarian movement likely; his subsequent tailoring of the *Fundamentals of National Reconstruction* to suit Soviet demands made the development of a flexible, liberal, political tradition most improbable.

6
Sun's Three Principles of the People: The Principle of Nationalism

Introduction

Sun Yat-sen's lectures on his Three Principles of Nationalism, Democracy and Livelihood were delivered in 1924. First enunciated in 1905, they had been developed by him into a programme which Sun had drafted in 1922 when the manuscript was destroyed by Ch'en Chiung-ming's bombardment of Sun's headquarters. Sun had no time to reprepare his lectures properly; he was terminally ill with cancer. He wanted not only to give his party a fully-fledged political programme, but also to distinguish it from that of the Communists who, after 1923, were able to enter the Party as individuals. Sun's Principles were designed, as he stressed at the end of his third lecture on democracy, to create the people's happiness which he had observed Western governments had been unable to achieve. It is a reflection on Sun's altruism that he was concerned with the happiness of the Chinese nation from which, as a dying man, he was sadly but nobly taking his leave.

'Two-Gun Cohen' has left a first hand account of how Sun Yat-sen delivered his lectures in Canton in 1924:

> He only marked them up in their final form towards the very end of his life. He must have realized that he hadn't long to live and was determined that as many people as possible should hear them from his own mouth. He lectured day after day to students, soldiers, shopkeepers, coolies, anyone who had enough intelligence to grasp his ideas, and a whole lot who hadn't. He knew his people and he kept his lectures simple, speaking a language that ordinary people could understand.[1]

In giving his lectures (in the packed hall of Canton Higher Normal School) Sun was making a heroic effort, being in pain with a low energy level (by the summer of 1924 he could eat only fruit)[2] which meant that his thoughts were not always as well-ordered as he would have wanted.

In his preface to the published version of his lectures on nationalism, writing in March 1924, Sun showed he was only too aware of the imperfections of his lectures; yet he did 'not have the time necessary for careful preparation nor the books necessary for reference'. His lectures were not in his view at all comparable to the material he had originally prepared. Sun therefore urged his comrades to: 'take the book as a basis or as a stimulus, expand it and correct it, supply omissions, improve the arrangement and make it a perfect text for propaganda purposes'.[3]

Shamefully, the Kuomintang never carried out his wishes. Sun's Principles remained in their flawed state providing his enemies with the ammunition of derision. They nevertheless became the 'vade mecum' of the Kuomintang and for a time the revered canon of New China.

Sun's lectures on the Three Principles were given weekly, beginning on 27 January 1924. In written form they each comprise over 20 pages of text. They are composed of six lectures on nationalism, six on democracy but only four on livelihood since Sun was unfortunately unable to finish them. The ideas expressed in the lectures in 1924 were obviously more expanded and complex than those expressed in 1906. The lectures were also more reflective, setting each principle in a detailed historical context and displaying knowledge of a wide range of subjects. Here each lecture of 25 pages will be presented as a précis of two pages.[4] At the end of each set of lectures there will be a commentary.

Lecture 1

Sun began his first lecture on nationalism by explaining what he meant by a principle (a 'chu-i' is often translated as an 'ism' in English). For him a principle was an idea that aroused a faith and thus released a power. Thus he was not lecturing for intellectual reception only but to inspire his audience with a belief that would become a driving force to accomplish his goal of making China a co-equal of the great powers in the world. Sun recognised that during the previous ten years the Three Principles were known by name but were not comprehended fully. Sun argued that his Principle of Nationalism was the doctrine of the state in China. However, it could not be the same in the West since there the state and the nation were not identical as they were in China. Unfortunately the Chinese people did not express loyalty to the nation but to their clans and families (Sun later wanted to build on this loyalty). Thus the Chinese people had become a sheet of loose sand.

States were usually moulded by force but nations were formed through the royal or natural way of blood, livelihood, language, religion and customs. The Han people had shared these common factors other than livelihood. They were thus a single pure race.

Compared with other nations China had the greatest population and the oldest culture, but was the poorest and weakest country owing to her disunity. She had become the fish and the meat while the rest of mankind was the carving knife and serving dish. Japan could be a model for China. The former's fiery national spirit and modernisations enabled her to sit at the Versailles Peace Conference as one of the Five Great Powers. In 1905 in the Russo-Japanese war Japan had smashed the Russian dream of world domination which the world had feared (this book has argued Sun expressed this Russophobia in 1897).

Since that time, however, Russia had experienced a revolution which Sun, perhaps over-optimistically, interpreted as meaning that Russia was now not aiming at world aggression but peace and justice. Because it aimed at destroying imperialism and capitalism there was now a global fear of Russia. Whereas wars had previously been between races there would now be struggles between the poor and weak on one side and the rich and strong on the other, with the Slavic race championing the former.

Inappropriate as it might seem today, Sun concluded by expressing concern that the Chinese population might fall behind that of the European powers who might then swallow her up.

Lecture 2

In his second lecture Sun reflected on what he called the force of natural selection by which many ancient families had disappeared. The Chinese had existed for longer than the four thousand years of authentic history. They were the world's largest and most civilised nation. Thus they could be said to enjoy the blessings of nature (Sun had a concept of nature that was like a life force and included the word 'Heaven' in its composition). However, the work of man could overcome Heaven. Nations were affected by economic and political forces as well as by nature.

Although China had been subjected to the Mongols and the Manchus the race had not been seriously injured. However, there was now the possibility that the Chinese population growth would not keep pace with that of the more powerful countries who might overpower her entirely.

Moreover China had already lost territory to foreign powers (particularly England, France and Japan) who might dismember her. Sun argued that his Revolution of 1911 had made the Powers aware it would be very difficult to take by force a people who could overthrow the Manchus. Economic domination was the more insidious method used. China had now become subjected to foreign economic imperialism in ways of which the Chinese were not aware: through the foreign control of China's customs; the invasion of foreign goods which resulted in indigenous handicraft industries collapsing and indigenous factories which were unable to export their goods profitably because of high export and internal duties. During the Great War, when foreign goods could not be imported into China, Shanghai mills prospered but they collapsed because of lack of protective tariffs when the War ended. The Chinese placed too much confidence in foreign banks which exacted excessive bank charges and yet paid little interest. The Chinese misplaced trust of foreign finance meant that Chinese paper money was unable to circulate in competition with foreign paper money. Foreign freight charges, concession profits and the business of speculation were further aspects of this subtle form of foreign economic domination. As a result of economic imperialism the Chinese people's problems were becoming more pressing, and the country's power weakening. Thus China was in danger of being exterminated by economic and political forces. Since China was subjugated by more than one foreign power, she was not just a colony, but a 'hypo-colony': in a worse position than if she were exploited by just one power.

Lecture 3

In his third lecture on nationalism Sun argued that nationalism was the precious possession that enabled a nation-state to perpetuate its existence and progress.

China had lost that precious national possession. Even the secret societies such as the Hung-men and San-ho-hui had reverted around 1905 to the pro-monarchical idea of the Protect Emperor Society which aimed at keeping the Manchu emperor on the throne. Yet these secret societies had been repositories for Chinese nationalism. When the Manchus subjugated China in the later half of the seventeenth century the Ming scholars first organised themselves into secret societies of nationalist resistance. However, the Manchu emperor inaugurated the examinations that caught the nationalist scholars in the net of government service. Therefore some of the nationalists, realising that the literati were not dependable, turned to the lower strata of society and organised the people whose homes were on the rivers and lakes. Thus the Ming veterans hid China's precious possession in the unlikely place of the roughest, lowest class of the Chinese. There it was transmitted in verbal codes by the secret societies. The Manchus meanwhile prohibited nationalist literature and they revised histories. When the Taiping Rebellion broke out the Hung-men supported it. However because of their ingenuity the Manchus were able to break up the secret societies.

Although the Chinese had lost their national spirit Sun pointed out that other oppressed peoples such as the Jews, Poles and Indians had not lost theirs. China had lost hers, Sun argued, because she had extended her Empire, taking in other states by the peaceful or royal way. Her nationalism then turned into cosmopolitanism as she tried to be supreme over other nations. As a result China could not resist the Manchus.

Sun was not against eventual cosmopolitanism but believed it must be developed after national unity had been achieved and not entered into imperiously. Sun illustrated his argument with a story of a coolie who bought a lottery ticket and hid it in his bamboo pole while remembering the number. When he discovered he had won the lottery and become rich he euphorically and prematurely threw the pole into the sea. Sun believed that the development of nationalism was essential to the continued existence of the nation. Sun asserted that Heaven's preservation of the four hundred million Chinese showed that it had not wanted them to be destroyed. Heaven wanted, Sun argued, the Chinese to further the world's progress.

In conclusion Sun upheld Lenin's idea of supporting the weaker nations. A united China could use Right to overthrow Might and then afterwards could discuss cosmopolitanism.

Lecture 4

In his fourth lecture on nationalism Sun showed the great impact that the Paris Peace Conference and the Russian Revolution had on him. His pride in China's anticipating modern political ideas and his desire to avoid unnecessary violence are also apparent.

Sun argued that many oppressed nations entered the First World War on the side of the Entente because President Wilson's proposal of the self-determination of peoples gave them the hope of future nationhood. China joined them in sending hundreds of thousands of labourers to work for the troops. However, after the War, England, France and Italy realised that Wilson's principle conflicted with the interests of imperialism. The Paris Peace Conference resulted in an unjust treaty that perpetuated the oppression of the weaker nations who nevertheless remained hopeful of independent nationhood.

The War had produced one benefit for mankind – the Russian Revolution. This had begun in 1905 but had not been accomplished. The war brought success to the Russian revolutionaries who were then invaded by the West after the war since they were determined to fight against imperialism and for self-determination. Therefore the weaker nations supported Russia and from its Revolution 'a great hope was born in the heart of mankind'.

Russia had broken with the other races but these, as Lenin warned, were subjugating the rest of the world. They were moreover attempting to dissuade small countries from their national aspirations under the guise of a false cosmopolitanism. True cosmopolitanism, Sun argued, was based on pacifism which was strongly traditional in China and was the reason why there was limited bloodshed during the Chinese Revolution of 1911.

Sun cautioned the Chinese young people against adopting ideas from the New Culture's cosmopolitanism. He urged them to take pride in the fact that peaceful cosmopolitanism, anarchism and communism were ancient Chinese ideals. In fact, observed Sun (in a possible attempt to differentiate the Kuomintang from the Communist party), pure Communism was not Marxism. Communism was practised during the Taiping Rebellion. Chinese political philosophy had been in advance of the West which had only progressed scientifically beyond China during the last two centuries. While China should learn from the West's scientific progress she should also take pride in the fact that her political ideas had been ahead of the West's.

Lecture 5

In his fifth lecture on nationalism Sun discussed the methods by which nationalism could be revived. The first was to awaken the Chinese to apprehension of their perilous position. The fact that she had not earlier appreciated she was in decline showed how understanding was difficult but action was easy. China had to understand that the foreign powers could subjugate China politically, economically and eventually with bigger populations.

The nearest country that could threaten China was Japan with its powerful navy which could easily smash her national defences within days of mobilisation. Here Sun showed an apprehension of Japan which had earlier not been apparent. Further afield the USA with more submarines, destroyers and an educated army could destroy China within a month. Britain, using land and sea forces from Hong Kong, India and Australia, could take over China within two months, while France, with her powerful airforce and using Annam as a base, could within a similar period annihilate China. However, China might not be destroyed by military force but by diplomacy: just a single day's joint decision between Britain, France, the United States and Japan. The Chinese could also be eliminated through economic domination as through limited population growth.

The means by which China could resist disaster were firstly to appreciate the dangers and secondly to unite. The Chinese could build on her family and clan structures, using them, after improving their internal organisation, to form a state. In foreign countries the individuals formed millions of separate units of the state. In China, uniting four hundred million separate units would be difficult; however, welding together four hundred clans would not be such a problem. In China, loyalty to the family and the clan was very strong, often resulting in clan feuding. From it must be developed loyalty to the state. Each clan could rally together all those who belong to it living in its neighbourhood, prefecture, province and eventually the whole country. The fact that there were only about four hundred surnames in China and that the practice of tracing ancestral lines was a strong tradition would facilitate this. Japan, Sun noted, had once united the interests of her feudal princes to form the great Yamato race. As to the economic subjugation of China, Sun advocated using Gandhi's policy of non-cooperation: refusing to work for foreigners, or to use foreign manufactured goods or banknotes, promoting native products, using only Chinese government money and ultimately severing economic relations with foreigners. This upholding of Gandhi's methods shows the strong pacifist leanings of Sun.

Lecture 6

Sun's last lecture on nationalism was delivered on 2 March 1924 in Canton. Sun began with a panegyric of China's ancient virtues. He believed that China had survived other races because of that high moral standing which had enabled her to absorb them. Only if China's ancient morality was recovered could China attain the position she had once had. China had still not lost sight of her old moral standards of Loyalty, Filial Devotion, Kindness, Love, Faithfulness, Justice, Harmony and Peace. Sun again showed concern that the cultural influence of the West had encouraged some Chinese to reject the old morality. Sun argued that the Chinese must preserve what is good in their past and throw away the bad. He deprecated the fact that loyalty had fallen into desuetude as some Chinese seemed to think the removal of the Emperor made it irrelevant. Sun however argued that loyalty to the nation was needed. Sun discussed each of the above-named virtues in detail, noting that Japan's sense of 'faithfulness and justice' in international matters was inferior to China's.

Sun urged that the Chinese recover not only their old morality but also their ancient learning and decried the decline of mental training. Moreover the Chinese should show more concern with their personal culture in the present as well as revere their national great achievement of the past.

In learning from the West scientifically China should learn from Japan's example and copy only the most recent of the West's scientific developments. In this way China would expedite her modernisation which, with a revival of her national spirit would enable her to be a great world power which could unify the world on the basis of her ancient morality and love of peace.

A comparison between Sun's Principle of Nationalism as expressed in 1905/6 and in 1924

In his Principle of Nationalism, Sun's emphasis on racial cohesion based on the concept of 'min-tsu' (meaning 'race') and not 'kuo chia' (with its territorial implications) remained the same from 1905 to 1924. Sun's theory of nationalism was predicated on the basis that a pure Han race existed.[5] This is a debatable assertion although it was more acceptable at the time when Sun was writing. Naturally Sun's nationalism was anti-Manchu in 1905; after the Revolution of 1911 this had become irrelevant and nationalism had been omitted from the programme of the Chinese Revolutionary Party of 1914. Sun probably restored it to being the first of his Three Principles partly owing to the intense patriotism engendered by the May Fourth Movement. As has earlier been discussed, the influence of the Bolshevik Revolution and Lenin's theory of imperialism, the Sun–Joffe agreement of 1923, as well as the fact that by 1924 Sun was losing hope of winning the support of the Western powers was apparent in his hostility to their imperialism. In 1906, Sun did state that foreign countries were looking at China with covetous eyes but he did not specify the countries, criticise their presence in China or give a detailed account of the nature of the economic and political subjugation of China by foreign imperialism. This is probably because in 1906 Sun still hoped to win the support of the foreign powers to his cause.

Sun's nationalism in 1905 was certainly revolutionary and involved violence although Sun did emphasise that the revolution should not result in revengeful killings and that bloodshed should be limited. In his lectures of 1924 Sun expressed admiration for Gandhi's methods of passive resistance to render economic imperialism financially non viable.[6] Thus Sun was still advocating the avoidance of unnecessary violence.

In his first lecture on nationalism in 1924 Sun argued that the Manchus had been absorbed by the Han people.[7] This was in contrast to his stand in 1906 when he argued that the Manchus were as strangers to the Han people. Nevertheless, after 1911 many Manchus did become assimilated into the Han race. However, there is no evidence to support the claim of Chang and Gordon that in 1924 Sun added: 'the equality of ethnic groups to the Principle of Nationalism'.[8]

In 1906 Sun took pride in the fact that China had such a large population. However in 1924 he was expressing anxiety lest China's population growth be outstripped by that of the other Powers.[9]

Sun's third lecture on nationalism in 1924 was concerned with the disappearance of Chinese nationalism into secret societies and with a warning against premature cosmopolitanism.[10] These points were not mentioned in his 1906 speech. Sun's fourth lecture was concerned with the Paris Peace Conference, the dashed hopes of the oppressed nations and their renewed hope in discovering that the Russian Revolution would aid them.[11] Since these historical events had not occurred when Sun gave his speech in 1906 they are obviously not discussed in it.

In 1906 Sun mentioned the problem of the Chinese lack of unity. In 1924 he emphasised this and also proposed a solution that the Chinese should build upon their clan structure to unite China.[12] He further stressed that his Principle of Nationalism was the doctrine of the state in China which it could not be in the West since the state and the nation were not identical as they were in China.[13] Sun did not state this in 1906.

In 1924 Sun gave a detailed discussion as to China's ancient values.[14] In 1906 Sun did remind the Chinese that they were an ancient and civilised people but he did not elaborate on their virtues. Also in Sun's lectures in 1924 there was a pronounced concern with natural selection; both that Nature had smiled on China[15] and also that she might be swallowed up by the foreign powers.[16] Sun's final concern in his lectures on nationalism in 1924 – that China should learn from the latest scientific and technological advances in the West while preserving pride in her own ethnic identity – was not mentioned in 1906.[17]

Thus Sun's six lectures on nationalism in 1924 were naturally far more detailed than the one he gave in 1906. Moreover, because of subsequent historical events his theory of nationalism in 1924 was emphatically anti-imperialist.

A critique of Sun's Theory of Nationalism

It is significant that Sun's First Principle was that of nationalism. He was actively concerned with this from the start of his political career, when he founded the Revive China Society in 1894. At this time his nationalism was of course anti-Manchu and not the anti-imperialism of 1924. Sun actually recorded an awakening desire to free his country when France defeated China over Annam in 1885:

> from the time of our defeat in the war with France, I set before myself the object of the overthrow of the Tai-Tsing dynasty and the establishment of a Chinese Republic on its ruins.[18]

It is however likely that growing up among ex-Taiping rebels, Sun developed a sense of anti-Manchuism much earlier.

Sun believed that nations exist and are identifiable by such factors as common blood, language, religion and customs.[19] Scholars who lived long after Sun, such as Elie Kedourie, have disputed the idea that nations do actually exist.[20] However, Sun's concept of a Chinese Han race was shared by other Chinese leaders and indeed many overseas Chinese who were particularly supportive of Sun's cause. At the time when Sun was writing the idea of the nation had become a vogue concept. Although close examination of the Chinese 'people' reveals differences of blood, language and customs, Sun's idea of nationalism made good political sense, for the Chinese were and still are a stronger nation for being united. Moreover it should be remembered that Sun's concept of nationalism, like that of many nationalist leaders, developed in reaction to foreign oppression.

In his lectures on nationalism in 1924 Sun's attitude to the Japanese, against which the May Fourth Movement's patriotism was partly directed was in fact ambivalent. In his first lecture Sun exalted the fiery spirit of Japanese nationalism as providing an example for the Chinese and prestige for all Asiatic countries.[21] However, in his fifth lecture Sun showed awareness of Japan's expanding army and navy as posing a possible threat to China.[22]

While Sun saw nationalism as an idea that could weld a people together and throw off a foreign yoke, he also saw it in another sense:

that of national pride and awareness of national identity. Sun sought to revive this national spirit which he believed the Chinese had once had, but lost in a premature cosmopolitanism.[23] Thus Sun was arguing that nationalism had existed before the nineteenth century. Scholars such as Elie Kedourie have disputed this.

Nevertheless, any discrepancy between these beliefs might be resolved by arguing that Sun was really describing ancient Chinese patriotism, not nationalism. This Chinese patriotism involved more a pride in achievements and culture than an awareness of nationhood and a desire for unity and independence as such. The sinologist J. B. Levenson has also argued that nationalism in the sense of loyalty to the 'kuo-chia' (or 'country') as opposed to loyalty to the 't'ien-hsia' ('under heaven') did not exist earlier in China. He has delicately traced the changing loyalty in China from allegiance to the latter (which was equivalent to Sun's cosmopolitanism) to loyalty to the former.[24] It was Sun's achievement to harmonise the ideas of 't'ien-hsia', 'kuo-chia' and 'min-tsu'. It was with this last, the idea of the common ancestor that Sun was primarily concerned.

Sun believed that the clan groups should unite and resist foreign domination, possibly by the method of non-cooperation. In playing on the Chinese ancestral loyalties Sun was wisely touching a raw nerve in the Chinese for a fear that could arouse the Chinese was that their ancestral lines might be extinguished by foreigners. The concept of nationhood might not be a concrete one for them but their familial loyalties on which Sun wisely wanted to build were very strong.

Sun also wanted to arouse in the Chinese a pride in these ancient virtues and achievements. He was undoubtedly right in stressing that other nations had not possessed China's ancient values (but wrong in stating that China had taken over other countries peacefully). It was this pride in her culture, Sun believed, that would enable China to learn from the West's scientific and technological achievements without her losing her ethnic identity.

Thus Sun, like the educator, Ts'ai Yüan-pei, the philosopher Feng Yulan and others, was arguing for syncretism: for 'the best in East and West'.

However, Sun did not argue that there was any wisdom in the West other than scientific progress and some political ideas. He came down heavily, nationalistically or patriotically on the side of China when reflecting on pearls of civilisation. As J. B. Levenson puts it:

> The quintessence of wisdom, political, economic and cultural, ancient and modern, Chinese and foreign, is not only commended to China

– it is attributed to China and to China alone, in the form of Sun Yat-sen's 'Three People's Principles'.[25]

Fortified by her ancient virtues and learning China could modernise technologically. She would then recover her national standing and be able to unify the world upon the foundation of her ancient morality and love of peace. China was to aid other disadvantaged nations of the world. These would also be helped to throw off imperialism by Russia. Sun lauded 'The Russian Revolution, a great hope was born in the heart of mankind.'[26] Indeed Sun's lectures on nationalism show an ardent support for Marxist-Leninism which had cooled by the time he gave his lectures on Livelihood later in 1924 when he argued that China needed foreign capitalism and not class-war. By that time he had read Maurice William's *Social Interpretation of History*.

However in praising both China's Confucian heritage and the Bolshevik Revolution in his lectures on nationalism, Sun was expressing ideas that later caused conflict and division within the Kuomintang.

To Sun nationalism held a nation together and enabled it to survive. He believed that this is what had enabled the Jews to continue as a stateless people for nearly two thousand years. He supported Zionism and thought that the Han Chinese were like the Jews in being a racial group with a common blood, religion and culture.[27]

Nationalism therefore to Sun was a positive cohesive force based on pride in culture and heritage: a powerful feeling to be aroused in the Chinese.

7
Sun's Three Principles of the People: The Principle of Democracy

Lecture 1

Sun opened his first lecture on democracy or 'Min Ch'üan Chu-I' given on 9 March 1924 with a discussion on the meaning of the phrase 'the people's sovereignty' or 'Min Ch'üan'. He argued that any unified body of men was called 'a people' and that sovereignty was power and authority extended to the area of the state. Sovereignty was the power to execute orders and to regulate public conduct. When 'people and sovereignty' were linked the result was the 'power of the people'. Government was of the people, by the people and controlled the affairs of all the people. The people's control of the government was the 'people's sovereignty'. It was with this that Sun was chiefly concerned in his lectures which in English are translated as being on the Principle of Democracy. Unfortunately, by March 1924 he had become quite ill and these talks show more digressions of thought symptomatic of a low energy level than do his lectures on nationalism.

Sun first endeavoured to show how the history of man on earth had progressed until the era of democracy had begun. Sun began by describing the initial formation of the earth and the emergence of human life on it. Initially men struggled together against wild beasts. When they had subdued them they had to struggle against the forces of nature. For this man called divine power to his aid and thence developed theocracies. Sun stated that Japan and Tibet were still theocracies. However, as states came into conflict with each other autocracies became the form in which states fought wars. But eventually the people wanted to throw off the control of their monarchs. This first happened in England with

Cromwell's revolution in the seventeenth century, but nevertheless the monarchy was restored in a modified form. A hundred years later the American colonies broke away from England, and became the first country to practise democracy. Ten years later the French Revolution occurred, although it was 80 years before it really succeeded since initially foreign states intervened and the monarchy was restored.

Sun devoted much time to discussing Rousseau's 'Social Contract'. He believed that his ideas of the popular right of freedom was a great contribution to governmental theory.

Sun argued that in 1924 the world had moved into an era of democracy. Although its seeds could be found in ancient Greece and Rome, yet Confucius also held democratic ideas. He said 'When the Great Doctrine prevails, all under heaven will work for the common good.'[1] Mencius had said 'Most precious are the people' and 'Heaven sees as the people see, Heaven hears as the people hear.'[2] Unprincipled monarchs who did not bring the people happiness should be removed. He saw even in his age that kings were unnecessary.

Sun believed that world history was moving towards republicanism. Russia and Germany had recently become republics. The Taiping Rebellion had failed because of the imperial ambitions of its leaders. Sun criticised Yüan Shih-k'ai for having similar aspirations and deplored the fact that there were still military leaders like Ch'en Ch'iung-ming (who had destroyed Sun's headquarters in 1922) who harboured imperial ambitions. Sun believed that republicanism was not only in keeping with the trend of world history but it was the form of government which could unite China.

Lecture 2

In his second lecture on democracy Sun emphasised, perhaps rather surprisingly, that his second Principle of Democracy was equivalent to the second idea of the French Revolution's slogan : 'equality'. The first idea 'liberty' was equivalent to Sun's first Principle of Nationalism since he meant by it national liberty. The third idea of the French Revolution slogan 'fraternity' was similar to Sun's third Principle of Livelihood.

In the West during the previous three hundred years the struggles were primarily for liberty which thus came to the forefront of the West's political lexicon. Western and Chinese youth criticised the Chinese for not having liberty or even a word for it. At the same time foreigners criticised the Chinese for being 'like a sheet of loose sand'. These criticisms were contradictory. The Chinese had too much liberty.

There was a Chinese phrase 'running wild without bridle' but that indicated excessive liberty.[3] To Sun liberty was the freedom 'to move as one wished with an organised group'.

Chinese students had extolled liberty with their cry 'Give me liberty or give me death' but they did not understand what they were talking about. In the West democracy had grown out of liberty which therefore had to be discussed. However, Sun differentiated liberty from democracy and argued that while China needed the second she had had too much of the first. Westerners' experience of particularly harsh autocracy had led them to extol liberty. The Chinese experience of despotism had been less odious and they had experienced its deleterious effects only indirectly since weak imperial rule had allowed foreign subjugation. The Chinese lack of emphasis on liberty did not mean that her political thinking was inferior to the West's but that her historical experience of autocracy was different from the West's. China now had to unify her people for the struggle for national freedom for which personal liberty had to be sacrificed.

Indeed in the West liberty had developed into evil excesses. Therefore the English scholar Mill had proposed his theory of limited personal freedom which did not encroach on others.

Sun's second Principle of Democracy was really the 'people's sovereignty' which meant political equality of all citizens. Thus it was equivalent to the French second slogan of equality. The goal of Sun's plan was 'for the happiness of our four hundred million people'.[4]

Lecture 3

Sun's third lecture on democracy was concerned with equality. This, during the French and American revolutions, had been closely associated with liberty as natural inalienable rights of man. Sun queried, however, whether equality was a natural right. His first lecture on democracy had traced the development of human rights from the primeval period to the present democratic era, but in it Sun had not identified any principle of natural equality.

Slightly digressing, Sun expanded on the lack of equality in Nature. Since the Chinese word for 'equality' is the same as that for 'level' Sun considered the lack of levelling things in nature other than water. The ground was only level when made so by man. Here, probably because his illness impaired his judgement together with a desire to be comprehended by the uneducated in his audience, Sun gave correct but infelicitous examples. He then held aloft an acacia[5] blossom from the vase in front of him and demonstrated that in Nature nothing was created the same, not even the leaves of the flower were identical, nor had any ever existed like them. Dissimilarity was the rule in Nature as was consequently inequality. Here again, possibly because of his low energy level, Sun did not consider how far broad similarities existed in Nature allowing for categorisation, neither at this point did he define equality.

Sun argued that Nature had not made men equal. However, autocracy had pushed natural inequality to artificial extremes. Sun drew a diagram to illustrate how society was divided artificially into a social hierarchy with the king at the top and the commoners at the bottom. The privileged classes had been cruel and unjust to the lower classes who, being ignorant, believed the former's teaching that they had the divine right to rule. In order to counter this doctrine the revolutionary scholars proclaimed that Nature had bestowed the rights of equality and liberty on man.

The idea of the natural rights of man lived on after it had successfully impelled the revolutions against the monarchs. Only recently had people doubted it. Sun drew another diagram to show what he called 'false equality' being imposed on men from dullards to sages. According to Sun every man builds up his career according to his natural endowments of intelligence and ability. If they were all kept down to the same level man could not make progress.

The true equality aimed at in Sun's revolution was that of giving everyone equal political rights.

In Europe social and political inequality had been more extreme than in China where social mobility was possible in a way that the European hereditary hierarchical system prohibited. Therefore in the West there was greater concern for liberty. This had sometimes been pushed to extreme limits with unfortunate results. For example intellectual leaders had in the West organised the labour unions so that they became powerful. However the unions were now expelling these leaders in the name of equality. Sun said there were signs of this happening in China but it was very important that the unions should retain their educated leaders.

Sun recalled that he had once suggested that the people could be divided into three groups: the discoverers, the promoters and the practical men. If these three groups could use each other in cooperation human civilisation would advance rapidly. When intelligent and able men were ready to use their talents for the welfare of others, religions of love and philanthropic enterprises would grow up. However, religious power and philanthropy alone could not remedy all evil. Therefore the Chinese must carry out a revolution, overthrow autocracy, raise democracy and level inequalities. The three categories which he had mentioned should have equal standing and work together in a spirit of service not exploitation. Those with greater intelligence and ability could make thousands of people happy; those with less intelligence could make hundreds of people happy; those with little intelligence or ability could still serve one another and make each other happy.

In this lecture's conclusion can be seen Sun's chief concern: to uplift the lives of the disadvantaged and to inspire the able to use their gifts to serve others. His ultimate goal was the creation of happiness.

Lecture 4

In his fourth lecture on democracy Sun considered the measure of people's rights won by Westerners by their struggle during the previous three centuries. After the War of Independence Hamilton's party had triumphed over Jefferson's in deciding for federalism in America with limited popular sovereignty and a division between the executive, legislature and judiciary. Because the USA had become strong and powerful many Chinese thought that federalism was the answer to China's problems. Sun disagreed, arguing that federalism would encourage the partition of China by the warlords. China's more than twenty provinces had in the past been united when the government had been good, disunited when there had been disorder. The American states had each had their own constitutions and governments before uniting in a federation. In order to copy the American historical model China would have first to divide up into separately governed states and then agree to unite and decide on a national constitution. This would be irrational and make the Chinese mere imitators of the West.

If federalism was properly applied to the Far East, China could unite with other Far Eastern countries in a federation.

The Americans initially achieved only limited suffrage, and as in Europe only recently had full universal suffrage been achieved. Sun emphasised that the French revolution was not immediately successful since it resulted in mob tyranny. Many of the educated and wise leaders were executed. No one dared say that the people did not have intelligence for fear of being regarded as counterrevolutionaries. The groups of violent followers who were left were devoid of clear vision and more easily manipulated. In their disenchantment many gave their support to Napoleon.

However eventually a tide of democracy swept over Europe with state after state taking the democratic road. In Britain the aristocracy had accepted the establishment of a labour party.

Germany had become united by Bismarck's military and political skill. A socialist movement in the late nineteenth century had begun to develop in Germany and should have developed alongside democracy giving rise to a socialist revolution as well as a democratic one. However Bismarck, through a policy of state socialism, weakened the cause of Marxist socialism. Nevertheless, since the First World War the German despotic government as well as that of Russia had been overthrown. Thus democracy in the West had progressed slowly with setbacks.

Sun noted that in some of the northwestern states of America many citizens enjoyed four popular rights: of suffrage, recall, initiative and referendum. The Swiss had achieved three of these (without the right of recall). Sun argued that any complete democracy should grant the citizens the four popular rights. Really all the West had achieved, save in a few areas, was representative government. China had tried this after 1911 but many of the representatives were financially corrupt.

Without the benefit of hindsight (and no doubt influenced by the Sun–Joffe agreement of 1923), Sun rashly asserted that Russia had developed not merely a representative government but an absolute government of the people. He did, however, acknowledge that there was no available data with which to assess it.

Therefore Sun concluded the West still had many problems with their democracy. If China could solve these problems she would be ahead of the West.

Lecture 5

In his last two lectures on democracy Sun endeavoured to find a solution to the problem of democracy. Because of the West's technological superiority over China many Chinese had attempted to follow the Western example politically despite the fact that the West's political advance had not equalled its technological progress. Plato's ideas of over two thousand years ago were still studied by Western scholars who thought they could learn from them. The recent growth of democracy in the West had not been achieved through thoughtful scholarship but by the masses of people moving with the tide. No fundamental method of directing democracy had been worked out beforehand so that Western peoples had met many innumerable difficulties on the road to democracy.

China must follow the world's tendency to democracy but not the Western pattern. Government was like an invisible machine based on the laws of psychology unlike a visible machine based on the laws of physics. However, psychology had only recently developed and had not greatly advanced.

Western governments did however offer experiences from which the Chinese could learn and Western scholarship on it did offer valuable enlightenment. An American scholar had argued that the greatest fear of modern democratic states was an all-powerful government which the people had no way of checking, but yet the finest thing would be an all powerful government in the employ of all the people and working for the welfare of all the people. The strongest government in Europe had been Bismarck's Germany but it had opposed democracy.

A certain Swiss scholar had said that since various nations had put democracy into practice, the power of government had declined. The reason had been the fear on the part of the people that the government might secure a power which they could not control. Hence the people had always guarded against giving their governments too much power. Therefore democratic countries should find a solution for this difficulty, but this would not be solved until the people changed their attitude to the government.

Sun agreed that the people's attitude to a strong government had to be changed; his solution was to make a distinction between sovereignty and ability. Under the republic the people would have sovereignty: they would be like the king. However, not all the citizens had intelligence and foresight. Those that had should be in the government which should be like a chauffeur driving the country like an automobile which was owned by the people. They gave orders for the destination but the chauffeur knew the best way of reaching it.

Lecture 6

In his sixth lecture on democracy Sun developed his metaphor of government being a machine. Westerners spoke of government as machinery and law as an instrument. Moreover many books on government and law were translations from the Japanese which designated government organisations as 'chi-kuan' (organs or bureau). 'Chi-kuan' in Chinese meant also machinery. It had come to replace 'yamen'. Therefore the image of a governmental machine was appropriate. Nevertheless manufacturing machinery was constructed from such material as wood and steel whereas political machinery depended on human beings.

Western political machinery had not kept pace with its advance in manufacturing machinery. The latter could be easily changed and discarded but political machinery could not be easily experimented with and change could involve a revolution. The United States, the pioneer nation of democracy, used practically the same constitution as a century ago yet it would not use machinery that had been made a hundred years earlier. Because of ingrained habits and social structures, machinery made up of human beings was more difficult to change. Western democracies were like early engines which could be advanced but not drawn back. Citizens could not control the men they elected to office whether they turned out to be worthy or incompetent. In machinery control and power were clearly separated. Initially when machinery was invented men did not dare use a machine with too much power for fear that it ran out of control. However, as the construction of machinery developed very powerful machinery could be easily controlled by one man. Now scholars and statesmen were talking of government as a machine and the people as the motive power in the government. In the autocratic era the king had been the motive power and a strong government organisation made it possible for the king to do as he wished.

Although in the democratic age the people were the motive power, they were reluctant to have a powerful government less it oppress them. Therefore there must be a distinction between sovereignty (which the people had) and ability (which the government had). The people should be like an engineer who controlled great machinery.

A high-powered, strong government, given China's large population and resources could achieve much. The people must have the four popular rights of suffrage, recall, initiating legislation and holding referenda. These would be the four controlling rights of the people for direct democracy.

In order for the government to be an effective administrative machine there must be a five-power constitution consisting of the powers of the executive, legislature, judiciary, censorship and civil service examinations. These last two organs were originally ancient Chinese institutions. Britain had eventually copied China's idea of civil service examinations. (In 1921 Sun had made it clear that he wanted political representatives as well as civil servants to be examined by the government organ of the Examination, and that the Control should have power to investigate corruption with the power of impeachment).[6]

In the sixth lecture Sun argued that Western political machinery 'still has many defects, and does not satisfy the desires of the people nor give them a complete measure of happiness'.[7] China with her five powers of government in operation would be able to achieve this.

A comparison of Sun's Principle of Democracy as expressed in 1905/6 and in 1924

In his theory of democracy in 1905/6 Sun did not expand on the whole history of democracy from man's early struggles with beasts and Nature, the developments of theocracy and autocracy and the eventual emergence of the era of democracy as he did in 1924. Neither in his earlier exposition on democracy did he discuss the ideas of Western thinkers such as Rousseau nor the American and French revolutions. However, in 1905/6 Sun did emphasise that China must be a republic since a monarchy causes factionalism. This idea was stressed again in 1924.[8]

The Five-Power Constitution was an important and unique concept in Sun's political thought. As early as 1904 he discussed it with Wang Chung-wei, a lawyer and later a close associate, in New York.[9] In 1905 he first used the phrase 'Five-Power Constitution' publicly when speaking to Chinese students in Brussels, Berlin and Paris. In 1906 he expounded on it, observing that in America there were politicians who were either stupid or corrupt.[10] America's division of powers was an improvement on Britain's unwritten constitution. However, from his study of Western constitutions he had concluded that the three-power constitution was insufficient for the best government. For this were needed two additional organs of government that had existed for centuries in China; the powers of examination and censorship. China's constitution would, therefore, consist of the Executive, Legislature, Judiciary, Examination and Control.

Although Sun was concerned about the problem of men without ability holding office, in 1906 he had not propounded his theory of the distinction between sovereignty (which the people should have) and ability (which the government should have). This was one of the most important new ideas in his theory of democracy as expressed in 1924.[11] Connected to this was his idea of direct democracy; the people were to run the government as easily as they might press a switch to turn on an electric light without understanding how the process worked.[12] Associated with this idea was Sun's further concept which he stressed in 1924: the emphasis on China's need for a strong government.[13] By 1924 Sun was emphasising that the Chinese already had too much liberty.[14] By 'democracy' he meant the 'people's sovereignty',[15] or 'political equality'; he warned that the French Revolution had resulted in mob tyranny which must be avoided in China.[16]

In 1905 Sun made no mention of the National Assembly; however by 1918/19 he did.[17] During the First World War Sun was probably aware that England's government, unlike Germany's, enjoyed the support of the people who controlled it, and that this contributed to her victory. The chaos of warlordism into which China had descended demonstrated to him the importance of the government being powerful yet controlled by the people.[18] Sun therefore propounded his theory of a Five-Power government and National Assembly which controlled it.[19] In 1924, in the *Fundamentals*, he reiterated the idea of the National Assembly having direct control, but in his lectures on the Principles of Democracy he omitted it.

Sun had asserted that when he was in the West in 1896–97 he had observed that Western governments had been unable to give their people full happiness. In 1906 Sun emphasised that the point of his revolution was to achieve this happiness.[20] He amplified this idea in 1924.[21]

A critique of Sun's Theory of Democracy

Sun Yat-sen's democratic programme for China has positive significance for those who would attempt to establish liberal democracy by revolution and those who would improve existing democracies. However, the programme also has some weaknesses, not least because it oscillates between elitism and populism, particularly when his *Fundamentals of National Reconstruction* and 'Principle of Democracy' are considered together. China's form of democracy was to be based on Sun's belief that men could be divided broadly into three groups: the discoverers, the promoters and the operators.[22] Sun's elitism was expressed in his belief that only those of special ability should govern.

However, at the same time Sun showed faith in the Chinese coolies and peasants by arguing that sovereignty should lie with them, and by expressing the populist belief in the people's direct participation in the government by means of election, initiation of legislation, referendum and recall.[23] Yet there is an ambiguity concerning the political power of the people. In local government it is clear that the people are to have the full rights of direct participation,[24] but with regard to government at the national level there was a contradiction in Sun's mind that was never resolved before his untimely death. In his 'Three Principles' Sun came down on the populist side and granted the people their full sovereign rights over the five departments of national government.[25]

However in the Programme for National Reconstruction Sun granted the four sovereign rights to the National Assembly or People's Congress which was composed of representatives from each district.[26] Thus, after his death, the Kuomintang was able to argue that the National Assembly had sovereign rather than administrative power. The 1936 Draft of the Constitution gave the four sovereign rights of the Five-Power government to the People's Congress. The latter therefore had the sovereignty which Sun had wanted to delegate to the people through direct democracy.[27]

The oscillation between elitism and populism was reflected in Sun's epistemology: on the one hand he argued that all can act without previous theoretical knowledge; on the other he argued for academically qualified politicians. He implied that he himself was one of the elite, possessing difficult theoretical knowledge which had been derived from practice but was given to the people in the form of his Three Principles and the Constitution before they practised liberal democracy.

That Sun meant his state to be a liberal democracy is shown not only by the system of checks and balances in the Five-Power Constitution (Figure 7.1), or by the four direct participatory rights of election, initiation of legislation, referendum and recall enjoyed by the people, at least at local level, but also by his declaration in the Manifesto of the First National Congress in January 1924 that liberal rights should be guaranteed:

> The people's right to freedom of assembly, of forming associations, of speech, of publications, of choice of domicile, of liberty of conscience, should be established by law.[28]

However during the period of tutelage, there was to be a Party dictatorship:

> After the political power has been wrested back and the government has been established, the Kuomintang must serve as the central organ for the administration of such political power, so that all counterrevolutionary movements will be suppressed. Only an organised party, and one with authority, can serve as the foundation of the revolutionary masses; only such a body can render this duty loyally to the people of the whole country.[29]

Therefore, the people, instead of learning through action, instead of having practical knowledge of a pluralistic state, of participation in a

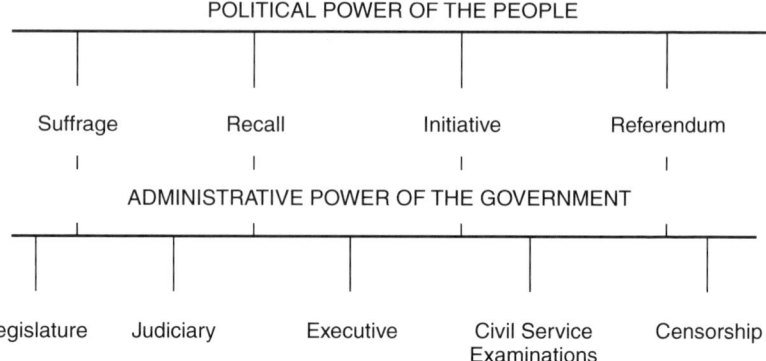

Figure 7.1 The Five-Power Constitution as outlined by Sun in his Principle of Democracy (*source*: Sun Yat-sen, *San Min Chu-1*, tr. Frank Price (Shanghai 1927) p. 354)

liberal democratic conversation, were to listen to the monologue of a one-party state and experience not politics in the sense of bargaining and compromise, but constitutional organisation.

Sun, however, was in a dilemma. China was in political chaos and order was needed to prevent his plans from being swept away. Sun was well-aware of the mob tyranny that resulted from the French Revolution; his mistake may well have been to exalt the Kuomintang above all else instead of subordinating it to the Constitution, legally limiting its powers. It was this weakness that the Kuomintang was able to exploit, enabling Kuomintang members to exalt their Party above all while claiming to be followers of Sun's Three Principles.

The Kuomintang implemented a distorted version of Sun's ideas in Taiwan, establishing a Five-Power constitution with also a National Assembly. This did not have direct democratic control over the Five-Power government but was part of the Kuomintang's dictatorial power over Taiwan. In the 1990s it became an unpopular and seemingly unnecessary institution, but it was not until the year 2000 that its powers were finally curtailed.

In his lectures on the 'Principle of Democracy', Sun argued simply that the people would have the four powers of direct democracy over the Five-Power government. However, he did not describe in detail how approximately four hundred million Chinese could control the government at national level through direct democracy. As has been argued previously, Sun had been greatly influenced by the model of

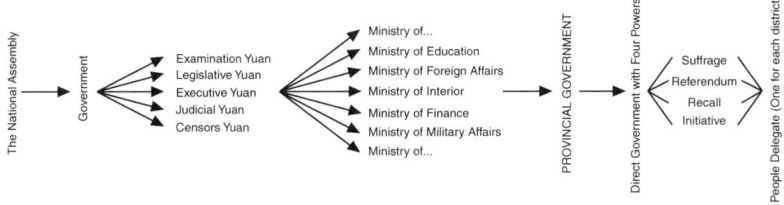

Figure 7.2 The Constitution as described by Sun in his *Fundamentals of National Reconstruction* (*source*: Sun Yat-sen, *Fundamentals of National Reconstruction*, (Taipe 1953) p. 51)

Cleveland City in the USA,[30] but this was direct democracy at the local level and not on a national scale. In his Principle of Democracy lectures Sun did not discuss direct democracy at the local level, however he did do so in his *Fundamentals of National Reconstruction* when he explained that each district was to elect its representatives to the National Assembly (Figure 7.2).

For further particulars of direct democracy on a national scale, Sun referred his readers to a book translated by Liao Chung-k'ai, *Government by All the People*. This was undoubtedly the work of that name by Delos F. Wilcox (published in New York in 1912) and translated by Liao Chung-k'ai in the Kuomintang organ *Chien-she* in 1919.[31] In the book, Wilcox suggested that the Electoral College in the USA under direct instructions from the people of the several states could exercise direct democratic rights over the government. However, he also argued that the people could control the government with their direct democratic rights without using the Electoral College.

There is value in Sun's ideas for modern democratic theory and practice. Direct democracy would obviate the undignified spectacle of voters taking to the streets to demonstrate against the government which imposed unpopular measures. Citizens would also feel encouraged to become better informed about political issues. There can be little doubt that the powerlessness of the electorate between elections is a flaw in contemporary democratic practice. Whatever may be the practical problems of implementing the people's direct democratic rights over the government, they cannot be insurmountable with modern technology. Sun was aware that Switzerland practised a partial form of direct democracy and queried whether larger states were not overly concerned about its cost.[32]

In support of Sun it could be argued that the price of policing mass protests should be weighed against the cost of direct democracy.

Whether it be desirable on a national scale for all issues, however, is another question. Sun himself argued for only people of the highest intellectual and moral calibre to be in the government. Presumably he would want the electorate to indicate to them whether it was dissatisfied with policies but not dictate the details.

Sun's distinction between sovereignty or 'ch'üan', which the people should have, and ability or 'neng' which the government should have, is the basis of his concept of the Five-Power constitution. This demonstrates Sun's originality of mind. It also shows his nationalism for he wanted China to have political machinery superior to that in the West. Moreover, he desired that the Chinese people have rights and happiness that in his view Western citizens did not have.[33] China might need to follow the West in developing her science and technology, but she could lead the West by creating political machinery more advanced than any in existence.

Sun was well-aware that Plato's ideas were still being studied by scholars.[34] Like him, Sun also wanted to devise a system that produced the best rulers, and his solution was to synthesise Chinese and Western constitutional ideas to add the ancient Chinese Examination and Control powers to the traditional Western three of the Executive, Legislative and Judiciary. All five should be separate and independent of each other. This system should ensure that only people of the highest intellectual and moral calibre should be in the government.

Sun's travels and studies had enabled him to make a critique of Western democracies. He was impressed with America's first written constitution, based on the three-power separation; however, he believed that it created too powerful an executive. Moreover, as he cogently argued in *The Fundamentals of National Reconstruction*, in Western democracies the influential 'demagogue', not the most capable statesman, was likely to come to power.[35] Sun's criticisms might well have additional pertinence today when politicians are greatly concerned with their public image and much of the parties' funds are devoted to public relations and salesmanship. Sun proposed that all candidates for elective office should be subject to certain tests of their abilities. However, it is not clear precisely what test might be designed. Nevertheless, this should not be regarded as an ultimate stumblingblock for the realising of Sun's dream in China. Examinations would certainly raise the standard of statesmanship in society. Indeed, the fact that the government in the USA is often weak because the presidents have little experience of the complexities of government and are manipulated by powerful pressure groups, should not encourage a cynical dismissal of Sun Yat-sen's criticisms.

Sun argued that Montesquieu's theory of the three separate powers, based on England's political customs and implemented by the USA which was then copied by Japan and other countries, was insufficient.[36] To strengthen his argument he referred to Western scholars who could also see the faults of the three-power system. Since the scholars wrote after Sun first pronounced on his Five-Power Constitution in 1905, they were not the source of his original ideas but buttressed them. In 1921 Sun referred to a Professor Cecil of Columbia University who published *Liberty and Authority* arguing for a four-power separation including a separate impeachment.[37] (In fact Sun meant Lord Hugh Cecil who was an Englishman and published an address on *Liberty and Authority* in 1910.) Sun also referred to John W. Burgess who in 1916 wrote *The Reconciliation of Government with Liberty* arguing in favour of the Chinese system of impeachment as 'a good device for adjustment between freedom and government'.[38] (It was he who was at Columbia University and in 1934 published a book on it.)

The examination system in China had a long history, beginning in the Han dynasty in the first century BC. It was gradually developed as the examination for administrators, although it stressed literary knowledge. Its qualification was very prestigious. The Chinese examination system influenced the West. At the end of the eighteenth century France and Germany introduced civil service examinations; Britain introduced them into India in 1855, and in England in 1870. All were arguably influenced by China.

Sun Yat-sen rightly concluded that the Chinese could be proud of originating the civil service examination. Although the West had improved on the Chinese form, Sun believed that it was defective in that the highest-ranking officials and none of the people's representatives had to take the examination. Sun proposed recovering the examination system from the West, with its improvements, but to make it independent of the executive.

It is, nevertheless, arguable that such an examination system will be biased in favour of the more educated classes and therefore the most wealthy. However, we do not have a detailed plan of the system Sun Yat-sen had in mind. Doubtless a method could be found to obviate the problem of the socio-economically and educationally impoverished parliamentary candidate from necessarily failing the examination.

Taiwan does have an Examination Yuan; its ensuring that her government consists of very highly qualified people could be a factor contributing to her economic success.

The second constitutional check that Sun Yat-sen esteemed highly as part of his Chinese legacy was that of the Control, which again dated back to the Han dynasty. The system consisted of officials who were to oversee the implementation of government policy and investigate corruption. In theory they could even criticise the Emperor. Understandably, Sun Yat-sen believed much could be gained by such a censorat system which could check governmental probity.

Taiwan has a Control Yuan to investigate political impropriety, but it has not been effective since it has been dominated by the Kuomintang which itself has been very corrupt. To be effective the Control Yuan needs to work within a liberal democracy and be staffed by an independent civil service. This is, however, difficult to develop.

Again Sun's ideas have relevance to modern political systems. The concept of a special authority which acquires expertise to investigate political corruption and has the power to bring the accused to justice is relevant not only to China, it is pertinent to Third World countries and indeed many Western states where political corruption is a seemingly intractable problem.

It has been argued that Sun's Five-Power Constitution, with its system of checks and balances, provides too many opportunities for blocks resulting in a paralysed government.[39] At the other extreme it has also been asserted that the Five-Power Constitution as implemented in Taiwan works harmoniously.[40] However, neither argument is correct. The latter argument was insufficiently critical possibly because its proponent had absorbed the one-party ideology that existed in Taiwan; the former is too pessimistic. It is true that gridlock already occurs in the three-power constitutions between the executive and legislature. However, this is partly because the latter decides by voting. The Examination and Control Yuans' decisions do not depend on voting. It is also true that party loyalties can vitiate the function of the Yuans. However, as emphasised before, this would not occur if the Yuans were staffed by independent civil servants. Whatever gridlock might occur, a vigorous Control Yuan as well as an Examination Yuan should produce politicians of high calibre and would be worth the price.

Sun's Five-Power Constitution is an original contribution to political theory, worthy of contemporary consideration. While many modern Chinese democratic thinkers concern themselves with liberty, Sun was at pains to stress that in China he believed it should mean: 'in having freedom of action within an organised group'.[41] Each individual must give up some of his personal freedom, submit to discipline and organisation, so that the state be strong and well-ordered. Thus it would be able to throw off its imperialist oppressors. National freedom should come before individual freedom. In seeing the individual essentially as part of a group and in putting the group before the individual, Sun was expressing a collective assumption that is more Chinese than Western. It is untrue to assert, as does Donald Treadgold, that 'Sun Yat-sen had himself owed nothing of great significance to the Chinese tradition'.[42]

Sun in fact did not concern himself with an essential idea in Western democracy: 'individualism' in the sense of the worth of each individual *per se* was a concept alien to Chinese thought – 'ko jen chu i' or 'individualism' in Chinese has selfish connotations. Sun believed that in China at the beginning of the twentieth century there was excessive personal liberty for the Chinese. They had to surrender some of it to the state for the sake of national liberty. Yet as in Confucian thought an emperor lost his heavenly mandate to rule the people if he misgoverned them, so the state in Sun's thought was answerable to the people. It is incorrect to argue as does Chester Tan that:

> In the voluminous writings of Sun Yat-sen, the nature of the state is hardly dealt with at all. At the same time, when the state was considered the supreme authority to which individuals should sacrifice themselves, especially to save it from foreign aggression and internal disorganization it was natural that the functions of the state were seldom discussed.[43]

Sun did describe the function of the state in its obligations to the citizen as well as the latter's duties to it. This aspect, however, perhaps significantly, was dealt with in the lectures concerned with the Principle of Livelihood rather than the Principle of Democracy. To Sun, the state had a specific welfare function; citizens had no obligation to it if it did not fulfil the functions of providing food, shelter, transport and clothing:

> It is essential that the state undertakes the responsibility for providing these necessities; anyone should be able to call the state to task if it does not provide enough of each.[44]

Such provisos, however, were ignored by the Kuomintang which thus distorted Sun's teachings.

Connected with this concern with the state's obligations to protect the citizens' social welfare, Sun argued in his lectures on the Principle of Democracy that democracy and socialism should have advanced together in the West: 'Socialism was originally closely related to democracy and the two should have developed simultaneously.'[45] It is significant that Sun spoke of the weapon of trade union strikes against capitalism in his Principles of Democracy; as has been noted earlier Sun probably became aware of the importance of the trade union's ability to give workers some power when he was staying in the West.[46] While some political theorists such as Frederick Hayek[47] have argued that capitalism and liberty are intrinsically linked, Sun would argue that the results would not create happiness for all the people: if his form of democracy and socialism were developed together, they would.

Democracy is a vague concept and Sun seemed well-aware of its ambiguity. It is to his credit that he attempted to create an original theory of democracy, tailored to suit China's needs, synthesising the best in Western and Chinese forms of government that would give the Chinese pride in themselves and might serve as an example to the rest of the world.

8
Sun's Three Principles of the People: The Principle of Livelihood

Lecture I

Sun finished his lectures on democracy on 26 April 1924; it was not until 23 August of that year that he began his lectures on livelihood. By that time, as will be discussed later, he had modified his views on Marxism.

Sun began by explaining that although the phrase 'min-sheng' as 'livelihood' was not new, few Chinese understood what it meant. It was equivalent to socialism, communism or the Great Harmony. The problem of livelihood had arisen just over a century earlier due to the rapid industrial developments occurring all over the world. When machinery was introduced many men lost their occupations and thus their livelihood. In order to alleviate this suffering a socialist movement developed in the West. However, it was unable to solve the problems it posed and there were disputes within the movement. Marx, relying on facts, founded scientific socialism which was to be distinguished from utopian socialism. Marx considered class war between capitalist workers to be inevitable and also the driving force of social progress.

Sun, however, believed the facts proved Marx to be incorrect. Socialised distribution (of water, gas and electricity) had reduced hardship for consumers. Heavy taxation of capitalists had enabled the state to take over the means of transportation and communication, to improve the education and health of the workers, and increase the productiveness of society. When the capitalists cared for the workers the latter increased their productivity. Society should progress through a harmonising rather than a clashing of the workers' and capitalists' interests.

Class war was not a cause of social progress; Marx was a social pathologist not a social physiologist. His ideas on surplus value had been contradicted by history. Marx had said that the capitalist would have to lengthen the working day, reduce wages and raise the prices of products. However, the successful Ford car factories in the USA had shortened the working day, raised wages and lowered the prices of their products. Moreover it was incorrect to argue that surplus value was created entirely by labour; it was the product of many factors in society, for example machines were the result of inventors' ideas and the effort in mining for metals with which they were made as well as factory labour. Thus material forces were not central to social history which pivoted on the problems of livelihood.

Lecture 2

Each country had to follow its own method in dealing with the problem of livelihood. The West should not be imitated because it had not solved its own problems and socialist parties disagreed with each other. The Kuomintang could solve the problem of livelihood in China by the equalisation of landownership and by the regulation of capital.

In the West capitalism had developed to such an oppressive level that the socialists might be obliged to adopt the Marxist method as class struggle. China was not yet so highly industrialised and therefore did not need these methods. The difference between the Principle of Livelihood and Communism was that of method rather than principle. In the West the problem of land value and unearned increments was very serious, but it was only just beginning to develop in China. Likewise, industry and commerce had not reached the levels of development reached in the West. It was important to solve the problem of livelihood before it was too late. The Kuomintang's policy was that the government should buy back the land if necessary; the landowners should be allowed to assess the value of their own land and pay taxes accordingly. If they undervalued their land they ran the risk of the government buying it back at their stated price. After the land values had been fixed a law should be passed ensuring that all increase in land values should revert to the community.

In China the equalisation of land ownership was a form of regulating capital. Other ways were to regulate private capital. The waterways and mines must be developed, and industry must be promoted. Initially China would have to borrow foreign capital to develop her communication and transportation facilities and use foreign experts to manage them.

Class war and the dictatorship of the proletariat were unnecessary. The min-sheng principle was Confucius' hope of a 'great commonwealth'.

Lecture 3

The food problem was the chief problem of livelihood. In China every year tens of thousands died of starvation. She did not produce enough food and had to import it. Nine out of ten farmers did not own their fields; their landlords received most of their production. The peasants should be liberated and given their own land to till. Moreover, agriculture should be improved by the use of machinery and fertilisers, rotation of crops, eradication of pests, manufacturing and transportation. Reforestation should be practised on a national scale to minimise droughts and floods for which rivers should also be deepened.

Sun began his third lecture by urging China to follow France's example of intensive agriculture. However, he later pointed out that the West had not yet solved its food problem since profit was still the only aim. The Principle of Livelihood should aim at the provision of nutrition for all the people. Moreover, it should also provide cheap clothing, shelter and means of travel for the people.

Lecture 4

In his fourth lecture, Sun dealt with the problem of clothing. However, this was his last lecture and therefore his ideas on shelter and travel were never heard (Chiang Kai-shek did write two supplementary chapters for an edition of the Three Principles but they were not actually on shelter and travel).

Sun argued that the problem of clothing had developed with civilisation. The sources of clothing material were silk, hemp, cotton and wool. China needed to improve her sericulture to catch up with the silk industries of other countries. She also exported cotton but bought it back as cotton goods. The Chinese wore foreign cloth which profited foreigners who controlled the Maritime Customs. Moreover, when Chinese cloth was transported in the interior of China it did not, like foreign cloth, warrant only one payment of likin tax, but one at every likin station. The Chinese should buy native products and boycott foreign cloth. Moreover, they should secure the control of the Maritime Customs. Chinese clothing should be protective, attractive, convenient and not hinder work. The State should establish clothing factories on a large scale, and everyone should be provided with clothing.

In return for the State's protection, the people should fulfil their obligation to work; the idle should be converted into honest labourers. When all men had a share in production there would be enough to eat and to wear, homes would be comfortable and the people would be content.

The development of Sun's Principle of Livelihood, 1905–24

Until 1905, Sun minimised his socialist sympathy partly for the sake of his foreign policy; later he exaggerated it for the same reason. Earlier he had wanted Western support, later that of Communist Russia. Nevertheless his socialism did really broaden in its scope. When Sun propounded his Principle of Livelihood in 1905 it bore no similarity to Marxism. He was chiefly concerned with the problem of urban rather than agrarian land reform through the solution of the single tax. As has been discussed in Chapter 2 he had been influenced by Henry George and probably other leading European socialists, and he had also witnessed the poverty and growing social conflict in the West. This, in 1912, he still believed would undergo a violent social revolution which China could avoid. He did not really concern himself with the regulation of capital until 1913 (although he had mentioned it to students in Paris in 1905). By this time he had been influenced by the brilliant Marxist Chu Chih-hsin.

As China industrialised, so the Principle of Livelihood was broadened. As the writer T'ang Liang-li observed:

> A Chinese industrial class had come into existence after the close of the Russo/Japanese war in 1905, when the victory of Japan started the Second Reform Movement in China. The introduction of the factory methods of production to China by foreign capitalists was made possible by the Treaty of Shimonoseki, in 1895. It did not take long for the new industrial processes to find favour with the Chinese moneyed men, who also started building modern cotton and silk factories, ran river and coastal steamers, and conducted modern banks and financial houses.[1]

No doubt influenced by the events of the First World War, when Sun systemised his thought during his stay in Shanghai from 1918–20, he introduced the idea of forced industrialisation.[2]

The success of the Bolshevik Revolution in 1917 had a profound impact on Sun. In 1923 he made the Sun–Joffe agreement with Soviet Russia which was the only country prepared to help him. By this agreement Sun was to receive financial and military aid from Russia in return for allowing the Chinese Communists to enter the Kuomintang on an individual basis. The Kuomintang was modelled on Leninist democratic centralised lines and Sun's political thinking complied more with Soviet Russia's outlook.

As Chinese capitalist industrialism was developing by 1923, the Kuomintang, according to T'ang Liang-li, was by then:

> on its guard against the evil of unrestricted capitalist industrialism. Thus, not only is the Principle of Livelihood to mean the equitable distribution of the land, through the instrumentality of taxation, and, if necessary, conditional expropriation, but private industries, whether Chinese or foreign-owned, which partake of the nature of monopolies or are beyond the power of individual investment, such as banking, railway and steamship undertakings, should be managed or controlled by the State, in order that private capital may not have the power to interfere with the economic life of the people.[3]

In 1924, Sun extended his land reform policy to include redistributing land to the peasants by government and law. Sun, however, was in a dilemma. He wanted to keep the support of those capitalists and landowners in the Kuomintang who were against Communism. In any case Sun's Christianity, Confucian values and kindness caused him to eschew the violent methods of the Communists. His solution was to emphasise that the methods of the Communists, 'the sharp knife of class struggle', were not those of the Kuomintang's. However, the long-term goals of the Communists were those of the Kuomintang's; Sun did not state how long-term these would be. In this he may have been influenced by clause 4 of the British Labour Party's constitution which stood for the common ownership of the means of production, distribution and exchange as a very long-term goal to placate the left wing of the party. He would have read about this in Maurice William's book which deeply influenced him and will be discussed later.

A critique of Sun's Principle of Livelihood

Sun's Principle of Livelihood was more humane than Communism; he rejected the latter's belief in violent social change, although appreciating that armed force was necessary to regain control of China. For him justice was seasoned with mercy. He believed in harmonising the interests of the workers and capitalists; that profits were the product not only of labour but of many factors; in initially only regulating private capitalism; and in building up state socialism and encouraging foreign capital. To him inequality was mainly caused by increased land values due to urban development. The solution to this was not class struggle but a single land tax, the revenue from which, together with future increments, could be used for the good of society; this would include Sun's projects such as cheap subsidised housing, food, clothing and transport for the poor.

In this Sun was influenced by Henry George and John Stuart Mill as discussed in Chapter 2. His idea that landowners should assess their own land value for taxation, risking it being bought by the government if it was priced too low was an ingenious and cheaply administered method of redistributing wealth and raising revenue. It may have been Sun's original idea, or he may have read about self-assessment in New Zealand in the nineteenth century (as observed in Chapter 2).

In his third lecture Sun expounded in detail his plans to solve the problem of famine from which millions regularly died. His policy was enlightened and remarkably responsible compared to the fatalistic indifference shown by Chinese governments to famine until the Communists came to power in 1949. Usually the governments in China were content to leave famine relief to foreign missionaries.[4] Sun planned to eradicate famine through land reform, giving land to peasants who would farm more effectively; through reforestation which would prevent floods and drought; and through the use of modern machinery, fertilisers, pesticides and improved transport.

It is significant that Sun spoke of land reform as part of his lecture on food production. This indicates he was not fully aware of the political importance of the peasants. Sun was concerned not to alienate those on the right in the Kuomintang, but he was also being pressured by the Soviet Communists to begin agrarian reforms.[5] Therefore, noting that nine out of ten farmers did not own their land, that this was unjust as well as inimical to efficient food production, Sun argued for agrarian reform through 'government and law'.[6] Whether this was possible is doubtful, although the landlords would have needed considerable military force to resist. Had Chiang Kai-shek concerned himself with agrarian reform and won the support of the peasants, who were the bulk of the population, he might not have lost the Civil War to the Communists who, under Mao's direction, gained the peasants' loyalty instead.

There has been much debate over how far Sun's Principle of Livelihood differed from Communism. I have discussed this elsewhere.[7] Suffice it to say here that he rejected the violent methods of the Communists, the class struggle, the dictatorship of the proletariat and dialectical materialism. Initially capitalism was only to be regulated and state capital built up; the long-term goal of the Principle of Livelihood was that people would 'share everything in the state',[8] but how far in the future this was Sun did not say.

Nevertheless Lenin's theories on imperialism did have an influence on his anti-imperialist outlook as exemplified in his lectures on Nationalism. Indeed in 1921 a minute was circulated to the British Foreign Office, Admiralty, War and Colonial Offices, stating amidst other information, that Sun Yat-sen was 'now credited with leanings to Bolshevism'.[9] This vague phrase was probably written to reinforce the already unsympathetic attitude of the Foreign Office to Sun.

Before Sun gave his lectures on Livelihood in 1924, he wanted an intellectual rebuttal of Communism from which he could differentiate the Kuomintang. He found it in Maurice William's *The Social Interpretation of History* which was published in the USA in 1921. The story of how the book came seemingly providentially into his hands is mysterious. The fact that Maurice William was an obscure American dentist is extraordinary.

The influence of Maurice William

In his first lecture on the Principle of Livelihood, Sun acknowledged his debt to Maurice William:

> Recently, an American disciple of Marx, named Williams [sic], after making a deep study of Marx's philosophy, came to the conclusion that the disagreement between fellow socialists is due to the defects in Marx's doctrines. He sets forth the view that the materialistic conception of history is wrong, that the social problem not material forces, is the centre which determines the course of history and that subsistence is the heart of the social problem. This social interpretation of history, he believes is the only reasonable one. The problem of livelihood is the problem of subsistence. The new theory of this American scholar tallies exactly with the Third Principle of our party. Williams's theory means that Livelihood is the central force in social progress, and that social progress is the central force in history; hence the struggle for a living and not material forces determining history.[10]

Sun goes on to argue that the Min-sheng Principle, which the Kuomintang had had for the previous twenty years, was equivalent to William's own theory. Because the Principle of Livelihood was different from Socialism and Communism in the West, the Kuomintang called it the Min-sheng

Principle. Thus Sun argued that his opinions had not been changed by William but merely confirmed. They were, however, considerably fleshed out by William's work since his lectures show the extent of William's influence. Nevertheless, it could be argued that Sun had only been confirmed in his own view and not dramatically changed by William's. As has been pointed out earlier, Sun Yat-sen was a most unlikely candidate for the Communist camp.

Sun's lectures on livelihood do draw heavily from William's work. Sun wrote for example that: 'Marx can only be called a social pathologist; we cannot say he is a social physiologist.'[11] Likewise William argued: 'Marx was a social pathologist. He studied social pathology and mistook the phenomenon he observed for the law of social biology. The manifestation of the class struggle are symptoms as pain, heat, redness and swelling in human pathology.'[12]

Sun referred to the disagreements over the nature of Socialism following the First World War, as did William. Sun even used William's phrase of 'fifty-seven varieties' to describe Socialism: 'A foreign proverb speaks of the 'fifty-seven varieties of Socialism' and one cannot tell which variety is real Socialism.'[13] William wrote: 'in former days, Socialists would smile at statements by non-Socialists to the effect that there seemed to be fifty-seven varieties of Socialism, but we can smile at that statement today.'[14]

Like William, Sun rejected not only the Marxist materialistic interpretation of history, the doctrine of class war, but also the theory of surplus value. Referring to the Ford factory in the USA, William argued that the products were the result of multitudinous factors, including the invention of machines, the manufacture of chemicals as well as managerial decisions and ideas.[15]

William argued that social progress developed when both capitalists and workers were regarded as having common interest as consumers and are not regarded as being in conflict as producers. Similarly Sun Yat-sen also used the example of the Ford factory in order to criticise Marxist theory of surplus value, asserting that: 'Marx gave all credit for production to the labour of the industrial worker and overlooked the labour of other useful factors.'[16]

Sun pointed out that contrary to Marx's theory, Ford factories raised wages, shortened the working day and reduced the price of cars. Working conditions in the factories had improved dramatically and the workers were insured against sickness, accident and old age. However, the factories, contrary to Marx's argument, had spread all over the world and were making a fortune.

Thus Sun Yat-sen was undoubtedly deeply indebted to Maurice William for giving him facts to support ideas which he already held. Nevertheless, as Schiffrin aptly remarked: 'Sun had not needed saving from an ideology he never believed in.'[17]

It would seem that William's work went to China possibly through the actions of a Chinese theological scholar who was studying in the USA. William published his book privately and endeavoured to sell it with little success in American bookstores. However, in 1921 the American News Company which had been given a sample copy received an order for William's book from one Timothy Jen, who was studying theology in the USA and was anxious to have a sound intellectual defence against Marxism when he returned to China.[18] In 1923, the company received an order for 40 copies from China and contacted William for an export price. There is no record from whom this order came in China nor how it found its way to Sun Yat-sen just as he wanted an intellectual justification for his rejection of Marxist methods and analyses. Thus during his lectures in August 1924, Sun referred frequently to William's book to buttress his arguments.

Maurice William himself was influenced by both German State socialism and the British Labour Party. He had most certainly read some of the writing of Sidney and Beatrice Webb. William observed:

> But, fortunately for the British masses, it is the non-Marxian Fabian society that has the ear of the British Labour Party and has played an important part in the framing of the reconstruction programme. This historic document is in harmony with the operations of the laws of social evolution and is therefore scientific.[19]

William was clearly impressed with the Labour Party's reconstruction programme published the same year in which he began to write:

> This programme of the British Labour Party has attracted international attention because it concerns itself primarily with social welfare, with the welfare of the consumer. So anxious is the British Labour Party to impress all with the fact that it is no longer a Labour Party in the sense that its principal concern is the welfare of the producer, that it feels called upon to reiterate again and again not a single one in this long list of proposals is in any sense a class proposal, which is perfectly true. The programme is consistently socialistic throughout and therefore in harmony with the laws of social evolution. It aims to accelerate social progress in the interests of the majority as social beings.[20]

British social democracy undoubtedly influenced Maurice William and the formation of his theory. It could therefore be argued that indirectly the British Fabian Socialists influenced Sun Yat-sen through the agency of Maurice William. Most certainly Sun Yat-sen read of the ideas of the British Labour Party and of Sidney and Beatrice Webb in particular, as expounded in Maurice William's book of which he had made a thorough study. (Sun moreover had probably had contact with Keir Hardie.) Therefore Sun Yat-sen's Third Principle which became an important part of the Kuomintang's programme was influenced not just by an obscure American dentist, but by some of the most influential socialist writers in twentieth-century Britain.

Sun believed his society would be an economic democracy: the state belonged to all the people, a government controlled by all the people, and the rights and benefits for the enjoyment of all people. Then China would realise not the Marxist dream but Confucius' hope of a 'Great Commonwealth'.[21] However, exactly when this Great Commonwealth would come about was not clear. This ambiguity is perhaps redolent of the programme of the British Labour Party in 1918 which possibly indirectly influenced Sun Yat-sen through Maurice William. Clause 4 of the British Labour Party's Constitution of 1918 called for the common ownership of the means of production, distribution and exchange. It was not clear, however, when this extreme form of socialism was to be implemented. The clause was partly a political device to keep together the socialists of varying viewpoints, and no doubt Sun Yat-sen used ambiguity as a similar device.

Desperate for Russia's financial and military aid and aware of China's growing industrialisation, Sun did show increased sympathy with the ideas of Russian Communists. However, Sun clearly aimed more for cooperation between the classes in China and did not desire to use one to violently crush the other. The pressure from the Soviet Union and his failing energy due to the fact that he was dying made it difficult for him to put over a coherent policy. His programme, however, was not less systematic than that of many social democratic parties in Europe. Indeed, he added to the valuable ideas that he gained from the West much of his own perception and reflection on the particular needs of Chinese development. It was a tragedy for China that this unusual and more peaceful synthesis of socialist ideas was not implemented.

Sun gave his last lecture on 24 August 1924. He then had to concern himself with military activities. In October he crushed the Merchant Volunteer Corps which was financed by his opponents in banking circles in Hong Kong and Canton. In November 1924 he left for a meeting with the warlords in Peking. On the way Sun visited Japan and suggested a mutual assistance pact, thus trying to break out of his dependence on Soviet Russia. However, in December 1924 it was clear that Sun was terminally ill with liver cancer. On 12 March 1925 Sun Yat-sen died in Peking and was mourned throughout the country. Memorial meetings were held in every major city.

Sun was succeeded as leader of the Kuomintang by Chiang Kai-shek who turned against the Communists. In 1927 Chiang ordered their massacre in Shanghai. During the same year Mao Tse-tung published his famous *Report on an Investigation into the Peasant Movement in Hunan*. He observed that several hundred million peasants would soon rise like a hurricane in revolt against their exploitative, miserable conditions. Some were already doing so. They should be the engine of the revolution.

Sun Yat-sen was only just awakening to the plight of the peasants in 1924. Had he lived longer in good health he might have diverted the peasant movement into a social revolution that was based not on class struggle but on mutual cooperation to the ultimate benefit of all. For this he needed foreign financial help so that he was not dependent on Soviet Russia, could gain power quickly and institute agrarian reform by peaceful, legal means. However, during his lifetime he had not received the foreign support that would enable him to implement his political thought.

Chiang Kai-shek neglected the peasants who were 80 per cent of the population. They supported the Communists who redistributed to them land taken from the landlords. Largely as a result, in 1949 Chiang's Kuomintang lost the civil war to the Communists. All hope of Sun Yat-sen's political thought being implemented in China was gone.

Before considering the impact of Sun's ideas on Kuomintang and Communist leaders as well as the Third World, two major spiritual and ethical influences on Sun will be considered: Christianity and Confucianism.

9
The Influence of Christianity on Sun Yat-sen

Sun Yat-sen's Christianity has been a subject of some controversy; it has been argued that Sun was not really a Christian but portrayed himself as such for political reasons. The evidence cited for this lies in the fact that Sun was not a churchgoer nor did he often celebrate Christian festivals.[1] Nevertheless, Sun told an audience in San Francisco, shortly before the Revolution in 1911:

> Our greatest hope is to make the Bible and Christian education, as we have known it, the means of conveying to our countrymen what blessings may be in the way of just laws.[2]

Was this a sham Christian referring to false convictions according to the demands of political expediency? The evidence points to the contrary. Obviously part of the answer pivots on the interpretation of what it means to be a Christian; and there are many differing opinions on this matter today, centring on belief in the divinity of Christ. Sun Yat-sen made no pronouncements on such theological questions, no doubt because in his day such issues were not popularly discussed. Since, however, Sun Yat-sen stated that he worshipped Jesus,[3] it can be inferred that he believed Jesus to be alive and worthy of worship. What then to make of Sun Yat-sen's failure to put in a regular church attendance? It could be argued firstly that Sun specifically eschewed the Christianity of the churches. He once asserted that: 'I do not belong to the Christianity of the churches but to the Christianity of Jesus who was a revolutionary.'[4]

This did not necessarily mean that Sun was not a Christian, merely that he could not accept ecclesiastical Christianity; and he has not been alone in this. Indeed, Sun Yat-sen's Chinese background is in itself an explanation for his rejection of ecclesiastical Christianity. In the China of Sun's boyhood there was an endemic hatred of the Christian churches. Moreover, ideas sown from the Taiping Rebellion still germinated notions that an alternative to ecclesiastical Christianity was feasible. These arguments will be returned to later.

The second argument concerning Sun's sincerity as a Christian pivots on the question of whether or not hypocrisy is to be found more in church pews than behind revolutionary flags. Obviously, quantitative studies are impossible but it is clear from observation and historical records that many people have led selfish and destructive lives while portraying themselves as Christians. Sun Yat-sen's life being one of greater vision, idealism and expenditure of time and energy to improve the lives of others, should surely mark him out to be a more distinctive and remarkable Christian than most. He was an unusual politician in that, having raised huge funds for his party, he amassed no personal fortune. In fact he died in poverty.[5] His idealism still shines from the first decade of the last century until today: a testimony to his amazing energy and personal magnetism which no doubt gained some of its messianic quality from his (as will be depicted) unconventional but inspiring faith. Sun indeed has been called 'the kindest of all revolutionaries'[6] which may have been partly induced by his belief in Jesus Christ, as well as his Confucian background. His renunciation of the Presidency of China in 1912 in favour of Yüan Shih-k'ai, as a sacrificial act which thus saved China more bloodshed, may also be interpreted as Christian gentlemanly conduct.[7]

Of course Sun Yat-sen emphasised his Christian beliefs to an American audience; naturally after being kidnapped in London he emphasised his Christian faith to arouse support. However, there is evidence that Sun Yat-sen was a regular reader of the Bible and discussed Christianity at length.[8]

Sun's reference to Christian beliefs as in: 'I am like the prodigal son and the lost sheep',[9] together with: 'The last shall be first' and the idea that China's salvation lay through faith (this time in Sun's ideas), indicate that Christian ideas were absorbed deeply into his unconscious and were expressed without deliberate contrivance. Moreover, at times Sun expressed allegiance to his faith when it was not in his vested interest to do so. There was no reason why Sun should equate the love described by Mo Tzu as the same as that of Jesus when he was talking to a Chinese audience.[10] In fact at the time when he was proclaiming his Christian beliefs, Christianity was being rejected by Chinese scholars as being both un-Chinese and unscientific. It is perhaps a little appreciated fact that Sun Yat-sen was a beacon for Chinese Christians, showing that Christianity could be the faith of a scientifically trained mind that also upheld many Chinese classical values. There was no need for Sun Yat-sen to draw attention to the fact that he was dying as a Christian. His family organised a Christian funeral for him in the face of opposition; there was no political capital to be achieved from this either, nor would such arrangements have been made for one of doubtful beliefs.

Sun Yat-sen's presentation of his Three Principles, indeed, resembled that of the missionaries in their endeavours to convert: this indicates how much he was influenced by them. Sun referred to his Principles as a faith by which the salvation of China could be obtained and put over his views as a proselytiser, to the extent that his apologist Judge Linebarger saw him 'as a missionary for secular ends' with an earthly gospel.[11] Later, after Sun's death, it is perhaps significant that the Kuomintang introduced the 'Monday service' in memory of Sun Yat-sen. This was a ceremony conducted in all schools and governmental offices 'reminiscent of Protestant forms of worship'.[12] Thus it would seem that the Kuomintang perpetuated the idea expressed, at times, by Sun himself: that he had been on a divinely inspired mission and thus, as the Kuomintang implied, worthy of reverential attention.

What then to make of Sun Yat-sen's reference to Confucian ideals and, above all, to his actually practising such ancient Chinese rules as, for example, addressing the last of the Emperors on the occasion of Sun's achieving the Presidency. Such utterances as: 'How could we have attained this measure of victory had not your Majesty's soul in Heaven bestowed upon us your protecting influence'[13] surely have no place in a Christian mind. Here it is possible to argue that Sun was not betraying his Christian faith nor holding the ceremony insincerely. Suffice it to say that most people are inheritors of traditional beliefs that remain with them and are not entirely discarded. Ancestor worship was a strong traditional belief in China, and it would have been ridiculous for Sun Yat-sen to have addressed the Christian God on such an occasion. It is also likely that Sun Yat-sen might have thought there might well be something in ancestor worship insofar as the communicable fate of the souls of the dead in Christian worship is not clear. Sun Yat-sen's speech was not in contradiction to his faith but a supplement to it; albeit that Sun may also have wished to please those of more orthodox Confucian persuasion. Indeed, as many Chinese Christians have shown, it was possible for Confucian and Christian ideas to jostle with each other in the Chinese mind just as most people's outlooks consist of mixtures of faiths and ideologies. Sun Yat-sen was an outstanding and articulate example of this. Thus Sun's frequent references to 'Heaven' or 'The Heavenly Way' seemingly indicating Confucian influence, is no contradiction of his avowed Christian beliefs.

What then may be said of Sun Yat-sen's divorce from his first wife whom he married out of filial duty, and marriage to his second wife, the beautiful Soong Ching-ling, daughter of the wealthy and influential Charles Soong? One can only sympathise with Sun's awakening to his predicament that he did not enter into his first marriage knowingly or wilfully. Moreover, in certain Christian churches, remarriage is not sinful. Sun was not a Catholic nor an Anglican and, as has earlier been evidenced, rejected ecclesiastical discipline. Furthermore, Sun Yat-sen's first wife agreed to the divorce.

The China of Sun's boyhood provided ample nourishment for antipathy towards Christian ecclesiasticism. More will be said later of the influence of the Taiping Rebellion on Sun Yat-sen, an influence that was certainly emphasised by the scholar Wu Yü-chang (who fought in the revolution of 1911 and later became President of the China People's University). Wu Yü-chang also vividly depicts in his *Recollections of the Revolution of 1911* how unpopular ecclesiastical Christianity was in the late nineteenth century. Wu asserts that the Western imperialists used Christianity as a cloak to legitimise their interests. Christians became involved in the Chinese government; and Chinese Christians relied on foreign missionaries to protect their interests so that any lawsuit involving Christians was regarded as a hopeless case. Above all, by the late nineteenth century the Christian churches had often become big landlords or money lenders.[14]

Therefore, there was particular antipathy between Chinese peasants and the church over lawsuits. The first 'church lawsuit' revolt broke out in 1863 between the people of Chongqing and the Church. In 1868, when the people of Yujang fought against the Church in the 'Church lawsuit of Yujang', more than 1000 people were killed or wounded. Other 'lawsuit struggles' followed. The Boxer Rebellion of 1900 attacked the churches and missionaries; its programme was to overthrow the Ching, restore the Ming, oppose foreigners and exterminate the churches. This Boxer Rebellion must have had a profound influence on Sun Yat-sen. It is to his credit that he did not discard his Christian beliefs at a time when they were associated with foreign imperialism. He might later have capitalised on anti-clerical feeling and gained support from the erstwhile supporters of the Boxers, but instead, he gave expression to a tradition of Christianity that originated in the Taiping Rebellion and which was profoundly to influence his thinking. The Taiping Rebellion gave Sun Yat-sen a model on which to base his belief that it was possible to be both a Christian and a revolutionary. Sun upheld the ideas of the Taiping Rebellion insofar as they were of the revolutionary Christian brand, and yet, at the same time, supported the ideas of the Boxer Rebellion by rejecting ecclesiastical Christianity.

Sun's Taiping Christianity

It is now necessary to consider the effect of the Taiping Rebellion on Sun Yat-sen. In order to do so it is pertinent to investigate at what point his Christian ideas took root. Much has been made of the influence of Christian modernism on Sun Yat-sen, and the orthodox version is that he was converted by Christian missionaries. Indeed, in 1879, Sun Yat-sen entered the Iolani School in Hawaii. This school was directed by the Anglican bishop Willis, who taught classes in Christian doctrine. Moreover, Sun would have had to attend services at the St Andrew's Cathedral.[15] Bishop Willis later claimed Sun would have been baptised had it not been for Sun's 'heathen relatives'. It will be later suggested, however, they were not so much heathen as 'anticlerical'. Then Sun Yat-sen transferred to an American Congregationalist School when it seemed Sun's attachment to Christianity developed. At this point, in 1883, Sun's brother Mei had him sent back to Canton 'when Sun Wen's conversion appeared imminent'.[16]

Back in his native village Sun, together with a friend, desecrated images to the local deity. His religious beliefs may well have been given a more militant and intolerant tone by his stay in Hawaii. Sun then decided to take up studies in Hong Kong where he enrolled in a Church of England school, studying the classics with a Chinese Christian minister, Ch'ü Feng-ch'ih, who was associated with the London Missionary Society.[17] In 1884 Sun entered the Government Central School and in the same year was baptised, together with his friend, Lu Hao-tung, who had aided him in smashing the village idols. The American Congregationalist missionary who baptised him, Dr Charles Hager, later helped him enrol in 1886 in the Canton Medical School, an Anglo/American missionary institution. After his baptism, Sun was given the name Yat-sen. Sun's brother, seemingly enraged at this behaviour, ordered Sun to return to Hawaii. There, however, Sun made many Christian friends, including the Reverend Damon, who helped raise sufficient funds for Sun Yat-sen to return to China and pursue advanced studies. It is reasonable to conclude that this support from Christians helped nurture the faith that led Sun to make a deathbed avowal of Christianity, unlike any Chinese leader before or since. Nevertheless, it will be argued that the seeds of Sun Yat-sen's

Christian belief had been sown even earlier in his life. It was from his boyhood that he learned of the possibility that Jesus need not be the Christ of the churches. It was this spark from the Taiping Rebellion that was to ignite in Sun a revolutionary brand of Christianity that upheld the name of Jesus, but rejected foreign ecclesiastical interference carried out in his Name.

Before the influence of the Taiping Rebellion on Sun Yat-sen is examined, it will be acknowledged that Sun was greatly affected by the Christian modernist missionaries who helped him. These missionaries in the first decade of the twentieth century preached that China needed a new social order, either through peaceful or violent means, and Sun himself declared:

> Where did the idea of Revolution come from? It came because, from my youth, I had intercourse with foreign missionaries. Those from Europe and America with whom I associated put the ideals of freedom and liberty into my heart.[18]

Donald Treadgold regards the Christian influence on Sun as being wholly of the modernist variety. He points out that, by 1911, such speakers as George Sherwood Eddy were drawing huge audiences in China with their Christian modernist message. Later Sun, as President, was an invited guest at one of Eddy's lectures.[19] Undoubtedly such a message did influence Sun. However, it will be argued that Christian modernism was not the original Christian influence on Sun's mind. The clue to his early awareness of Christianity lies in Treadgold's reference to Sun's 'false claim that his father was a Christian'.[20] Schiffrin also believed that this claim was false. He refers to Sun's telling a Dr Manson, who had found him trustworthy, that he was a born Christian and not a convert.[21] Schiffrin believes he said this in order to 'establish his "bona fides" in this quarter'. This, however, does not seem a convincing argument. A born Christian is not more respected than a convert.

In *The Japanese and Sun Yat-sen*, Marius B. Jansen suggests that Sun might actually have been a Christian before going to Hawaii.[22] He quotes Sun in 'My Reminiscences' (*Strand Magazine*, London 1912, XLIII: 301) in which Sun says:

> I had led the life of any Christian youth in my class, except that from my father's conversion to Christianity and his employment by the London Missionary Society, I had great opportunities of coming into contact with English and American Missionaries in Canton.

Jansen points out, however, that few Western biographies follow this, although Wittfogel (Berlin, n.d.) in *Sun Yat-sen* does, and George Soulie d'Morant, *Soun Yat-sen* (Paris, 1932)[23] adds to it by asserting that Sun's parents took refuge in Macao during the Taiping Rebellion. According to Jansen, one of the most careful Japanese accounts – Hatano Kenichi's *History of the Chinese Nationalist Party*[24] – considers this quite dubious. Jansen concludes: 'Sun was frequently contradictory in his various memoirs'.[25]

However, Jansen may well be right in casting doubt on the generally accepted idea that Sun was a Christian convert. Indeed, more evidence that he was not can be found in T'ang Liang-li's *Inner History of the Chinese Revolution*. T'ang states that Sun's father was converted to Christianity during the Taiping Rebellion,[26] although he also retained his beliefs in the household gods and other aspects of Chinese traditional religious beliefs. If this is true, this would explain why Sun said that he was born a Christian. Why then should Sun's father recall him from Hawaii when he found he was becoming converted to Christianity as Treadgold asserts?[27] The answer to this lies partly with Schiffrin's more detailed work in which he states it was Sun's brother who recalled him.[28] Further, T'ang also says Sun's brother recalled him because he was 'in danger of being completely Westernised'.[29] T'ang was well-placed to know personal facts about Sun since, as the representative in Britain of the Central Executive of the Kuomintang, and as Political Private Secretary to some of the most prominent revolutionaries, T'ang had access to personal reminiscences and confidential documents. If T'ang is right, Sun Yat-sen, born two years after the Taiping Rebellion, imbibed from his father an unconventional Christianity. His uncle, also an old Taiping rebel, educated him. As a child Sun started calling himself Hung Hsiu-ch'üan and wanted to become a second Rebel Emperor. Treadgold indeed also states:

> Sun more than once thought of himself as another Hung Hsiu-ch'üan, and it appeared that indeed Protestant modernism was as faithfully reflected in his thought as Protestant fundamentalism was in Hung's.[30]

Treadgold, however, does not consider that in his childhood Sun may have been influenced by the revolutionary Christian ideas of the Taiping Rebellion. Referring to Sun's words the day before he died: 'I am a Christian; God sent me to fight evil for my people. Jesus was a revolutionary, so am I,' Treadgold asserts 'It is a statement inconceivable for a Chinese Christian to have made thirty years earlier before modernism changed the face of Protestantism everywhere.'³¹ It was not inconceivable that a child of a Taiping rebel family could have had such ideas fifty years earlier. Sun's debt to Christian modernism should not be underestimated, but a possible debt to Taiping unconventional Christian relatives should also be considered. Nor need his father and uncle have been influenced by Hung Hsiu-ch'üan's madness. Among Taiping rebel leaders was Hung Jen-kan who had been much influenced by the missionary and scholar, James Legge, who, as Treadgold points out, preached 'the compatibility of much of the original Confucian ethic with Christianity'.³² It was a similar syncretism that Sun Yat-sen was later to expound.

Sun's strong admiration for the Taiping Rebellion can be seen by his preface to a book written by Liu Ch'eng Yü and published in 1904. Sun claimed that official Chinese historians have forged documents about the Taiping Rebellion, written fabricated accounts of the uprising and belittled Hung Hsiu-ch'üan, believing success to be the only criterion of exceptional ability. Subsequent generations therefore did not understand the Taiping Rebellion about which Mr Liu had discovered new information concerning heroic achievements. Sun concluded that: 'If later generations, after reading this book, follow their great ideals and continue their struggle, I will be honoured and gratified.'³³

A summary of Sun's Christianity would perhaps be that it was originally and continuously of the Taiping Revolutionary variety; it also incorporated the anti-clerical attitude of the Boxer Rebellion, although Sun did not attack the Christian ecclesiastical organisation of which he was dismissive. Sun's Christianity also embraced Darwin's theory of evolution and accommodated many conflicting Chinese values.

Sun's sincerity

The eclectic nature of Sun's Christianity may well have given rise to scepticism among certain conventional Christians. For example, at the time of the Canton Plot in 1895, the British Consul in Canton was informed that missionaries doubted Sun's sincerity as a Christian.³⁴ This, however, as Schiffrin points out, was no doubt because the Christian missionaries were anxious lest they be associated with Sun Yat-sen's activities and Christianity be linked with subversion in the Peking official mind. Memories of the Taiping Rebellion and its Christian associations might be awakened. Indeed, German missionaries at this time specifically told their converts not to engage in revolutionary activities. However, the missionary who baptised Sun Yat-sen and who was closest to Sun at this time, Dr Hager, believed in Sun's sincerity.³⁵ It is true that Sun never abandoned certain Confucian ideals, such as those of Love, Loyalty and Justice, but these ideas were not incompatible with Christianity but rather part of it. Indeed, Sun believed that Mo Tzu's ideas of universal Love and that of Jesus were the same.[36] (How similar they were in fact is debatable. Herrlee G. Creel argues that Mo Tzu's concept of Love lacks any emotional content. It differs, therefore, from the Christian ideal. However, Creel himself quotes Mo Tzu as saying that: 'If everyone loved every other person as much as he loves himself... would there be anyone who was not affectionate?'[37])

Sun's own life was distinctive in its kindness. After Sun was released from the Chinese Legation in 1896, Dr Cantlie received from Sun's friends in Canton and Hong Kong a large tablet with an inscription on it which he was at first unable to decipher. However, with the help of Sir J. S. Lockhart the full meaning was clear. It was: 'Blessed are the merciful.'[38]

Sun Yat-sen himself was known as a merciful person. Morris Cohen, Sun's bodyguard, for example, recounts several incidents of Sun's kindness and mercy which may well have stemmed from Sun's faith:

> The strangest of the humble folk I ushered into Dr. Sun's office was a spy who'd been caught by our counter-espionage and sentenced to death. By all the rules his life was over except for a walk to the execution ground. Then he would kneel down and the executioner would put the muzzle of a Mauser pistol against the base of his skull and blow out his brains.
>
> We usually managed to keep this sort of event from the Doctor's knowledge, but someone slipped up this time and he got to hear of it and insisted on talking to the man himself. He saw him quite alone. Everybody was turned out of the room including me, so no one knows what passed between them. Presently his bell rang and he sent Mah Sang for the head of Intelligence and told him, 'This man will work for me in future!'[39]

Sun often showed his aversion to killing. In his speech in 1906 he emphasised there would be no revenge killing against the Manchus. In his Sixth Lecture on Nationalism in 1924 Sun stressed the ancient Chinese saying: 'He who delights not in killing a man can unify all men.'[40]

Cohen recounts how Sun would stroll amongst the coolies in Canton, listening to their problems. Sometimes he would even financially arrange for a child's schooling. When he saw a beggar he would invariably send Cohen to give him a hand-out.[41] Yet Sun himself accumulated few personal possessions, having little to bequeath other than a library on his death.[42]

Both Wong and Schiffrin were concerned with whether Cole, the porter at the Chinese Legation, had been rewarded for helping Sun to escape.[43] This question may be resolved by Morris Cohen's account of how, at the end of his life, Sun recalled Cole's help and asked one of his supporters to trace Cole via Scotland Yard to see if he were well.

> Eugene Chen did so and the Metropolitan police tracked him down and found that he had died in the meantime but that his widow was still alive. The news reached Dr. Sun just before he left for North China on his last journey, and one of the last orders he ever issued in Canton was for the payment of a pension to the old lady for the rest of her life.[44]

Sun's Three Principles is redolent of Christian believing. As has earlier been pointed out, Sun argued that his Principles would inspire faith that would be the salvation of China and elevate her above the other powers. In the words of Christ he said 'The last will be first.'[45] That Sun was able to use such phrases shows his knowledge of the New Testament. In his third lecture on Nationalism Sun discussed the possibility that Jesus' teachings did contain some ideas of political revolution. Further, Sun believed that Jesus had had to face the problems of revolutionary leaders like himself: those of betrayal by people who believed the cause was lost and those of supporters trying to gain powerful positions if the movement was victorious. Sun referred to the account in St Matthew 20 verse 21when the mother of James and John asked Jesus ignorantly for their right to sit in positions of honour with Him.[46] Sun's awareness of the contents of the New Testament was considerable.

On being released from captivity at the Chinese Embassy, Sun wrote to a Chinese Christian friend:

> I am like the prodigal son and the lost sheep ... I owe everything to the great favour of God. Through the Will of God, I hope to alter the political way. I hope you will not cease to write to me about the Way of God.[47]

Sun certainly found the political mission to be religiously inspired: 'God has sent me to China to free from bondage and aggression and I have not been disobedient to the Heavenly Mission.'[48]

If some missionaries in China did cast doubt on Sun Yat-sen's sincerity as a Christian in order to safeguard their own community, they themselves were not acting as true Christians. Sun Yat-sen's Christianity may have been unconventional: for that reason it may have been the more sincere. Certainly Sun seems to have been inspired by a 'strange vigour': an unusual charisma that was characterised by unselfishness. Ultimately, Sun Yat-sen's impact has been greater than that of the missionaries in China. His life is one to which Christians can refer the Chinese today in an attempt to reawaken respect for Christianity.

Had Sun Yat-sen received the Western support he had needed in 1911 to remain as president, China would have had a Christian leader who may have had a dramatic impact on the future not only of China but of the rest of the world.

10
The Influence of Confucianism on Sun Yat-sen

There has been much debate as to how far Sun was influenced by the teachings of Confucius and Mencius, despite the fact that in his lectures in 1924 Sun emphasised that the Chinese in their eagerness to modernise should not abandon their ancient morality of Loyalty, Filial Devotion, Kindness, Love, Faithfulness, Justice, Harmony, Peace and personal refinement and culture. These Confucian ethics, he believed, were superior to Western values.

Sun's classical learning

First the manner in which Sun acquired his classical learning will be examined. On this subject there are differences of opinion. According to T'ang Liang-li, Sun went to study at the age of seven at an evening school run by his uncle at the village temple. He:

> soon got into trouble for asking too many questions and for remonstrating about the futility of the Chinese classics, the meaning of which was then above his comprehension. It should be noted that in the traditional Chinese school, learning consisted of the mechanical repetition of classical Chinese texts without any explanation from the teacher. No arguments on the part of the pupil were tolerated, and strokes with the whip were frequently distributed to troublesome boys.[1]

Nevertheless Ying-shih Yu argued that Sun Yat-sen was deeply versed in the Chinese classics before he came to the West:

> In 1886, when he was a student at the Canton Hospital Medical School, he is reported to have read Confucian classics and dynastic

histories assiduously in his spare time. A complete set of the dynastic histories was found in his dormitory room. At first his schoolmates believed that he had purchased the set only for decoration; to their surprise, they soon discovered that he was familiar with the contents of many of the histories. Only then did they begin to realize that his ambition went far beyond the pursuit of a successful medical career.[2]

Further Ying-shih Yu asserts that in July 1924 Sun donated a set of the 24 histories and a set of the *Ssu-pu pei-ya* (*Essential Works of the Four Categories*) to the library of the Whampoa Military Academy.

However, Ying-shih Yu's account is derived from 'Kuo-fu nien-p'u' which was published in Taipei (in 1965) and which may contain exaggerations of Sun's classical scholarship in keeping with Taiwanese ideology.[3] In particular it seems to clash with Sun's own humorous admission about his study of the classics in a speech he made in July 1916 to Cantonese parliament members in Shanghai:

> I had mimicked the pupils of our school in reading the Four Books and Five Classics, only to forget them later on. But I believed it was necessary to know history in order to bring about political reform and to understand history, it is necessary to know the language. So, I read the English translations of our Four Books, Five Classics and history. And what do you know! I understood them after a while.
> (The audience roared).[4]

It is possible that Sun acquired a detailed knowledge of the Chinese Classics by reading them in English under the guidance of Professor Graham in the British Museum.

However an idea that might reconcile these conflicting records of Sun's early classical education may be found in Schiffrin's account that in 1889 in Hong Kong Sun had:

> transferred to Government Central School (later called Queen's College), a respected secondary school that offered instruction in Chinese and English. Earlier, he had begun studying the Chinese classics with Ch'ü Feng-ch'ih, a Christian minister connected with the London Missionary Society. Although there are conflicting opinions concerning Sun's Chinese education... it seems fairly certain that he did not undertake serious classical studies until this later period.[5]

It is possible at this stage that Sun's study of the Chinese classics was in a bilingual form.

Whatever the truth concerning the extent to which Sun at this time could study ancient Chinese texts in the original, there can be little doubt that he became greatly interested in K'ang Yu-wei's textual scholarship and ideas on reform in the early 1890s.

Between 1892–4 Sun had rented space for his medical clinic in a bookstore in Canton which was frequented by K'ang Yu-wei with whom Sun several times tried to arrange a meeting. K'ang however rebuffed him, informing him that he had to apply in writing to be one of his students.[6] By his actions Sun demonstrated his early interest in K'ang Yu-wei's thought.

In 1888 K'ang Yu-wei had completed his study of the Forged Classics of the Hsin Dynasty, showing that all the Old Text classics were forgeries and reinterpreting the New Texts. In 1896 K'ang finished his *Confucius as a Reformer* which legitimised K'ang's argument for reform. In 1901–2, K'ang's thought culminated in his 'ta-t'ung shu'. In his 'great commonwealth' national and familial boundaries were to be erased and the government was to be representative; the ideal political system of Confucius and Mencius was to be democratic. In 1890, Liang Ch'i-ch'ao had come to study at K'ang Yu-wei's academy. By 1898 he had rejected K'ang Yu-wei's idea of preserving Confucianism as a religion and of mystifying Confucius.[7] However, he did agree with K'ang Yu-wei's idea of Confucius as a reformer, with the central idea of the Modern Text school that the authorship of the Spring and Autumn Annals was Confucius himself and that the Kung-yang text, through the oral transmission of Confucian teachers had preserved Confucius' original teaching. Liang emphasised the democratic aspect of Confucius' and Mencius' teaching. Until 1898 Liang interchanged Mencius' political ideals with democracy, despite the fact that Mencius obviously assumed absolute power for the ruler and no protection for the citizen's liberty.

It is therefore unclear as to how far Sun was influenced by the work of K'ang Yu-wei when he spoke in 1897 of the Celestial Empire being a time when:

> the people had a voice in the Celestial Kingdom's public affairs, and when there is said to have been enough of prosperity and contentment to make the phrase more or less descriptive of reality.[8]

These ideas may have been influenced by Sun's early classical studies, his Taiping background or K'ang Yu-wei and Liang Ch'i-ch'ao's teachings.

Like K'ang Yu-wei Sun was deeply critical of the Chinese educational system which produced students whose main achievement was a useless literature and literary style of composition. However, by paying much attention to the need to reform education Sun was showing a Confucian-centred concern. He was too, by deprecating the value of degrees often obtained through bribery, obviously helping to nourish his own self-esteem with regard to his self-study of the classics and the literati's depreciating him.

It was probably with much pride and pleasure that Sun in his preface (in 1904) to Liu Ch'eng Yü's book on the *History of the Taiping Heavenly Kingdom's War* wrote of well-known Chinese literati who, because of the Manchu's domination, had become ignorant of Chinese moral laws and sense of honour. Above all he claimed they did not really understand the Spring and Autumn Annals at all.[9] In this idea Sun may well have been influenced by K'ang Yu-wei and Liang Ch'i-ch'ao. In this passage Sun also uses Confucian terminology when asking whether Heaven did not dislike the Ching government.

Whatever Sun's debt to K'ang and Liang, he did not acknowledge it. This is hardly surprising since he bitterly opposed K'ang Yu-wei's 'Protect the Emperor Society'. In 1903 Sun attacked K'ang for supporting the Emperor whom he believed would not save China and would deny the Chinese their rights. He saw Liang as not being able to decide between revolution and reform:

> in *'Xin Min Cong Bao'* he sometimes said he was a revolutionary, sometimes he said he was a royalist. He also said he loved his own people more than the emperor, sometimes he said he loved the truth more than his teacher K'ang. He was like a patient talking in his sleep.[10]

Sun called both K'ang and Liang traitors in his speech. Such an adversarial approach is not conducive to acknowledging an ideational influence.

It is of significance, however, that Mao Tse-tung showed that K'ang had influenced him memorably, because therefore it is reasonable to assume that Sun was also deeply influenced by K'ang's ideas. Mao wrote:

> The family appear in the latter period of primitive communism. It will vanish in the future, thus completing the cycle. In his Universal Harmony 'Ta-T'ung' K'ang Yu-wei realized his point.'[11]

Sun in his lectures on the Principle of Livelihood expressed his desire of achieving 'Ta-t'ung' that some scholars have seen as being communism.

Yet Sun's 'Ta-t'ung' was not Marxist. His rejection of class conflict and his desire to reach social goals through more cooperative and harmonious methods than those advocated by Marxists might well have been inspired by Maurice William's writings, but might also have been influenced by Confucius' teachings. Indeed Sun expressly stated that he hoped to achieve: 'Confucius' hope of a great commonwealth.'[12] Sun's 'Ta-t'ung' was not Mao's; nor indeed was it K'ang's: for Sun was strongly in favour of the family as a 'social unit'. This fact is perhaps another reason why Sun saw no reason to acknowledge K'ang's influence. For Sun the family was an essential part of nation building. In his fifth lecture on Nationalism he argues:

> As I said before, China has had exceedingly compact family and clan groups and the family and clan sentiment of the Chinese is very deep-rooted...
> As I see it, if we take these fine sentiments as a foundation, it will be easy to bring together the people of the whole country...In the West the individual is the unit.... in lawsuits, no questions are asked about family conditions, only the morals of the individuals are considered. The individual expands immediately into the state; between the individual and the state there is no common, firm, social unit. So in welding the citizens together into a state, foreign countries do not have the advantage that China has.[13]

Sun, moreover, in this passage shows an emphasis on Confucian loyalties with loyalty to the nation replacing that to the Emperor. 'I think that in the relation between the citizens of China and their state, there must first be family loyalty, then clan loyalty, and finally national loyalty.'[14]

It is significant that Sun's discussion of traditional virtues was part of his lecture on Nationalism because Sun's evidenced nationalism was based on a pride in China's past. This pride Sun wanted to awaken in the Chinese people, and with it a confidence and a cohesive will to throw off the foreigners under whose subjugation as well as that of the Manchus 'our ancient morality has been asleep, our ancient learning has been asleep'.[15]

Sun upheld traditional virtues in his teaching, cited Confucius as authority for his key ideas, and showed the traditional nature of his thought by his concern, not with the state, but with culture and not so much with changing the laws as with changing men's hearts by educating them in moral principles. Instead of the Emperor, Sun's party was to act as the tutelary body. Here, Sun's teaching can be seen to be in the Confucian as opposed to the Legalistic tradition.

Some of Sun's interpretations of Confucius – his rejection of passivity and his democratic ideas, for example – were unconventional and he may have been showing here the courage that he showed in many situations in his life. He showed a similar lack of orthodoxy in his Christianity. Despite Sun's emphasising the value of China's heritage there has been some debate over the extent to which it influenced him. I have examined this elsewhere.[16]

The Confucian revolutionary

As Sun was concerned with a culture, not with a nation-state as a focus of nationalism, he could be described as a Confucian revolutionary. To Sun, the justification indeed for his revolution was partly Confucian, in that the ruling dynasty had lost the Mandate of Heaven. His society would be in accordance with the 'Will of the People' with which Heaven acted. In January 1923, Sun wrote:

> The term Ko-ming, or Revolution was first used by Confucius ... the Principles which I have held in promoting the Chinese Revolution were in some cases copied from our traditional ideals, in other cases modelled on European theory and experience and still in other formulated, according to original and self-developed theories.[17]

Sun was both overthrowing foreign oppression by Western means and justifying it in Confucian terms of the Heavenly Mandate. Thus, on his deathbed, Sun addressed the Central Executive Committee of the Congress of deputies of the USSR in terms which were hardly those of a Marxist dialectician:

> It is the will of Fate that I must place my uncompleted work in the hands of those whom because they remain true to the principles and teachings of my Party, are my real followers.[18]

Sun frequently exalted Chinese and other Asiatic cultures as being based on the Wang-tao or Royal Way, unlike that of Western culture which was based on 'pa-tao' or the rule of Might. The Wang-tao suggests the brotherhood of man. In his famous speech in Kobe, Japan on 28 November 1924, Sun argued for the traditional values of the Asiatic Royal Way:

One may say, therefore, that Oriental civilization is one of the rule of Right. Since the development of European materialistic civilization and the cult of Might, the morality of the world has been in decline.[19]

Sun, despite the Sun–Joffe Agreement of 1923, was not happy with the essentially violent methods used by the Russians. It is true that in 1924 he may well have been making his speech about Pan-Asianism in Japan to win Japan as an ally and break out of his dependence on Russia. Nevertheless, he may well have felt a genuine repugnance for Marxist violent methods because of his Confucian culture, and an obvious affinity with the Japanese because of their Confucian history.

Sun's idea of the brotherhood of man extended to neighbouring countries:

> A common phrase in ancient China was 'rescue the weak, lift up the fallen'. Because of this noble quality, China prospered for thousands of years and Annam, Burma, Korea, Siam and other small states, were able to maintain their independence. As European influence spread over the East, Annam was overthrown by France, Burma by Great Britain, Korea by Japan. If we want China to rise to power, we must not only restore our national standing, but we must also assume a great responsibility towards the world.[20]

It was in this sense of a common interest with smaller countries in imposing imperialism that the Confucian idea of brotherhood can be seen. In that Sun urged China to revive her national spirit and: 'Unify the world upon the foundation of our ancient morality and love of peace, and bring about a universal rule of equality and fraternity'[21] he was advocating a Confucial global community, not a Marxist one.

Sun was influenced by a Confucian heritage which may still be seen in China. Her ancient emphasis on ethical education, or morality, could still be detected under the Communist regime until the 1990s. Her example of concern for 'spiritual nourishment' and ethical standards such as purity, fidelity and honesty did impress foreigners. That this Confucian ethos of emphasis on ethical education could have emerged under the Communist regime shows how strong is the undercurrent of China's Confucian past. To argue that someone such as Sun Yat-sen who openly advocated upholding China's ancient values as an example to the world, was not greatly influenced by its Confucian tradition, is to ignore the subtle power of centuries of refining culture. Moreover, Sun's emphasis on the Chinese need to polish their manners and cultivate themselves, was essentially a Confucian idea. Sun himself was an unusual revolutionary in that his gentlemanly compassion was self-evident. Indeed, as has been noted before, he has been called 'the kindest revolutionary'.[22] This kindness may partly have been based on Sun's Confucian background emphasising benevolence, brotherhood and peace. His concern in his political thought with an Examination Yuan for politicians arguably also shows the value Confucianism placed on education.

Sun Yat-sen believed that China should revive her pride in her Confucian past which included learning that could lead to world peace:

> China has a specimen of political philosophy so systematic and so clear though nothing has been discovered or spoken by foreign statesmen to equal it. It is found in the 'Great Learning: 'search into the nature of things, extend the boundaries of knowledge, make the purpose sincere, regulate the mind, cultivate personal virtue, rule the family, govern the state, pacify the world.' This calls upon a man to develop from within outward, to begin with his inner nature and not cease until the world is at peace. Such a deep all-embracing logic is not found in or spoken by any foreign political philosopher; it is a nugget of wisdom peculiar to China's philosophy of state, and worthy to be preserved.[23]

China was to learn from the West with regard to science and technology but to treasure her own unique 'learning' which created her identity and from which the West might also learn. It is this attitude that China might well adopt today when she is puzzling over the next problem of how to modernise without Westernising. Indeed at the end of 1991 it was reported that Confucianism was again being examined in Chinese academic circles with official approval. Scholars were arguing that the non-feudal essence of Confucianism can be a positive aid for general social morality.[24] Moreover, Herman Kahn has actually suggested (with regard to Taiwan) that the Confucian ethic of working hard for the group (usually the extended family) is superior to Western values as a basis for a modernising industrialising society.[25]

Eventually Sun wanted not only to establish a 'Grand Union' with other minorities which would be peacefully assimilated into a civilisation but also to build a peaceful global community. Exactly how this was to be achieved is not clear but Sun's ideal may be regarded as a worldwide version of the Great Harmony with China setting a powerful moral example.

A final comment on Sun's Confucianism might be on Sun's calligraphy for which requests were frequently made during his lifetime. Two-Gun Cohen records how Sun's favourite maxim was the classical maxim 'T'ien Hsia Wei-Kung' (All under Heaven belongs to the People): 'He worked fast, in a free, dashing style quite different from the careful correctness of other scholars.'[26] In his speedy calligraphy Sun showed a possibly Western approach to time.

The significance of Sun's thought lies perhaps in the impact he had on later Chinese political leaders as well as other revolutionaries. This will be examined later. Both the Chinese Communist and the Kuomintang parties have claimed to have taken up Sun's mantle, probably because of the ethical association of his name as well as the value of some of his political ideas. It was the Kuomintang that emphasised the Confucian heritage of Sun's thought. The impact of this last on Chiang Kai-shek as well as his supporters will now be examined.

11
The Development of Sun Yat-sen's Political Thought by Chiang Kai-shek

After Sun Yat-sen's death in 1925, General Chiang Kai-shek became the leader of the Kuomintang after a power struggle. He claimed to have taken up Sun's mantle but in fact distorted his teaching.

Chiang Kai-shek did not implement Sun Yat-sen's ideas partly because he himself had different values. Chiang laid greater emphasis on the importance of Confucian teaching than did Sun Yat-sen; he had not travelled in the West, as had Sun Yat-sen and had not experienced liberal democracy at first hand. Moreover, Chiang was less sympathetic with the lot of the socio-economically underprivileged than was Sun Yat-sen. His party, the Kuomintang, was comprised of many wealthy landlords and merchants who were not concerned with improving the lot of the peasants and workers. Above all, Chiang Kai-shek was fanatically anti-Communist, unlike Sun Yat-sen.

Chiang' anti-Communism

Had Chiang Kai-shek been more sympathetic to socialist ideas the future of China under the Kuomintang might well have been different. However, Chiang Kai-shek's view of Soviet Communism turned into antipathy when he visited Soviet Russia at Sun Yat-sen's request in 1923. In *Soviet Russia in China* Chiang asserted that whilst studying Soviet Russia's party, political and military organisation from September until November in 1923, he came to the conclusion that the Soviet Union wanted to use the Kuomintang as a vehicle for its own designs on China. Its goals and methods, moreover, were inimical to the implementation of Sun Yat-sen's Principles in China. Interestingly he concluded:

> Most of the Russian leaders holding responsible party and government positions who express regard for Dr. Sun and sincere desire to cooperate with China in her national revolution were Jews, the only exceptions being Kamenev and Chicherin who were Russians. These Jews, long in exile in other European countries during the Tsarist days, had returned to Russia only after the Revolution of 1917. This aroused my special interest. I found that men like Trotsky, Zinoviev, Radek and Joffe, were, comparatively speaking, more concerned with the question of cooperation between the Kuomintang and the Russian Communist Party. Joffe, however, lost his influence shortly after his return to Russia from China.[1]

Chiang Kai-shek, therefore, in a letter circulated among members of the Kuomintang's standing committee said that:

> According to my observation, the Russian Communist Party is not to be trusted... Chinese Communists in Russia always speak of Dr. Sun slanderously and with suspicion.
>
> The Russian Communist Party, in its dealings with China, has only one aim, namely, to make the Chinese Communist Party its chosen instrument.[2]

Chiang Kai-shek stated that he felt so disillusioned with the Chinese Communists' increased influence in the Kuomintang during the First National Congress in January 1924 that he left Canton for his native home Chekiang, declining his appointment as Commandant of the Whampoa Military Academy. He took up his post, however, in April 1924 after persistent persuasion from Sun Yat-sen.

Despite Chiang's evident disillusionment with Soviet Russia, however, it is interesting to note that he was not among the group of Kuomintang leaders who were vociferous in demanding the exclusion of Chinese Communists from the Kuomintang in 1925 after Sun Yat-sen's death. Sun Yat-sen himself had to contend with criticisms from within his Party over his admission of Communists to the Kuomintang. After his death the gulf between those for and against Communist participation in the Kuomintang widened, particularly as the Communists were active in stirring up workers to strike against foreign exploitation and organising peasants into activist organisations.

Their activities harmed the merchant and landlord elements in the Kuomintang. Possibly the turning point came for Chiang Kai-shek in 1926 when he believed he had just managed to foil a plot, inspired by the Soviet Union, to transport him to that country so that he could not obstruct the Soviet Union's activities in China. Certainly, a split came at that time between him and the pro-Soviet group of the Kuomintang over military strategy. In January 1927 in Nanchang, Chiang Kai-shek overruled the pro-Soviet group who wanted military progress northwards while he wanted to move to Shanghai and Nanking. Both Mikhail Borodin (the chief Comintern representative in China) and Chiang Kai-shek publicly criticised each other. In January 1927 the Communist Central Committee reports declared:

> The Right Wing of the Kuomintang is daily becoming more powerful ...there is currently an extremely strong tendency within the Kuomintang to oppose Soviet Russia, the Communist Party, and the Labour and Peasant movements.
> The tendency towards the right is due first to the belief of Chiang Kai-shek ... and that the greatest enemy at present is not imperialism but the Communist Party ... [3]

It was this evident hostility that culminated in the massacre of the Communists in Shanghai in 1927. It was a hostility that had not been felt by Sun Yat-sen and which made the implementation of his Principles unlikely.

Chiang Kai-shek most obviously departed from Sun Yat-sen's *San Min Chu-I* with regard to his Principle of Livelihood. There was little that was socialist under the Kuomintang despite the extreme poverty of the peasants and workers in China for whom Chiang had little sympathy.

One essential problem in endeavouring to understand Chiang Kai-shek's thought is that most of his books and speeches were ghost-written. However, as the distinguished political scientist Chester Tan has observed, Chiang Kai-shek's *China's Destiny* which was 'ghosted' for Chiang Kai-shek by Tao Hsi-sheng (a former professor at Peking National University) begun in November 1943, and eventually after an initial edition published in revised form in January 1944 to become the Bible of the Kuomintang, could be regarded as expressing Chiang's viewpoint.[4] In it Chiang constantly expresses repugnance for Nazism and Fascism and upholds Sun Yat-sen's Principles. Chiang Kai-shek argued that Sun's:

Nationalism is based on emotion, Democracy on law and the People's Livelihood on reason. We secure national independence through increased national emotion, we lay the foundation of democracy through the firm establishment of government by law, and we solve the problem of the people's livelihood through the adjustment of the surpluses and deficiencies in the public and private economy according to fair and uniform laws of reason. In this way, emotion, reason and law are each assigned their proper place. This is how and why the Three People's Principles are comparatively more complete and enduring and more far-reaching yet easier to carry out than other doctrines.[5]

Here can be seen, perhaps, how little feeling Chiang Kai-shek had for the socio-economically deprived classes compared with Sun Yat-sen's more concerned approach. Chiang Kai-shek argued that ancient Chinese political philosophy paid particular attention to the relationship between emotion, reason and law.[6] Thus he saw the Three Principles as being basically influenced by ancient Chinese political thought, whereas Sun Yat-sen saw them as a synthesis of Eastern and Western thought.

In 1934, Chiang Kai-shek launched his New Life Movement, designed to revive the practice of Confucian virtues of propriety, property, rectitude and honour in Chinese life. Chiang Kai-shek indeed leaned far more towards Confucianism (which he regarded as superior to any other philosophy in the world[7]) than did Sun Yat-sen, and criticised political leaders for accepting foreign political theories which: '... only caused the decay and ruin in Chinese civilization and made it easy for the imperialist to carry on cultural aggression'.[8]

Indeed, in contrast to Sun Yat-sen who upheld many of the ideals of the Taiping Rebellion and even likened himself to its leader, Chiang Kai-shek showed admiration for the Chinese leaders who, with Western military aid, crushed the Taipings. The leaders were Tseng Kuo-fan, who represented the landed interests, and Li Hung-chang, the leader of the new comprador class. Chiang admired their 'Confucian' outlook.

In 1931 the Japanese had invaded Manchuria. As they seemed likely to invade all China the Communists tried to negotiate a United Front with the Kuomintang against the Japanese. However, Chiang believed that the Communists were a greater threat to China than the Japanese and was against cooperation with the former. Therefore rebel generals in his own army kidnapped him at Sian in 1936 to force him to agree to the United Front. Chiang Kai-shek recorded in his *Diary* the events at that time. One of his generals, Chang Hsüeh-liang said:

> You, the Generalissimo, certainly have a very high character, but there is one defect, namely, that the Generalissimo's thinking is too old and too much inclined to the right.[9]

Curiously, Chiang Kai-shek had a spiritual experience when he was kidnapped, just as Sun Yat-sen had had one when he was kidnapped in 1896 at the Chinese Embassy in London. During the morning of 22 December 1936 Chiang was reading the Bible and came across the unusual passage from Jeremiah, xxxi, 22, which in the Chinese version read: 'Jehovah will now do a new thing, and that is, He will make a woman protect a man'.[10] To Chiang's astonishment, in the afternoon his wife arrived to see him. He did not know that she had bravely come to Sian and charmed her way through his captors, acting as a conciliator.

Chiang eventually agreed to the United Front against Japan which began its bloody invasion of China in 1937. It is arguable that Chiang was already, in late 1936, planning to resist Japan but the Sian Incident clinched the issue and Chiang's position as leader of China was strengthened.[11]

Chiang's repression

It is possible that Chiang Kai-shek did originally intend to implement Sun's Principle of Democracy in China but it was difficult to do so while he was involved in war. In private correspondence to Paul Linebarger, Chiang said that the *San Min Chu-I*: '... is a type of democracy particularly suited to China. In its general features, I think, it is similar to Western democracies.'[12]

In 1936 the National Government promulgated the 'May 5th Draft Constitution', based on Sun Yat-sen's concept of the Five Powers and giving the National Assembly the powers of election, recall, initiative and referendum. The National Assembly which had the power to adopt it was scheduled to convene in November 1937. However, the Japanese invasion caused this to be postponed, rendering the implementation of democracy in China even less probable.

In 1941 Sun Yat-sen's son, Sun Fo was expressing anxiety over the absence of democracy thus:

We must remember that, in the first year of the Republic, we had parliament and provisional councils. But were the representatives elected by the people? The so-called democracy we had then was, in fact, bureaucracy. Min Ch'uan Chu-I in which the Kuomintang was professed to believe for scores of years, is the only road to real democracy... Democracy will be only an empty term if we fail in the establishment of local self government, for only through local self government can the spirit of real democracy be promoted in this country.[13]

Sun Fo observed that the period of party tutelage, beginning with the reorganisation of the National Government and the institution of the Five Yuan system, in October 1926, had lasted for 15 years. That was far beyond the time limit assumed by Dr Sun Yat-sen when he mapped out the three-phase plan for China's political evolution from autocracy to constitutional democracy. Sun Fo argued that his failure to implement the decisions of the party resulted from the incompetence and inexperience of the rank and file of the party membership. However:

a more important cause existed. This was the die-hard attitude of certain party members who consciously reject the party dogma that party rule during the period of tutelage should be subjected to any limit. What they want is indefinite prolongation of the one-party regime in order to build up a strong unshakeable political machine of, by, and for themselves.[14]

Sun Fo believed that such party members feared that once the period of tutelage terminated, rival groups such as the Communists would seize power.

Perhaps the most damning aspect of Chiang Kai-shek's regime was his use of the secret police and the army to kill and imprison those whom he believed were his enemies. How far he himself was personally responsible for the repression is difficult to evidence. Nevertheless, one of the most articulate criticisms of what was deemed to be Chiang Kai-shek's perversion of Sun Yat-sen's thought was made in 1946 by Professor Chang Hsi-jo, Head of the Political Science Department at China's famous South West Federated University in Kunming and a member of the Kuomintang and People's Political

Council. In January 1946, before about 7000 students and visitors he said:

> The Kuomintang still claims it is a 'Revolutionary Political Party' but, in reality, it has long since become something to be revolted against... Legally the Kuomintang can be said to be a government. Morally, it is simply a bandit. The Kuomintang holds political power by force and guns... We honour Dr. Sun Yat-sen as 'the Father of the Nation' but his principles have been exploited for selfish gain. How his spirit must protest this cruelty and shame.[15]

Professor Chang said that the Kuomintang talked about Three People's Principles continuously but did not implement them:

> The only right the people have is the right to attend the weekly Kuomintang memorial meetings, to bow to the Kuomintang flag, and to read Kuomintang principles. They have nothing else. I need not talk about the principle of the people's livelihood. The streets are filled with beggars. The soldiers live worse than the beggars. The streets are filled with them for everyone to see.[16]

Referring to Sun Yat-sen's period of tutelage, Chang asked rhetorically if anyone had ever heard of any training being undertaken to prepare the people for their political rights: 'The real purpose of 'tutelage' is to postpone constitutional government indefinitely.'[17]

Moreover, nothing has been done to limit capital or equalise land ownership:

> Look at the war profiteers. Did anyone ever try to limit their capital? How do they propose to equalize ownership of the land? Maybe they are waiting until the peasants can no longer afford to plant their crops because of the heavy land tax.[18]

Chang wittily attacked the failure of the Kuomintang to convene a People's Assembly:

> Dr. Sun's will, which called for the convocation of a People's Assembly 'in the shortest possible time' was written in 1925. 'The shortest possible time' is already twenty years. No wonder that foreigners complain that the Chinese idea of a unit of time is very long.[19]

Chang concluded that the only successful undertaking of the Kuomintang was thought control.

However, in the same year, Chiang Kai-shek did introduce the draft constitution to the National Assembly in November 1946. In it Chiang showed how much he had been influenced by Sun Yat-sen's own elitist belief that only those with special ability could govern. In his speech to the National Assembly he said:

> The significance of the Founding Father's five-power constitutional system lies in its distinction between sovereignty and ability. We must fulfil two conditions before we can implement and develop this five-power system. First, the people exercising political powers must possess the ability and habits to maintain and safeguard the five powers. Secondly, the government exercising administrative powers should adhere to the boundaries of those powers so as not to encroach on political powers. Otherwise the spirit of the Founding Father will be violated... If the five-power system is realized today, will the people be able to protect their political powers from being encroached upon? My answer to this question is negative.[20]

Thus, using Sun Yat-sen's argument that 'the people' were not then able to protect their political powers under a fully-fledged Five-Power Constitution Chiang Kai-shek argued that the National Assembly was to be given the right in 1946 only to elect and recall the President and Vice President of the Republic, but not the other high ranking officials. The powers of initiative and referendum could only be exercised after these two powers had been employed successfully in one-half of the counties of the whole country and after the National Assembly had instituted regulations and implemented them. Since these powers of initiative and referendum were thus rendered ineffective Sun Yat-sen's plan for popular democracy was therefore shelved.

Chiang Kai-shek did contribute to the realisation of Sun Yat-sen's Principle of Nationalism by fighting to free China from foreign domination and exalting her cultural heritage. However he failed to implement Sun's Principles of Democracy and Livelihood.

12
The Development of Sun Yat-sen's Ideas by Wang Ching-wei, Hu Han-min and Tai Chi-t'ao

Sun Yat-sen's Principles did live on after his death, embodied in their written unpolished form, and in the minds of his professed followers. However, because inevitably the latter were different in personality from Sun Yat-sen, they gave varying emphases in interpretations of his thought. Their differing values, interests and concerns, the changing external circumstances to which they had to respond have resulted in dissimilar interpretations of Sun Yat-sen's thought. Indeed, the differences of opinion between the varying factions within the Kuomintang after Sun Yat-sen's death were united only by a common professed allegiance to Sun Yat-sen. It is significant of Sun's achievement that others wanted to capitalise on the positive associations of his name. In a society like that of China, where originality is often condemned as being too individualistic, and where for this reason new ideas are often introduced disguised as traditional developments, it was to Sun Yat-sen's credit that he was able to graft new ideas on to an old tree whilst lopping off many of its branches, so that new, yet not entirely unfamiliar, fruits would be brought forth.

The mixture of old and new, Eastern and Western ideas did result in differing interpretations being given to Sun Yat-sen's thought by his followers. Chiang Kai-shek was the most famous of these but another who, had he won the power struggle after Sun Yat-sen's death might well have implemented a more 'left-wing' version of Sun Yat-sen's thought, was Wang Ching-wei.

Wang Ching-wei

Whilst showing 'leftist sympathies', Wang Ching-wei differentiated Sun's Three Principles from Marxism which he rejected. He upheld Sun's view of attempting to implement social change through legal and peaceful methods where possible; he eschewed the extremely violent methods of the Communists.[1] Wang criticised the Communists for ignoring the real economic and social conditions of China and disseminating the doctrine of class struggle creating disorder and confusion. He argued that people were arbitrarily divided into classes and that mass killings became an acceptable political method. He emphasised that the Sun-Joffe agreement had rejected Soviet methods for China.[2]

Perhaps Wang's most moving and vocal defence of Sun's teaching occurred when he took up the pen against Hu Shih's criticism of Sun's ideas on thought and action. Wang said:

> Unlike Mohammed who preached his sermons with the Koran in one hand and a sword in the other, Dr Sun hoped that all his followers should convince themselves as to why they were following him. It was their hearts that he wanted to conquer not their bodies. He wanted no obedience that did not voluntarily come from his followers.[3]

Moreover Wang did not agree with Hu Shih that Sun Yat-sen's programme overlooked a Bill of Rights. As Wang Ching-wei pointed out, Sun Yat-sen had said that: 'In the History of the Chinese Revolution (1923) directly a 'hsien' has been cleared of all reactionary influences, the Military Government should promulgate a Bill of Rights and establish local self-government.'[4] He believed it was clear that:

> Dr Sun would have been no more in favour of the personal dictatorship of Mr Chiang than any of us are. Dr Hu Shih is right in finding fault with the Nanking Government, but he is wrong in charging the crimes perpetrated by Mr Chiang Kai-shek to the account of Dr Sun Yat-sen.[5]

While Wang Ching-wei rejected the Marxist dogmatic advocacy of class struggle together with their methods which he believed lowered them to the level of 'bandits'[6], Wang did show a far greater concern with the impoverished than did Chiang Kai-shek:

> It is said that labourers such as the coal miners are the worst used of all human beings. This remark if applied in Europe or America may be

correct. But, in China, are there any people who are so ill-used as the Chinese soldiers? They suffer hunger, thirst and cold: alive, they have no food, no shelter; ill, they have no medicine, no nursing; dead, they have no coffins, no graves. They lead a beggar's – nay, a dog's – life.[7]

And again:

> It is useless, however, to talk about the revolution and the emancipation of the people if the most elementary human rights, the protection of life, property, and livelihood, cannot be guaranteed to the people. Without these, the people are in virtual slavery. Political rights can only develop on the basis of securely protected personal rights.[8]

Unlike Sun Yat-sen, Wang Ching-wei stressed the importance of mass organisations:

> China's pressing need at the moment is the supply of suitable leaders for the mass organizations, who will refuse to be the marionettes of the militarists and politicians. They must be of independent mind, with a broad outlook and a clear understanding of the needs of the Chinese people...[9]

Wang Ching-wei, however, while stressing the need for mass organisations, as did the Communists, emphasised that ultimately liberal democracy must be implemented. In this he also opposed Chiang Kai-shek's government and stressed that Sun Yat-sen was against one-party government: 'The suppression of political parties other than the governing party would be contrary to the letter and the spirit of Dr Sun's manifesto.'[10] Wang pointed out that in Sun's programme for national reconstruction:

> Three months after the completion of the general election, the national government shall hand over its governing authority to the government elected by the people... which cannot but mean a 'freely' elected government. It therefore follows that if the Kuomintang has the confidence of the people, it will continue to exercise government authority. Failing this, the Kuomintang will be replaced by some other political party. There can be no doubt about this.[11]

Wang Ching-wei blamed the Kuomintang faction led by Chiang Kai-shek for splitting the party and driving out the Communists who then unleashed the tidal flood of the peasant revolt which should have been controlled by the Kuomintang:

> To make matters worse, in the Fall of 1926, the Communists in Hunan gathered together the lumpen proletariat for the purpose of seizing political power in the villages, under the slogan of 'down with the country bosses and the wicked gentry'... And, in consequence of the decision of the Kuomintang's expelling the Communists from the party, the Communists merged into the lumpen-proletariat, being at present hardly distinguishable from the ordinary bandits.[12]

So keen was Wang Ching-wei for Party unity that he argued strongly that the pro-Western Hills group be allowed to return to the party provided that it admitted its mistakes. (In 1925 this group had broken from the Kuomintang and had met initially in the Western Hills near Peking, near the initial resting place of Sun Yat-sen's body. The group claimed they were upholding Sun Yat-sen's teachings. They argued that Borodin's relationship with the party should be ended, and Wang Ching-wei suspended for six months from party membership.) Wang Ching-wei nevertheless said:

> The Western Hills members have committed many mistakes, but who can maintain the leftists have not? We must have the courage to repent and not attempt to conceal our own shortcomings by blaming others.[13]

Indeed, Wang Ching-wei was deeply concerned that a strong national front be maintained to achieve China's emergence from the status of a quasi-economy to that of equality with the great powers: 'A united national front is imperative lest the perpetual state of war should exist between the workers and the entrepreneurs, between the shop assistants and the shopkeepers, between the peasants and the landlords to the detriment of all concerned.'[14]

It would seem possible, then, that had Wang Ching-wei led the Kuomintang he might have got together the different factions and vested interests until an implementation of Sun's Three Principles had been achieved. Certainly he was far more attentive to the question of mass movement than was Chiang Kai-shek or even Sun Yat-sen had been; at the same time he was prepared to negotiate with the 'right-wing' Western Hills group. Wang Ching-wei's ability to compromise, for which he has often been criticised, may have been the very political quality needed to steer the Kuomintang through the difficult period of the 1930s and 1940s.

As it was, Wang Ching-wei was always obliged to play second fiddle to Chiang Kai-shek. Having lost the leadership struggle to Chiang after Sun's death, Wang left for France in 1926. He returned the next year to oppose Chiang Kai-shek's Nanking Government with his Hankow Government which also claimed to uphold Kuomintang principles. In 1932 Wang decided to work with Chiang Kai-shek, as President of the Executive Yuan in the latter's government, in order to oppose the Japanese invasion of Manchuria. However, in 1938 Wang urged peace negotiations with the Japanese and finally collaborated with them; setting up his government in 1940 with Japan's support. In 1944 Wang died in Japan, having, it might seem to have taken his idea of flexibility too far. However, it could be argued that, had it not been for the unyielding presence of Chiang Kai-shek, he would not have taken the actions that he did. Further, he might well have found a way of negotiating a Pan-Asian agreement with the Japanese instead of yielding to them or subjecting China to a bloody massacre.

Probably while Wang Ching-wei had earlier urged that peace with Japan was essential, in view of China's weak and disunited state, his mind was finally made up in March 1939 after his secretary and friend Tseng Chung-ming, was assassinated in a room where Wang Ching-wei was thought to sleep, by presumed members of Chiang Kai-shek's Blue Shirts. One week after the assassination, a Hong Kong newspaper announced Wang Ching-wei's intention of making peace with Japan:

> Not only for the sake of comforting my friends, who will never leave my mind, but, even more so, for the sake of the nation whose existence depends on this policy.[15]

Wang Ching-wei, at this time, still defended Sun Yat-sen's Principles and endeavoured to clarify to the Japanese that Sun's Principle of Livelihood was not Communism.[16] Moreover, Wang insisted on flying the Nationalist 'Blue Sky and White Sun' flag that Sun had pressed for even before 1911, and thus angered the Japanese who felt that their soldiers might fire on Wang's areas of occupation. Because of this, Wang finally agreed to fly a yellow triangular pennant below it. The flag disagreement was perhaps symbolic of Wang Ching-wei's determination and belief that he was always upholding the principles that he and Sun had fought for since the beginning of the century. His claim that he was negotiating peace in the interest of China should not be dismissed as mere opportunism. There was validity in his claim that negotiation was better than subjecting a weak China to destruction. Wang had been educated at Hosei University in Japan and spoke fluent Japanese. He no doubt had some affinity with the people. Had he been in a strong position, leading the Kuomintang, he might have been able to negotiate a Pan-Asian alliance along the lines approved of by Sun Yat-sen.

Wang Ching-wei had a brilliant intellect to which even Sun Yat-sen, 17 years his senior sometimes deferred. A Japanese journalist once described Wang Ching-wei's powers of oratory thus:

> He always spoke in a very low voice in small groups. He was very polite, would address you by your full name. But in a crowd of three thousand, he was just like a crazy lion. He was a great orator.[17]

Wang Ching-wei clearly had a superior intellect to that of Chiang Kai-shek and no doubt superior political agility. It was a tragedy for the fate of Sun Yat-sen's Three Principles that Wang Ching-wei did not take over the leadership of the Kuomintang after Sun's death.

Tai Chi-t'ao

The second Kuomintang leader who will be considered had a very different outlook from that of Wang Ching-wei. Tai Chi-t'ao was known as a 'Rightist' and was most certainly a traditionalist. After Sun Yat-sen's death in 1925, Tai Chi-t'ao wrote *The Philosophical Foundation of Sun Yat-senism*, to be followed in the same year by *The National Revolution and the Kuomintang*. The chief objective of the works was to distinguish the Kuomintang's ideology from Communism which did not acknowledge the nationalism that Sun Yat-sen stressed. Furthermore, in *The Path for Youth* published in 1928, Tai Chi-t'ao urged young people to study, emphasising the difficulty of knowledge rather than the ease of action. Tai Chi-t'ao stressed the importance of law and discipline in society, in contrast to the Communists at that time.

Tai Chi-t'ao's challenge to the Communists was met by their leader, Ch'en Tu-hsiu who, in August 1925, defended the Communists' motives in joining the Kuomintang. He argued that Tai's works were being exploited by reactionaries, which was certainly true. Undoubtedly Tai Chi-t'ao, a close friend of Chiang Kai-shek, helped bring about a split within the Kuomintang by giving ideological backing to those whose vested interests were threatened by the Communists. This split was physically first manifested when a group of Kuomintang veterans met in the Western

Hills, near Peking and demanded the expulsion of the Communists from the Kuomintang.

Tai Chi-t'ao emphasised the Confucianist influence in Sun's thought. In his *Philosophical Foundation of Sun Yat-senism*, for example, Tai argues that Sun himself said that his thought was based on Confucianist teaching.[18] More specifically, ignoring the Western influence in Sun's Principle of Livelihood, Tai claimed that it was rooted in the Confucian idea of benevolence.[19] Nevertheless, this did not mean that Tai Chi-t'ao was 'Rightist' as he was sometimes portrayed. He pointed out that Sun Yat-sen had emphasised that the Revolution was carried out for those who had endured much suffering.[20] He was aware, too, that the working class, unlike the merchants, lacked a political platform.[21]

The question of Confucian influence in Sun Yat-sen's thought has been discussed in Chapter 10 of this book, where it was argued that Sun Yat-sen was indeed influenced by Confucius, yet at the same time was greatly impressed with Western ideas. This latter influence was almost ignored by Tai Chi-t'ao. The reasons for this are difficult to fathom. It is true that Tai Chi-t'ao did not travel to the West and was therefore less susceptible to its influence than was Sun Yat-sen. However, not all Chinese revolutionaries who wanted to implement ideas from the West had travelled there. Moreover, Tai Chi-t'ao came from a poor family. His was not the background that required a conservative interpretation of Sun's thought out of self-interest. Tai Chi-t'ao did recall that Sun reconfirmed to him on his deathbed that his thought was essentially rooted in Chinese traditional thought,[22] but it is impossible to ascertain whether this insensitive conversation ever took place. Indeed, even if Sun had 'reconfirmed', it would seem that he may have assented to ideas which he did not, at that time, understand. Moreover, Tai Chi-t'ao was surely able to work out for himself whether Sun's ideas were essentially traditionalist. The need for Sun's affirmation was indicative of Tai Chi-t'ao's lack of confidence in his own personal judgement, which is not an uncommon phenomenon in collectivist societies. The event also shows how important Sun's works were to the Kuomintang and also their complexity.

Tai Chi-t'ao was an unstable man who attempted suicide in 1922 and then, seeing Buddhist lights as he was drowning, embraced that religion after he was rescued.[23] His instability may explain his unbalanced interpretation of Sun's thought, for such a mind might be less able to evaluate a complex ideational system. But why did he come down on the traditionalist side? The answer may lie in Tai Chi-t'ao's strong nationalist feeling which of course involved a pride in China's Confucian past. Tai Chi-t'ao believed that nationalism was the principle that needed to be understood most clearly since it was important to prevent the country from collapsing completely.[24] Tai believed that China should be welded together, and, like Sun, believed that the Kuomintang would be able to solve the problem of the national minorities. He argued in particular that under the Ming Dynasty the Tibetans had enjoyed a degree of political autonomy. The Manchus had oppressed them. In the nineteenth century the British endeavoured to stir up Tibetan nationalist feeling against China, and the Tibetans identified the Kuomintang with Manchu rule. However, once they had perceived the difference they would want to be part of China.[25]

It is of significance that Tai argued that the Revolution was not creating a hiatus with China's past. It was restructuring a state that had survived past changes.[26] This idea echoed the notion in Sun's speech of the 1911 Revolution at the Ming tombs: 'The cicada has shed its shell.'[27]

Tai's emphasis showed his need to have roots in the past and to find continuity in disruptive change. It reflected also Tai's essential traditionalism. Tai perhaps felt more intellectually secure in holding on to China's traditional thought. Moreover, by 1925 the Communists within the Kuomintang were showing their concern more with the fate of the working masses than with China's national identity and independence. It is perhaps understandable that Tai Chi-t'ao should have thought to turn the Kuomintang emphatically away from their ideas.

It has been argued that Tai Chi-t'ao was so disturbed by Sun's death that he adopted a conservative approach to the latter's thought. Herman Mast III and William G. Saywell argue that:

> It was the trauma of Sun's unexpected death in 1925 at a critical juncture of the Revolution that shaped in part Tai's conservative redefinition of Sun's thought. The prospect that psychology might offer insights into such a momentous bond is of course intriguing.[28]

However, as the authors go on to state, Sun's and Tai's writings yield few facts about a personal relationship. They state that Tai attached himself to Sun who dominated people in 'high Confucian patriarchal style'. The authors assert:

> Sun's passing was an anguishing blow to Tai, and it sharpened his sense of insecurity about the Revolution in two ways. First, it eliminated the prime source of restraint that he depended upon to keep all aspects of the Revolution within acceptable limits. Thus, Tai's attempt to make Sunism into a cult represents something more than just an

obsessive concept of apostleship. He was also trying to fill the void that Sun left with an appropriate, distinctive ideological centre that would hold.[29]

Mast and Saywell additionally argue that Tai was concerned lest the 'centrifugal revolution would disintegrate and destroy his bosom friend, Chiang Kai-shek'. Certainly, Sun's death no doubt added to Tai Chi-t'ao's feelings of insecurity. However, it is important to stress that Tai had always been an ardent nationalist. When in Japan, in his youth, Tai was inspired by the power of Japanese nationalism which he felt could serve as a model for China. Later he was sceptical of the Sun–Joffe Agreement of 1923 since it seemed to involve Russian imperialist designs on the Chinese nation. Partly because of this and aware of the Kuomintang's interests, he opposed Borodin's programme for radical social reform in 1923–24. Tai Chi-t'ao's ideological stance was already apparent before Sun's death. It is most likely that Tai Chi-t'ao swung strongly to the traditionalist path in 1925 when confronted with the alternative way down which the Communists seemed to be dragging the Kuomintang, as Mast and Saywell point out. Initially Tai Chi-t'ao welcomed the nationalist fervour of the May Thirtieth Movement in 1925, but he was then horrified at the excesses of class struggle that the Communists encouraged. Tai Chi-t'ao was no doubt writing in response to political events as well as endeavouring to secure himself by anchoring his thinking in Chinese tradition. His instability might explain the extremity of his lopsided interpretation of Sun Yat-sen's thought.

Hu Han-min

The third Kuomintang leader who will be considered is Hu Han-min. He was one of Sun Yat-sen's most trusted colleagues and was appointed acting head of the Cantonese regime when Sun left it in 1924 for Peking. However, Hu, like Wang Ching-wei, lost out to Chiang Kai-shek in the power struggle for the leadership after Sun's death. Hu initially supported the Sun–Joffe Agreement. However, later, like Tai Chi-t'ao and others, he opposed Communist influence to the Kuomintang because it did not nurture Chinese nationalism and was a channel for Russian influence in China. Nevertheless, as will be shown later, Hu Han-min by no means accepted Tai Chi-t'ao's interpretation of Sun Yat-sen's teachings either.

A member of the T'ung Meng Hui in 1905 in Tokyo, Hu Han-min edited the party's journal *MinPao* from 1905 to 1906. In it Hu drafted the anti-Manchu *Six Great Principles of the MinPao*. He also took up the literary cudgels against Liang Ch'i-ch'ao's accusation that Sun's Principle of Livelihood would necessarily involve violence. Like Sun, Hu was much influenced by Henry George's deprecation of the landlords' obtaining profit from the unearned income of the land. Hu interpreted Sun's programme of land rights as being equivalent to land nationalisation.[30] This he believed would prevent gross land profiteering which, not yet a major problem as it was in the West, would eventually become one if urgent steps were not taken to obviate it. Hu was also possibly responsible for the introduction of the idea of the state regulation of capital.[31] Thus Hu was greatly concerned with the implementation of the Principle of Livelihood, unlike Chiang Kai-shek. Indeed, when Hu was Governor of Kwangtung from April 1912 to June 1913, he did try to implement Sun's equalisation of land rights, which involved landowners making current assessments of their land. However, as the Kuomintang were forced to leave office in 1913, this scheme was never implemented.[32]

Although initially Hu Han-min supported the Kuomintang's alliance with the Communists, with whom he had some sympathy, he later, by 1927, opposed the Russian influence in the Kuomintang. Hu believed, as did Sun Yat-sen, that the Principle of Livelihood had much in common with Communism, but that it denied the validity of nationalism, and its method of class struggle was unacceptable and unhistorical. While rejecting Marxism, however, Hu also rejected Tai Chi-t'ao's interpretation of Sun's writing. To him Sun was unique, as was Marx, Confucius and Buddha:

> To state it simply: Sun Yat-sen only is Sun Yat-sen, Marx only is Marx: similarly, Confucius and Buddha only are Confucius and Buddha: none of them can be compared to Sun Yat-sen.[33]

In 1928, as an official in the Nanking Government, Hu wrote, *The Interrelationships of the Three Principles of the People* in which he argued that Sun's ideology was the supreme revolutionary ideology.

Resenting Chiang Kai-shek's right-wing military dictatorship, Hu resigned from Chiang's government in 1931. Hu had been President of the Legislative Yuan and, in order to implement Sun Yat-sen's programme of national reconstruction, Hu endeavoured to negotiate a loan from the United States which would have strengthened his position against Chiang's Executive Yuan. Because of the ensuing tension, Hu had resigned in February 1931, only to be placed under house arrest by Chiang Kai-shek ostensibly for his own protection.

After his release in October 1931, Hu eventually made his way to Hong Kong where, in 1933, he founded the *San Min Chu I Monthly*. Through it Hu attacked Chiang Kai-shek for betraying Sun's Principles: Chiang's dictatorship was not Sun Yat-sen's prescription for political tutelage and appeasement of the Japanese was a betrayal of Sun's Principle of Nationalism. Hu also responded to speculation on whether Sun believed in materialism or idealism. Hu argued that Sun was not concerned with such questions; however, he did reject the materialistic interpretation of history. Perhaps elaborating on Maurice William's interpretation of history, Hu argued that the motivation force in society is the desire to live. Changes in the mode of living, not production, cause historical change. It is 'Life' ['Sheng'] that is operative, not material phenomenon ['Wu'].[34] After people have struggled for survival they desire to possess more and more material things: this causes social division and change. Hu therefore rejected the Marxian materialist view of history, substituting human will, desire and greed for the dialectic.

In 1935, Hu Han-min went to Europe for health reasons. In 1936, invited to rejoin the Kuomintang Government, he returned to China but died of a stroke in May 1936 at the age of 56. His death occasioned national mourning.

Hu Han-min was another Kuomintang leader who might well have led the party more effectively and in accordance with Sun Yat-sen's ideas than did Chiang Kai-shek. His concern for the implementation of the Principle of Livelihood contrasts with Chiang Kai-shek's more 'Rightist' attitude. As with Wang Ching-wei, it could be argued that had Hu Han-min led the Kuomintang instead of Chiang Kai-shek, the Three Principles might well have had a different future. Hu Han-min had some of the visionary sense and capacity for reflection that Sun Yat-sen had said should characterise the leaders of the Revolution. It was this intellectual capacity that Chiang Kai-shek sadly lacked.

13
Sun Yat-sen's Three Principles and the Chinese Communist Party

In 1980, Teng Hsiao-p'ing in a speech at a meeting of cadres called by the Central Committee of the Communist Party of China commented:

> China always used to be described as 'a heap of loose sand'. But when our Party came to power and rallied the whole country around it, the disunity resulting from the partitioning of the country by various forces was brought to an end.[1]

The phrase 'loose sand' was Sun Yat-sen's criticism of what he saw as excessive libertarianism then prevailing in China: '...it is everybody's liberty which is making us a sheet of loose sand and that if all are united in a strong body we cannot be like loose sand'.[2]

Like Sun Yat-sen, Teng Hsiao-p'ing (and Mao Tse-tung before him) believed that the political stability and cohesion of China was more important than political liberalism.

The United Front

Historically, the Chinese Communist Party (CCP) did give Sun Yat-sen's Three Principles its (at least professed) support through participating in the United Front. From 1924–27 the CCP formed the United Front with the Kuomintang (KMT) because the Comintern had instructed it to do so. It had decided that the KMT represented the interests of the bourgeoisie which could play an important role in the initial stage of the revolution and struggle against imperialism. The KMT allowed the Communists to join it on a personal basis but ended the United Front in 1927 with a bloody massacre when it decided that the Communists were trying to split the KMT. The CCP then decided that the revolution had changed from the United Front stage to that of 'agrarian revolution' in which the peasants were to be mobilised.[3]

The Communists, under attack from the Kuomintang, needed to form a safe, secure base. In 1934 they embarked on their famous Long March northwards from Kiangsi, arriving in 1935 at Yenan where Mao consolidated his leadership. But the threat of aggression from the Japanese (who had invaded Manchuria in 1931) revived the idea of the United Front. In 1936 the CCP and the KMT discussed its possibility but Chiang Kai-shek opposed it. However, at the end of the year, rebel generals in his own army arrested him and forced him to change his mind.

The CCP's offer to collaborate with the KMT had caused anxiety among some CCP members. Therefore, a national conference was held in May 1937 by the CCP to discuss this policy. At the meeting, Mao Tse-tung declared that the Communists' programme was more radical than the Three People's Principles but not in conflict with them. The CCP and KMT could therefore collaborate to struggle for 'the three great objectives of national independence, democracy and freedom, and the people's livelihood and happiness'.[4]

In July 1937 the Japanese invaded China from Manchuria. The following September final agreement on collaboration was reached between the KMT and CCP, and the latter pledged that: 'The San-min-chu-i enunciated by Sun Yat-sen are the paramount need of China today'.[5]

At the Sixth Plenum of the CCP in 1938 Mao went further:

> The anti-Japanese national united front is backed up by two parties, the KMT and the CCP. Of these two, the KMT is the first major party. It is unimaginable that the war of resistance could be launched and carried on without the KMT....It has a historic tradition in the San Min Chu I and two successive great leaders, Dr. Sun Yat-sen and Mr. Chiang Kai-shek... In the conduct of the war of resistance and organization of the anti-Japanese national united front, the KMT has occupied the leading hardcore position... We think the KMT has a bright future.[6]

At the Sixth Plenum Mao Tse-tung also remarked that 'both Sun Yat-sen and Chiang Kai-shek are our teachers' in comprehending that 'political power grows out of the barrel of a gun'.[7] It is possible to argue that Mao Tse-tung and his party were supporting the KMT merely out of opportunism and that Mao was insincere.

However, in 1937 Mao told the American journalist, Agnes Smedley, that the Communists had been able to support the Kuomintang from the first United Front because they believed the Three Principles were relevant to China's present needs.[8] Mao pointed out that the policy of the second United Front did not mean that the Communists had abandoned the class struggle but were aware that China's nationalist needs at that time were of supreme importance.[9]

To Mao Tse-tung the second United Front was a collaboration to defeat the Japanese; the goals of the CCP and KMT were attuned to this goal. But the ultimate objectives of the CCP were more far-reaching than those of the KMT. The latter's goals of social reform were only a stage along the road to the Communists' destination.

In 1937, one of the Communist leaders, Liu Shao-chi condemned the Kuomintang for not implementing Sun Yat-sen's Principles for which Liu implies respect:

> Although the Kuomintang reactionaries memorize the 'Three People's Principles' and recite Sun Yat-sen's Testament, in actual fact they bleed the people white with taxes, practise corruption and slaughter, oppress the masses, are opposed to 'those nations who treat us as equals', and go so far as to compromise with or surrender to the national enemy.[10]

In January 1940 Mao Tse-tung outlined his concept of the state when the Communists initially came to power. It was not to be the dictatorship of the proletariat but a:

> joint dictatorship of all anti-imperial and anti-feudal people led by the proletariat, that is, a new-democratic republic, a republic of the genuine revolutionary, new Three People's Principles with their Three Great Policies.[11]

This New Democracy was a direct result of the United Front experience. While it did not involve the implementation of Sun's Principle of Democracy with its Five-Power Constitution, its economic programme was drawn mainly from Sun's Principle of Livelihood:

> The republic will take certain necessary steps to confiscate the land of the landlords and distribute it to those peasants having little or no land, carry out Dr. Sun Yat-sen's slogan of 'land to the tiller, abolish

feudal relations in the rural areas, and turn the land over to the private ownership of the peasants'.[12]

Thus the economy of the New Democracy was to be based on Sun Yat-sen's Principle of Livelihood to which Mao Tse-tung deliberately referred in his quotation.

However, the Communists were not prepared to implement Sun's idea of allowing landowners to assess their property for taxation and then risk governmental compulsory purchase at the low price they might set to avoid high taxes. It is possible that Sun Yat-sen had in mind that compulsory governmental purchase with low compensation would be the main method of transferring land to the peasants. For Mao, more drastic and non-compensatory methods were justifiable. Earlier in 1939 Mao had held that the:

> new democratic revolution is basically in line with the revolution envisaged in the Three People's Principles as advocated by Dr. Sun Yat-sen in 1924...The Communist Party of China was referring to the...Three People's Principles...when in its Manifesto of September 22, 1937, it declared that the Three People's Principles, being what China needs today, our Party is ready to fight for their complete realization. These Three People's Principles embody Dr. Sun Yat-sen. Three Great Policies – alliance with Russia, co-operating with the Communist Party and assistance to the peasants and workers. In the new international and domestic conditions, any kind of Three People's Principles which departs from the Three Great Policies is not revolutionary. (Here we shall not deal with the fact that, while communism and the Three People's Principles agree on the basic political programme for the democratic revolution, they differ in all other respects).[13]

Mao's interpretation of Sun's thought derived from its format after the Sun–Joffe agreement in 1923 when Sun gave his ideas a communist dressing. Mao did not advocate the full implementation of Sun's ideas, for, as has been earlier pointed out, the Five-Power system was not part of the programme and Mao's land reform programme was more radical than Sun's.

Another CCP leader, Liu Shao-chi, did advocate the study of Sun Yat-sen's theory of democracy although he characterised it as bourgeois. In 1942 he urged:

we must carry out education inside the Party as well as among the people. It is necessary to assign some comrades to study democracy as practised by the bourgeoisie during their revolutions (by the French, the Americans and Dr. Sun Yat-sen) and by the proletariat of the Soviet Union to study the New Democracy to be practised.[14]

Liu Shao-chi also observed that democracy would probably be established first at local and then at national level which was in fact the sequence enunciated in Sun's policy. In 1940 he declared:

Because some persons in the Kuomintang are unwilling to institute democracy, it is difficult, for the time being, to democratise the central government. However, democracy has already been realised in a number of places in China, and these democracies can serve as well as the local foundation for a new democratic republic – a republic based upon the Three People's Principles. In our country the actual institution of such a republic may have to proceed from the localities to the central government and then to all parts of the country.[15]

In March 1940 Mao Tse-tung outlined a report for the Communist Party's senior cadres in Yenan on the problems of tactics in the anti-Japanese United Front.[16] Mao asserted that the pro-European and pro-American 'big bourgeoisie' faction in the United Front was trying to suppress the Communists under the guise of uniting with them against the Japanese. Mao urged that in their propaganda the Communists should stress carrying out Sun Yat-sen's Testament by arousing the masses for united resistance to Japan, implementing the Principle of Nationalism by firmly resisting Japanese imperialism, and striving for complete national liberation and the equality of all nationalities within China; carrying out the Principle of Democracy by granting the people absolute freedom to resist Japan and save the nation by introducing governmental elections at all levels, and by establishing the revolutionary democratic political power of the Anti-Japanese National United Front; and carrying out the Principle of the People's Livelihood by abolishing exorbitant taxes and miscellaneous levies, reducing land rent and interest, enforcing the eight-hour working day, developing agriculture, industry and commerce and improving the livelihood of the people. It is of significance that while the Principles of Nationalism and Livelihood bore resemblance in Mao's description to Sun's ideas, his description of the implementation of the Principle of Democracy without the Five-Power constitution and liberal democracy did not.

After the war against Japan ended in 1945, civil war broke out again between the KMT and the CCP. The latter emerged victorious in 1949. It is a tribute to the positive associations of Sun Yat-sen's name that probably in order to encourage unity among the Chinese mainlanders, Mao Tse-tung in 1949 declared that the Communists, having triumphed over the KMT were now fulfilling the ideals of Sun Yat-sen. It was not only that the Communist victory meant that the Chinese people 'have begun to stand up' but as Mao continued:

> For more than a century, our predecessors never paused in their indomitable struggles against the foreign and domestic oppressors. These struggles include the Revolution of 1911, led by Sun Yat-sen, the great pioneer of China's revolution. Our predecessors instructed us to carry out their work to completion. We are doing this now.[17]

The Communist state

The Communist state established in 1949 was defined as a 'people's democratic dictatorship' and not a 'dictatorship of the proletariat'. On 30 June 1949 in a speech on the People's Democratic Dictatorship, Mao argued that this was the true realisation of Sun Yat-sen's Principle of Democracy:

> Chiang Kai-shek betrayed Sun Yat-sen and used the dictatorship of the bureaucrat-bourgeoisie and the landlord class as an instrument for oppressing the common people of China. This counterrevolutionary dictatorship was enforced for twenty-two years and has only now been overthrown by the common people of China under our leadership. The foreign reactionaries who accuse us of practising 'dictatorship' or 'totalitarianism' are the very persons who practised it. They practise the dictatorship or totalitarianism of one class, the bourgeoisie over the proletariat and the rest of the people. They are the very persons Sun Yat-sen spoke of as the bourgeoisie of modern states who oppress the common people. And it is from these reactionary scoundrels that Chiang Kai-shek learned his counterrevolutionary dictatorship.[18]

Mao Tse-tung went on to argue that the transition to socialism from New Democracy depended on the alliance of the workers and peasants (which made up about 90 per cent of China's population) and the urban petty bourgeoisie. The people's democratic dictatorship needed the leadership of the working class revolution.

Nevertheless, like Sun Yat-sen, Mao Tse-tung in 1949 did not wish to destroy capitalism although unlike Sun Yat-sen his policy clearly was only a temporary stage on the road to socialism. He believed, moreover, that Sun Yat-sen was quite wrong in believing that the bourgeoisie could lead the revolution:

> Sun Yat-sen advocated 'arousing the masses of the people' or 'giving assistance to the peasants and workers'. But who is to 'arouse' them or 'give assistance' to them? Sun Yat-sen had the petty bourgeoisie and the national bourgeoisie in mind. As a matter of fact, they cannot do so. Why did forty years of revolution under Sun Yat-sen end in failure? Because in the epoch of imperialism the petty bourgeoisie and the national bourgeoisie cannot lead any genuine revolution to victory.[19]

Mao Tse-tung argued that state power could not be abolished in 1949, because imperialism, domestic reaction and classes still existed. Like Sun Yat-sen Mao wanted China to progress into the Great Harmony, but unlike Sun, Mao meant by this phrase a classless society where the state had withered away.

Mao Tse-tung's interpretation of Sun Yat-sen's ideas relied heavily on those expressed at the end of Sun's life when he had had to accept Russian support:

> Throughout his life, Sun Yat-sen appealed countless times to the capitalist countries for help and got nothing but heartless rebuffs. Only once in his whole life did Sun Yat-sen receive foreign help and that was Soviet help. Let readers refer to Dr. Sun Yat-sen's testament; his earnest advice was not to look for help from the imperialist countries but to 'unite with those nations of the world which treat us as equals'. Dr. Sun had experience, he had suffered, he had been deceived. We should remember his words and not allow ourselves to be deceived again. Internationally, we belong to the side of the anti-imperialist front headed by the Soviet Union, and so we can turn only to this side for genuine and friendly help, not to the side of the imperialist front.[20]

Mao therefore argued that the alliance with the Soviet Union was a fulfilment of Sun Yat-sen's last testament: a fulfilment that Chiang Kai-shek had failed to carry out.

In recognition of the continued existence of classes in China the idea of the United Front was continued in that it was allowed to represent the eight small parties including the Revolutionary Committee of the Kuomintang. However, the parties were not associations for mass political representation nor mobilisation.

In 1956, a prominent supporter of the Three Principles, Madame Sun Yat-sen remarked that the Communists 'have not only transferred Sun's life-long dreams into reality, but have achieved much more than Sun's ideals'.[21] Madame Sun Yat-sen had sided with the Communists who had rewarded her after 1949 with a palatial house and other forms of special treatment. It was to the advantage of the Communists to have the support of the wife of Sun Yat-sen since it gave the Communist revolution the addition of respect and prestige of association with the idealism of the Father of Modern China. How far, however, Madame Sun Yat-sen's summary of the Communists fulfilling even more than Sun Yat-sen's dreams went is debatable. The CCP did unite China and gave the poor work, cheap housing, free education and healthcare. However, the Communists did not introduce the period of political tutelage which for Sun Yat-sen was all important. The institutions through which Sun Yat-sen had wanted to establish radical democracy were not implemented. Sun had not believed in class conflict and his policy of land reform was milder and more gradualist than that of the Communists as was his attitude on the regulation of capitalism.

Under Mao Tse-tung the far reaching programme of collectivisation and nationalisation went far beyond Sun Yat-sen's aims. Moreover, the atheism and socialist realism that was promulgated as part of the Communist policy was directly contradictory to Sun Yat-sen's beliefs.

In 1956 Mao relaxed the Party's control on free speech, launching a campaign with the slogan 'Let a hundred flowers bloom, a hundred schools of thought contend.' He expected the intellectuals would constructively criticise the considerable achievements of the Communist Party and make some Communist officials less arrogant. The problems that Hungary and Poland had faced with their intellectuals would be avoided. However, the intellectuals' criticisms of the Communist Party were so devastating that Mao felt obliged to stop the 'Hundred Flowers' campaign. He introduced instead the Anti-Rightist campaign (1957–58) by which the harshest critics of the Communist Party lost their jobs and were sent to the countryside or to jail. Sun's ideas of developing democracy at the grassroots where the peasants could discuss local issues would have avoided this mistake.

Sun's Three Principles and the CCP   149

The Anti-Rightist campaign silenced any possible critic of Mao's next policy, with tragic results. In 1958 Mao launched his Great Leap Forward to enable, as he hoped, China to speedily catch up with the West's economic development. The agricultural collectives were merged into huge communes. As a result of mismanagement, drought and officials' falsifying statistics millions of Chinese died from starvation (estimates vary from eight to thirty million deaths). The statisticians and economists who could have offered sound advice on the Great Leap Forward had lost their jobs or were intimidated by the Anti-Rightist campaign. The tragedy would have been avoided if Sun's methods of democracy had been introduced.

The Sino-Soviet split during the early 1960s erased the last aspect of Sun's Testament that the Communists had claimed to be implementing. The chaos and destruction of the Cultural Revolution, which lasted ten years from 1966, would have been impossible under Sun's political system. In 1966, symbolically, Sun's shrine in his native province was defaced. He was accused of making a 'bourgeois' revolution.[22]

The eventual overthrow of the Gang of Four and the coming to power of Teng Hsiao-p'ing saw China becoming more stable and with a new policy agenda of modernising agriculture, industry, defence and science and technology that might have met with Sun Yat-sen's approval.

In 1979 Teng Hsiao-p'ing urged that the CCP promote the patriotic united front and work for Taiwan's early return in order to accomplish national reunification.[23] The next year Teng Hsiao-p'ing made clear that he believed that some of the 'democrats' on mainland China were in fact working for the Kuomintang secret service:

> There are still factionalists around as well as newly emerging elements who engage in beating, smashing and looting. There are also hooligan gangs, criminals and counter-revolutionaries who carry on underground activities in collusion with foreign forces and the Kuomintang secret service.[24]

Teng deplored 'bourgeois liberalisation', and in 1981 argued that:

> Without Party leadership there definitely will be nationwide disorder and China would fall apart. History has shown us this. Chiang Kai-shek was never able to unify China, The keystone of bourgeois liberalization is opposition to the Party leadership. But without Party leadership there will be no socialist system.[25]

Democracy

In June 1989 Teng Hsiao-p'ing showed that he was prepared to enforce this policy bloodily when he crushed the pro-democracy movement probably thinking that the chaos of another student-led Cultural Revolution was beginning. It is also possible that the Party leadership did believe that, as Teng Hsiao-p'ing had suggested in 1980, that the Kuomintang secret service was inciting the students. Even local Beijing residents and students suspected 'agent provocateurs' in their midst, encouraging violent action.[26]

It was not clear what kind of democracy the students wanted when they began their demonstrations on the 70th anniversary of the May 4th Movement. Their use of a model of the Statue of Liberty as the Goddess of Democracy indicated American inspiration. However, their cries of 'long live democracy, down with corruption' suggested that they believed liberal democracies did not connive at corruption.[27] Sun Yat-sen's awareness that corruption did occur in democracies led him to emphasise that the ancient Chinese institution of the Control Yuan would be essential to Chinese democracy which could be superior to that in the West.

Sun Yat-sen's name was symbolically cited by both sides during the pro-democracy demonstrations in 1989. Beijing city authorities objected that the Goddess of Democracy was blocking the spot where a portrait of Sun Yat-sen was hung on national holidays.[28] On the pro-democracy movement's side a student from Wuhan University wrote a small character poster as an open letter to the Central Committee of the Chinese Communist Party on 28 April 1989:

> The forerunner of the Chinese democratic revolution, Sun Yat-sen, held that officials are supposed to be the 'servants of the people', but what we have now is exactly the opposite. Foreign presidents who come to our country are bewildered by the sight of police cars opening up a path for our state cadres when they venture out.[29]

Indeed in the USA, after the crushing of the pro-democracy movement, Chinese dissidents quoted Sun Yat-sen in their fundraising speeches rather than Mao Tse-tung.[30] This, of course, may partly be because they appreciated that the former Chinese leader had a more positive image in the USA than the latter.

Perhaps the most unkindest cut of all to be delivered against the Chinese communist system using the weapon of Sun Yat-sen's thought was that from a teacher at the People's University. On 12 May 1989 in a big character poster he wrote:

> It is tragic that in its ideology, the political system of centralized power presumes the goodness of human nature, for in fact it is the evil side of men that has been fostered and developed to its fullest extent by this system. For example, people tend to lie, fight among themselves – to be, in effect, nothing but a 'heap of loose sand'.[31]

Teng Hsiao-p'ing had proudly proclaimed that the CCP had given China cohesion so that Sun Yat-sen's phrase could no longer be used critically to describe her (in the speech quoted at the beginning of this chapter). Now even the stability and cohesion that was the rationale for the curtailment of liberty in China was being questioned – and questioned with the words of Sun Yat-sen.

However, while there are still Chinese citizens demanding democracy it seems that the overriding concern is for stability and avoidance of chaos into which China has been plunged at great cost during the twentieth century.

In China since the late 1970s democracy at grassroots level has, in fact, been developing in the wake of economic reforms. Elections are held for village and urban residential committees every three years. In the villages the candidates, who do not have to be Communists, are questioned at meetings by the peasants on their programmes for the area. The voter turnout is about ninety per cent. Villagers have the right to petition for the recall of committee members during their time of office. This was a right which Sun had stressed was important. However, when in 1999 four elected officials tried to oust a corrupt Communist Party secretary, they were arrested.[32] This local democracy was legally formalised in the 1980s. The National People's Congress enacted the Village Committee Law in 1987 and the Urban Resident Committee Organisation Law in 1989.

Sun Yat-sen wanted China to democratise upwards from the local level, but China has not stated she is following any of his ideas. In fact one of the reasons for the local democracy was that the peasants were objecting to perceived oppressive taxation and local official corruption. Nevertheless, China's pattern of democratisation may follow that of Taiwan's which implemented Sun Yat-sen's method of first developing a thriving local democracy under a strong one-party government.

The CCP gave China after 1949 a unity she had not known since China collapsed into warlordism in 1916. The Communists greatly improved the working conditions of the poor, and gave them sickness benefit, pensions, cheap housing, free healthcare and education: life chances of which the poor of China could only dream before 1949. However, this was achieved through much repression.

Had Sun Yat-sen not died in 1925 at the age of 58 but lived to see his ideas implemented, there would have been no need for the excesses of communism; the labour camps, the millions of deaths of the Great Leap Forward and the brutish chaos of the Cultural Revolution. The poor would have been given land and social security under Sun's programme. All the Chinese would have enjoyed local democratic rights which would have gradually expanded until the whole country was democratic.

The CCP was the party which could, and did, best help the poor in China in 1949, since the alternative was the KMT under Chiang Kai-shek. However China's tragedy was that the leader who could have benefited China the most, Sun Yat-sen, died without receiving the Western backing that would have enabled him to do so.

14
The Implementation of Sun Yat-sen's Three Principles in Taiwan

The implementation of Sun Yat-sen's Three Principles in Taiwan has always been part of the Kuomintang's political rhetoric. In practice, however, only a distorted version of the Principles has been implemented.

The USA's use of atomic power in 1945 resulted in Japanese surrender to the Allies and her withdrawal from Taiwan which she had controlled for the previous fifty years. In 1949 the island was taken over by Chiang Kai-shek and his Kuomintang troops who had lost the battle against Mao Tse-tung. The government established by Chiang Kai-shek in Taipei was that of the minority of the Chinese mainlanders over the majority of the Taiwanese (in February 1947 the Kuomintang had bloodily suppressed thousands of Taiwanese). In theory, the Kuomintang sought to implement Sun Yat-sen's Principles; in practice it did not due to the political exigencies of its situation – the constant threat of Communist insurgence, the unfailing dream of retaking the mainland and the tailoring of Sun's principles to suit the Kuomintang.

The implementation of Sun's Principle of Livelihood in land reform

The first major change introduced by the Kuomintang was that of land reform. In part it could be seen as a move to implement Sun's Principle of Livelihood. In 1926 the Kuomintang had begun to implement land reform in mainland China. Landlords were obliged to reduce rent by 25 per cent, which meant that most rents would not be more than 37.5 per cent of the total annual crop yield. In 1930 this was stipulated as the maximum rent by the central government's new Land Law. However, due partly to the Civil War, this was not implemented.

In 1949, in Taiwan, the Kuomintang introduced the land reforms which it had not successfully brought about on the mainland. In Taiwan, two-fifths of farmers did not own the land they tilled, had no security of tenure and had to pay more than 50 per cent of their harvest as rent (this is still the situation in Asiatic countries such as the Philippines where land reform cannot proceed because of corruption).[1] In Taiwan, however, the circumstances were unusual in that the reformers came from the outside with military support for their economic reforms. The Governor of the Province of Taiwan in 1949, General Ch'en Ch'eng, was determined to carry out the land reform programme and eventually to practise the teaching of Dr Sun Yat-sen concerning the people's livelihood. However, as Chen himself pointed out, there were reasons not so much of ideology as political expediency that required the implementation of Sun's Principle of Livelihood:

> To safeguard the island as a base of operations for national recovery, we required social stability and the first prerequisite had to be satisfactory solution of the problem of the people's livelihood.[2]

This unrest was more likely to break out because of the closure of preferential Japanese and Chinese mainland markets for Taiwanese farm producers.

The first step of the Kuomintang's land reform programme was to extend lease tenure to a minimum of six years and to reduce farm rentals to a maximum of 37.5 per cent of the average crop yield of the previous three years. This gave an immediate boost to tenant incomes. The second step was the sale in 1951 of public land in easy instalments to 156 000 families at a price fixed at 2.5 times the annual crop price. The final stage was to limit individual land holdings, with dispossessed landlords reimbursed with government land and stocks.

Because of the rent reduction the value of land dropped. In 1952 a piece of tenanted land was worth only one-third of its price in 1948.[3] Therefore landowners had to sell cheaply to the benefit of the tenants. The government's land-to-the-tiller programme began greatly to increase the number of tenant farmers who became owners of small farms, and by 1988 only 6 per cent of farming families worked land that they did not own, either fully or in part.[4] According to the GINI-index of land concentration in selected countries, Taiwan has a higher equity in the distribution of land ownership than Colombia, India, Mexico, Philippines and the UAR.

Sun Yat-sen had asserted that: 'when the Min-sheng Principle is fully realised and the problems of the farmer are all solved, each tiller of the soil will possess his own field – that is to be the final fruit of our efforts.'[5]

The Kuomintang's implementation of its land reform programme has been one of its most outstanding achievements and implemented one of Sun Yat-sen's most important policies. It has played an important part in making Taiwan become one of the fastest growing economies in the world. It made the peasants more efficient, and machinated agriculture released more labour into the industrial sector of the economy. Large landowners were compensated with stock in state-owned light industries. Some were impoverished by the compensation but others used it to become Taiwan's first industrial capitalists together with refugee businessmen from the mainland.[6]

Taiwan moved from being primarily an agricultural country to an industrial one. In 1952 agriculture's share of gross domestic product was 32 per cent and industry's share was 22 per cent; today, agriculture accounts for less than 6 per cent of GDP and industrial output for about half.[7]

However, Sun Yat-sen's idea that the land could be compulsorily purchased at a price set by the owner for tax assessment has not been implemented. Moreover, it was not until the enactment of the 'Land Tax Law' in July 1977 that all the laws, rules and regulations concerning the collection of the land value tax, agricultural land tax and land increment tax were consolidated. The Ministry of Finance of the Republic of China has claimed:

> Based on the concept that 'the increment of the land price should belong to the public' contained in the theoretical framework of 'Equalization of Land Rights' advocated by Dr. Sun Yat-sen, the founding father of the Republic of China, the land value increment tax was designed to impose a heavy burden on the natural incremental value of land for the purpose of curbing speculation and monopolies in land. The said theory contends that the value of the natural increment of land is attributable to social development rather than result of labour or capital investment, and therefore it should be shared by the general public through the mechanism of the land value incremental tax.[8]

Nevertheless, Taiwan's system of land tax, derived from Sun Yat-sen, has contributed considerably to her economic success, yielding a large proportion of her public revenue, possibly enabling her to ride the storms of economic crises in Asia during the 1990s.

The implementation of Sun's Principle of Livelihood in the industrial sector of Taiwan's economy

In his lectures on the Principle of Livelihood, Sun Yat-sen argued: 'Our minsheng principle aims at the destruction of the capitalist system'.[9] He asserted that the goals of Communism and his Principle of Livelihood were the same: only the methods were different. Eventually China would reach the stage:

> When the people share everything in the state, then will we truly reach the goal of the Minsheng Principle, which is Confucius' hope of a 'great commonwealth'.[10]

Taiwan has not destroyed capitalism; rather it has developed it to become, in capitalist eyes, an economic miracle. It could be argued that for Sun Yat-sen the harmonising of social interests was far more important than whether there existed capitalism in his future society. Indeed it is not clear whether capitalism would have been destroyed or not. Sun argued: 'If most of the economic interests of society can be harmonized, the majority of people will benefit and society will prosper'.[11]

It is possible that Sun Yat-sen would have approved of the general raising of living standards of all classes in Taiwan through the public–private form of economic cooperation which has involved both the benefits of competition and governmental intervention and avoided one group's exploiting another. Indeed, the Republic of China (ROC) expressed its aim to 'narrow the gap between the rich and the poor' and to achieve 'an equitable sharing of the fruits of the growing economy'.[12] In 1953 in Taiwan 'the average per family income of the top twenty per cent was fifteen times that of the bottom twenty percent: by 1979 this ratio had been reduced to 4.2 times'.[13]

Sun Yat-sen would perhaps have conceded that Taiwan's method of industrialising was preferable to the Communist's achievement: a conclusion to which many Communists themselves had reached by the end of the 1980s. Moreover, Taiwan is not mainland China. Sun said:

> The different countries of the world because of varying conditions and various degrees of capitalistic development, must necessarily follow different methods in dealing with the livelihood problem.[14]

Indeed, Sun did not make clear his stand on capitalism. He argued that his Principle of Livelihood was to be implemented by the equalisation of landownership, the regulation of capital,[15] the building up of state capital and the initial borrowing of foreign capital.[16]

Initially the Kuomintang in Taiwan did carry out land reform according to part of Sun Yat-sen's plan and endeavoured to build up state capital and borrow foreign capital. However, gradually the ROC increased privatisation until today most capital is privately owned (although the great capitalists that Sun Yat-sen deprecated are very few in number such as Wang's 'Formosa Plastics' or Chang Yung-fa's 'Evergreen Line' – the world's largest container shipping line).[17]

The chief reason for the ROC's stress on the privatisation of capital is the probable chief reason for Taiwan's economic success: American economic aid and investment. Taiwan achieved her 'miraculous' economic transformation although she possesses few natural resources because of many factors: the energetic application of the mainlanders, who brought management skills to the Taiwan and realised that building Taiwan's economy was their last chance; the Japanese legacy of an infrastructure of roads and communications and a basic educational system, albeit in Japanese; the political stability provided by the Kuomintang and the presence of the American fleet in the Taiwan Strait (sent at the outbreak of the Korean War); but, above all, American aid and investment played a vital part in Taiwan's economic development.

Under the provisions of the China Aid Act of 1948, the United States began a programme of direct economic aid to Taiwan which it had previously been helping through the United Nations Relief and Rehabilitation Administration. Economic aid was intended to prevent economic instability and a subsequent Communist takeover. The comparatively small amount of aid ($48 million) was administered by the Economic Cooperation Administration (ECA).[18] However, the outbreak of the Korean War in 1950 resulted in the United States greatly increasing its economic and military aid to Taiwan. The aid ceased in 1965 after Taiwan had received roughly $1.5 billion from the USA.

The USA was influential in encouraging Taiwan to transfer public enterprises to private hands. In 1953 Taiwan began the first of a series of four-year economic plans for 'import substitution industrialisation'. This need to replace imported goods by those domestically produced was an idea stressed by Sun Yat-sen in his Principle of Livelihood. It was out of deference to his ideas that even during Taiwan's second Four-Year plan, the Kuomintang government still emphasised state enterprises.[19] The mainlanders, moreover, did not fully trust local Taiwanese entrepreneurs and the private sector in Taiwan did not seem worthy of the state's development.

However, American aid gave the USA an influence over the economic policies of Taiwan it would not otherwise have had. According to a report published by the ROC–USA Economic Council: 'This influence was used to raise the importance of development as a policy goal and to promote greater reliance on market forces and the expansion of the private sector'.[20]

American aid to Taiwan was channelled through the USA Agency for International Development (AID) which encouraged the development of private enterprise in Taiwan by withholding funds to support the public sector.[21] The AID entrusted, in particular, the implementation of its policy to J. G. White Engineering Corporation of New York which had an office in Taipei and was responsible not only for developing the glass, fibre and plastics industry, but also the textile industry. It was this industry that Sun Yat-sen, in his fourth lecture on the Principle of Livelihood, had emphasised must be developed. Sun wanted to develop China's textile industries to solve China's clothing problem, making her independent of foreign imported clothing and substituting for these her own exports. He expressed his concern over the cotton industry in China:

> Lately, however, foreign cloth of a better quality than the native cloth, and quite inexpensive, has been imported into China, Chinese have preferred the foreign to the native cloth, and so our native industry has been driven to the wall.[22]

In Taiwan during the 1950s, J. G. White Engineering consultants developed the cotton industry in Taiwan, providing American aid for the purchase of American cotton for which they paid Taiwanese spinners to spin and Taiwanese weavers to weave.

It is likely that the American cotton producers saw in Taiwan the cheap labour that would satisfy these demands. Taiwan benefited from the employment and exports thus produced. Therefore, the dovetailing of interest in the USA and Taiwan resulted in the development of an industry which had been of prime concern to Sun Yat-sen. However, Sun wanted the textile industry to be a state enterprise, whilst American aid ensured that it was in private hands.

Sun Yat-sen would also have approved of the development of the canning industry in Taiwan, which exported such quantities of canned pineapples and mushrooms to the USA that during the 1960s the American mushroom industry protested at lower priced competition from Taiwan.[23] In his third lecture on Livelihood Sun observed:

Recently a new method has been introduced in the West. The food is first thoroughly cooked by boiling or baking, then put into cans and the cans sealed. No matter how long the food is kept, it has a fresh flavour when taken from the cans.[24]

The textile industry went from strength to strength. In 1957 with aid from the Agency for International Development the China Man-made Fibre Corporation was established, producing polyesters, nylon, rayon and acrylic fibres. In 1980 it achieved fourth place in the world in artificial fibre production. The consultants J. G. White were again responsible for encouraging the venture.[25]

In 1957, PVC resin production was begun and became the highly successful source of Taiwan's export industries in shoes, upholstery and travel goods.

In 1961, the Stanford Research Institute was asked by the ROC[26] to recommend potential industries for development. Its recommendation of the electronics industry resulted in a booming exportation of transistor wireless sets and TV sets. American expertise as well as aid and investment had again helped and influenced Taiwan. By 1965, 24 US electronics companies were operating in Taiwan, taking advantage of the cheap labour available. However, the Taiwanese also began electronics operations in their own right. One of them became a Taiwan-based multinational with subsidiaries in the USA, Singapore, Hong Kong and England. This was possibly due to managerial skills of the Chinese mainlanders.[27] It is evidence that Taiwan was not merely a base of cheap labour for the USA; the educational system left by the Japanese and developed by the Kuomintang probably helped the Chinese to learn new technical skills quickly.

Today, the major export industry of Taiwan is that of electronics. This was also something that Sun Yat-sen could not have foreseen but of which he would no doubt have approved. However, it involves much capital investment both from the USA and Japan (as well as from Overseas Chinese), an investment of which Taiwan does not seem likely ever to be independent. Of this Sun Yat-sen would not have approved since he believed that foreign capital investment should be encouraged but only in the early stages of China's development.

When Taiwan graduated from American aid in 1965 she was second after Japan in Asia in per capita income and had one of the highest rates of gross national product and industrial production in the world. She also had, however, one of the highest population growth rates and rising unemployment. She had to sustain her economic growth and for this needed foreign investment. Before Taiwan ceased to receive American aid she implemented a programme to encourage foreign investment which further developed private sector enterprise.

Thus the ROC enacted the Statute for Investment by Foreign Nationals (in 1954, amended 1959); the Statute for Investment by Overseas Chinese, enacted in 1955, amended in 1960 and the Statute for Encouragement of Investment enacted in 1960 and amended in 1965. The main features of the legislation to attract foreign investment were the exemption of newly-formed corporations from income tax for a period of five years, and the limiting of corporate income tax to a maximum of 18 per cent. The programme to encourage foreign investment was developed after consultation between US and Chinese officials and promulgated in Taiwan with the expectation of further US aid.[28]

In 1966 Taiwan opened the Kaohsiung Export Process Zone, a custom-free enclave in the harbour of Taiwan's second largest city to attract foreign companies which would want to use the low-cost labour but also to produce for the export market. By the next year, 26 companies were operating in the zone and providing over 400 000 jobs. By 1969, foreign investment in Taiwan amounting to around $505 million had been made, the bulk of it by the USA, Japan and the Overseas Chinese.

In 1972 the government launched 10 major projects including an integrated steel mill, a shipyard, a new port, a north–south superhighway, nuclear power plants and an expansion of the petrochemical industry which supports the textile industry. This state enterprise greatly facilitated the development of the private sector and the trend to privatisation has continued. In July 1989 the Executive Yuan established the 'Task Force for the Privatisation of Public Enterprises' which included the China Petrochemical industry.

Thus Taiwan has moved away from public enterprise and towards further privatisation because of American influence which has also been partly responsible for Taiwan's economic success.[29] There has, however, been much controversy over the extent to which the USA has been responsible for Taiwan's success and how far the latter country has been dominated by the former.[30] Obviously, Sun Yat-sen would not have approved of Taiwan being subjected to American economic imperialism.

The USA undoubtedly played an important part in the ROC to develop private enterprise, just as it has been partly responsible for Taiwan's economic achievement. Given the personality of Chiang Kai-shek, however, and his expressed views against helping the impoverished,[31] it is possible that Taiwan would have become more concerned with private enterprise even without huge amounts of American aid, investment and influence. However, it must be remembered that the ROC did not lose control of the economy. The private enterprise sector developed only as part of a series of government controlled four-year plans. These encouraged, first, labour-intensive enterprise to create employment, then turned to capital-intensive industries. Governmental policy encouraged, first, import substitution industrially, and then its export orientation.

Moreover, as has already been mentioned, the great capitalists that Sun Yat-sen deprecated are few in number. Most of the businesses in Taiwan are small family firms (out of the 706 500 business enterprises registered in 1983, some 98.6 per cent were classified as 'small' and 'medium' – meaning that their operating capital was less that NT $40m). As the *Economist* remarked:

> Taiwan authorities make sure that not too many links of the industrial chain are held in a single group. The producer of polyvinyl chloride does not also make the plastic buckets and shiny raincoats. In Taiwan there is no equivalent of South Korea's 'chaebol' and Japan's 'zaibatsu' industrial agglomerations that wield an extra-governmental power.[32]

In contemporary Taiwan, state enterprise accounts for only a tenth of industrial output for nearly all the 'strategic' parts of the economy; such as China Steel, Chinese Petroleum and Taipower. The Taiwan government has also continued its influence by developing more export-processing zones as in Nantze and Taoching in 1970, and in 1981, Hsinchu, a science-based industrial park where government support and incentives, five-year tax holidays, venture capital from the state and low-interest loans are special attractions for foreign investors.

However, it must be acknowledged that although the ROC has encouraged foreign investment through tax incentives, it has also done so through lax employment and environmental protection policies of which Sun Yat-sen would have disapproved. In his lectures on Livelihood Sun showed a medical awareness of the importance of the environment.[33] Likewise, Sun showed knowledge that forestation is a method of preventing floods[34] and drought.[35] Sun would no doubt have condemned Taiwan's corner-cutting method of industrialising at the expense of environmental health which has resulted in Taiwan's having the world's highest incidence of hepatitis B.[36]

162 *The Political Thought of Sun Yat-sen*

As to the lax employment-protection laws in Taiwan that have attracted foreign investment, it is arguable that Sun would not have approved of them. A. James Gregor, for example, argued that:

> Sun early recognised that one of China's advantages was its abundance of cheap labour. China could attract foreign and domestic private venture capital with its low-cost labour.[37]

Gregor based his argument on Sun's work *The International Development of China*. Yet the whole thrust of Sun's reasoning in his lectures on Livelihood was that the interests of capital and labour should be harmonised. The capitalists must care for the workers; if they gave them better working conditions they would become more productive. Therefore Sun would have argued that as soon as the companies in Taiwan could afford to improve their workers' conditions, especially their wages, they should do so. Gregor concluded that:

> There is some evidence that multinationals, given the passivity of government agencies, have been less than diligent in protecting the health of their workers. It appears, moreover the multinationals are not rigorous in meeting the requirements of Taiwan's Labor Union Law – in fact, most unions that do exist among multinationals give every appearance of being 'company unions'.[38]

Gregor went on to observe that the only realistic way by which employees could be protected was by resolute government intervention. When Gregor was writing (in 1981) there was no evidence of this. In fact in 1984 Taiwan did enact its Labour Standards Law; however, Sun would probably have declared this to have been long overdue.

The question of cheap labour is linked to Gregor's argument that: 'Sun insisted that China's development required foreign capital investment, the transfer of foreign technology, and the assistance of foreign expertise.'[39] In his lectures on Livelihood Sun certainly believed this to be initially necessary. However, in his lectures on Nationalism he had earlier warned against foreign economic domination. It is arguable that Sun would not have approved of the extent of American influence on Taiwan's economy. He would have objected to the fact that the workers in Taiwan had even less employment protection than that obtained in the USA. Gregor is an American scholar who has shown admirable patriotism in arguing that Taiwan's (American influenced) economic development has implemented the ideas of Sun Yat-sen. However, in his *Essays on Sun Yat-sen and the Economic Development of Taiwan* (written with Maria Hsia Chang), he unfortunately shows lack of appreciation of the sources for Chiang Kai-shek's thought. Thus Gregor argues that:

> in 1943, when Chiang Kai-shek took it upon himself to write a brief account of 'Chinese Economic Theory' he simply reiterated Sun's plan of economic development predicated on the necessary resolution of the land problem.[40]

However, Chiang Kai-shek's work (ghosted by Tao Hsi-sheng) showed respect not only for Sun Yat-sen but for the 'clerical Fascist', the German economist Othmar Spaann.[41] This indicated how far Chiang Kai-shek's economic theory was to diverge from Sun's form of socialism. Chiang indeed had little sympathy for the socially unfortunate.

This uncritical approach to Chiang Kai-shek's slanted version of Sun's economic theories has resulted in Gregor declaring:

> The fact is that more than 'some aspects of Sun Yat-sen's Three People's principles can be read into nationalist rule on Taiwan' – the entire programme was not only infused with the developmental spirit characteristic of his ideology, it embodied most of its critical programmatic components.[42]

Later, Gregor argues that Taiwan had satisfied: 'the essentials of Sun's social goals'.[43]

This, in fact, is untrue. Those who are old, sick, frail and impoverished in Taiwan have little protection. This directly contradicts the ideals of Sun whose theory of state protection for all led to his need to distinguish his goals. Gregor rightly argues that Sun would have approved of Taiwan accepting American aid while avoiding dependency. It is true that Sun saw the tutelary state as having an interventionist role. In *The International Development of China* the state is to manage the entire economy in an indicative planning sense. However, Gregor neglects to mention that Sun, in the Principle of Livelihood, saw the state as being the protector and provider for the needy. In Taiwan it is the family that is the protector of its members, not the state. The employees of the government (such as civil servants and teachers) and of prosperous companies are protected against adversity as are now also most of their dependants. However, for families that are impoverished and who fall into even harsher circumstances, such as the death of the breadwinner or the burden of an elderly

164 The Political Thought of Sun Yat-sen

relative falling ill, there is little to alleviate the prolonged anguish of the family. One recourse has been that of child prostitution. Possibly due to the publicity given to the darker, grimmer side of Taiwan and partly due to the fact that Taiwan is becoming more prosperous, the government is now considering a more comprehensive system of social security. That this at present does not exist evidences that Gregor is incorrect in arguing that Taiwan has fulfilled Sun's social goals.

The implementation of Sun's political ideas in Taiwan

The Kuomintang's land reforms in the 1950s also promoted the implementation of another of Sun Yat-sen's ideas: the encouragement of local democracy. It made the peasants independent of the landlords and gave the farmer an interest in local government.

In 1950 the Kuomintang held meaningful local elections which initiated the process delineated by Sun Yat-sen which was to develop democracy first locally, then nationally. However, democracy was not implemented in Taiwan at a national level until 30 years later. It was delayed for longer than Sun had planned.

Nevertheless democracy has been effected from local government upwards in accordance with Sun Yat-sen's wishes. Indeed, the fact that in local government Taiwan has had greater vitality than in most countries would have met with his approval. From 1950 onwards regular local government elections were held in which the peasants who had benefited from the Land Reforms actively participated. The official parties of the KMT, the Young China Party and the China Democratic Socialist Party only were allowed to be represented. However, in 1977 the 'tang-wai' (or 'outside party') emerged and played the role of an opposition party in local elections.

Under the Constitution, the ROC government is divided into four main levels: central (ostensibly for all China), provincial, county/city and town/borough. Elections take place every four years for the county and city governments, councils and mayors. The counties are divided into villages and townships which have similarly elected representatives, conferences and mayors. The cities are divided into districts whose chief administrator is appointed by the city mayor. The villages and townships are divided into 'small villages' or 'communities'. These 't'sun' or 'li' also elect their administrators for four-year terms and are divided into neighbourhoods which are the basic unit of self-government. These 'lin' appoint their heads on the recommendation of the 'li' or 't'sun' chief to the village or township office. Thus regular elections have taken place since 1950 throughout the levels that make up Taiwan's local government, giving the country a firm basis of local democracy.

Democracy at a national level was, however, a long time in coming. For 30 years the Kuomintang governed Taiwan as a one-party dictatorship. The fear of a Communist invasion and the Kuomintang's reluctance to relinquish its aim of retaking the Chinese mainland meant that Sun Yat-sen's Principle of Democracy was shelved. Sun Yat-sen's East–West synthesis of political institutions was established (the Executive, Legislative, Judicial, Examination and Control Yuans), but Sun's idea of democracy was not implemented.

In 1979, on 10 December, Human Rights Day, Taiwan's second-largest city, Kaohsiung, witnessed violent demonstrations against government oppression. Some of the protesters were tried and given lengthy prison sentences. At the trial the defence argued that the Republic of China had violated Sun Yat-sen's Three Principles.[44]

A year earlier the ROC had prepared for national elections. However, because of the USA's decision in 1978 to derecognise the PRC, the Taiwan government, insecure at the loss of its powerful ally, decided to defer the election. At the same time the United States' derecognition of the ROC triggered off much criticism of the undemocratic nature of the one-party state and the futility of the dream of re-taking the mainland. The journal *Formosa Magazine* led criticism of the political system which finally erupted in the outbreak of the Kaohsiung riots. While the government cracked down on the protesters it also decided to hold the postponed national election on 6 December 1980. This was the first national election in Taiwan's history. Although it had not held national elections for nearly 30 years after taking over Taiwan, the ROC claimed that Sun Yat-sen's Three Principles were the basis of its political system. In order to assess that claim and that of the Kaohsiung protesters it is necessary to refer briefly to the history of Taiwan's constitution. This was promulgated by the National Government on the Chinese mainland on 1 January 1947, the culmination of many years of constitutional redrafting.[45]

The Constitution became effective from 15 December 1947. In 1948 the National Assembly convened at Nanking and elected Chiang Kai-shek as President of the ROC. Because of the Civil War in 1948 the National Assembly adopted the 'Temporary Provisions for the Duration of Mobilisation to Suppress the Rebellion' which strengthened the President's emergency powers at the expense of the Legislative Yuan, as did the enactment in 1949 of the Emergency Decree which activated martial law.

The Temporary Provisions remained in force until 1991, the Emergency Decree until 1987, greatly curtailing the implementation of Sun

Yat-sen's political ideas. The perceived communist threat resulted in constitutional restrictions on the Taiwanese citizens rights to freedom of expression and of association. Moreover, because of what was initially regarded as the Kuomintang's temporary sojourn in Taiwan, no attempt was made to include the indigenous Taiwanese in the political leadership of the country. During the 1970s, however, Chiang Ching-kuo (Chiang Kai-shek's son and successor) made a special effort to accelerate the recruitment of the Taiwanese into the Kuomintang. By 1976, five Taiwanese were members of the Party's Central Standing Committee (its highest decision-making organ). Initially the ROC government meant mainland domination over the Taiwanese who were, however, encouraged to participate in local government.[46]

Moreover, the actual personnel in the government institutions that arrived in Taiwan in 1949 remained in their posts for decades without re-election because of the 'national emergency'. Of the 2961 National Assembly members elected in 1947, 1393 were still serving in 1971; of the 759 members of the Legislative Yuan, 434 remained; and in the Control Yuan, of the 180 in 1949, 69 remained in April 1971.[47] To fill the gaps, the 1966 Temporary Provisions authorised the President to hold elections for the vacancies that had occurred from natural wastage.

Taiwan had therefore been a one-party state since 1949 for a longer period, it could be argued, than Sun Yat-sen had envisaged. Moreover, he believed that political tutelage must include other parties. Neither was he anticommunist as was the ROC. It was against this background that the Kaohsiung riots in 1979 broke out. When the ROC finally decided to hold a national election in December 1980, it still banned all other parties other than the Kuomintang, the Young China Party and the Democratic Socialist Party. Candidates not belonging to these parties could stand as 'tang-wai' or independent candidates.

The non-party candidates attacked the KMT as being corrupt, oppressive, nepotist, undemocratic and with a poor human rights record. Both they and KMT candidates expressed concern over housing and welfare. In the National Assembly contest the KMT won 82 per cent of the seats, and in the Legislative Yuan the KMT won 80 per cent.[48] However, some of the most articulate non-party candidates won the most outstanding victories. There was no serious criticism of vote-rigging, and the free voicing of other criticisms, moreover, showed an easing of the KMT's repression.

President Chiang Ching-kuo was aware that Taiwan had to adapt to pressures both economic and political, from abroad and at home. No doubt, too, the downfall of President Marcos in the Philippines and the discrediting of President Chun in South Korea made him appreciate that he might suffer a similar fate. In 1987 the Emergency Decree was lifted. In that year there were some 1800 street demonstrations, almost all ignored by the police.[49] Taiwan's two major newspapers had been liberalised and other newspapers were allowed to publish in competition. Books could be bought in Taiwan that had been published on the mainland, which the Taiwanese were able to visit.

In September 1986 in Taipei, the 'tang-wai' movement (which had begun as an unofficial opposition party during the 1977 local elections) declared itself the 'Democratic Progressive Party'. In January 1989 it was legalised along with the more than 20 other parties by the Law on Civic Organisations. Taiwanese-born President Lee Teng-hui who succeeded Chiang Ching-kuo in January 1988 continued liberalisation.

Sun would not have agreed with the ROC's policy of hostility towards the Chinese Communists. However, in 1991 the ROC officially ended the 42 years' state of war with them, ceased referring to them as 'bandits' and lifted the remaining temporary provisions. China's agreement with Britain in 1984 to take back Hong Kong inspired Teng Hsiao-p'ing to offer Taiwan the same 'one country, two systems' solution. Taiwan's response has been three 'noes': no contact, no negotiation and no compromise with the Communists.

Nevertheless, thousands from Taiwan now visit the mainland through Hong Kong, with trade now worth more that $1 billion a year, with the balance running in Taiwan's favour. Yet some Taiwanese do not want unification with the mainland and are calling for independence. Indeed it has been argued that the recent moves towards democratisation in Taiwan have taken place so that in any future unification with the mainland the KMT would appear more attractive to the mainlanders than the Communist party.[50]

In 1992 the Kuomintang introduced a complete overhaul of the election process to the National Assembly where there had remained elderly members of the party who had been originally elected in mainland China over 40 years previously. Under the new system all members of the National Assembly were to be elected every six years. The Kuomintang veterans were retired.

Until 1996 the National Assembly had the right to elect the President of Taiwan and to alter the constitution. However, in March 1996 in response to popular pressure the constitution changed and the President of Taiwan, Lee Teng-hui of the KMT, was directly elected. The members of the Legislature are elected every four years. Nevertheless, the Kuomintang still dominates the mass media.

The electorate has the right to recall the representatives as Sun Yat-sen recommended, but this does not seem have happened at national level. At local government level sufficient popular demand for recall is usually the result of campaigning by the representative's political opponents.

The Examination and Control Yuans were an important part of Sun Yat-sen's constitutional model. However, they have not been able to play the full part in Taiwan's political life that Sun Yat-sen would have wished (for example the Examination Yuan cannot set its own examinations for politicians). Nevertheless, all national and local government officials must have their educational qualifications scrutinised by the Examination Yuan. The Control Yuan, in theory, investigates government corruption. The Examination and Control Yuans are concerned with the qualifications and probity of civil servants not of the political representatives, other than the President or Vice-President against whom the Control Yuan can initiate impeachment proceedings. However, there does exist a Central Election Committee that fulfils this task of vetting the members of the Legislative Yuan and the National Assembly. There is a distinct preference for selecting candidates with high educational qualifications. About two-thirds of the members of Taiwan's government have PhDs; Sun would have approved of this, having once expressed contempt for electoral systems that allow, 'A wagon-driver to be elected at the expense of a PhD candidate'.[51]

The Examination Yuan, by ensuring highly-qualified government officials and representatives, may have played a part in Taiwan's economic success. The same cannot be said of the Control Yuan. It used to be part of the long, corrupt dictatorship of the Kuomintang which would have been against Sun's wishes. The Control Election Committee is controlled by the Minister of the Interior who used always to be a Kuomintang member. Thus it could not stop bribery by Kuomintang ministers. Therefore in August 1993 a new break-away party from the Kuomintang was formed: the Chinese New Party. It included six members of the 161 member Legislative Yuan. The dissidents criticised the Kuomintang for its concern with 'big money politics' and lack of internal democracy. It believed that the Kuomintang was becoming increasingly corrupt partly out of the need to finance electoral campaigns. A former Finance Minister Wang Chien-shien commented:

> KMT policy favours the rich and especially those rich people who do not make money in an honest way. The KMT has more than $40 billion in real properties and it controls much of the media.[52]

After the legislature election in 1992, several KMT candidates were indicted of vote fraud. The extent to which the KMT bribed voters is not known. Under the martial law which lasted until 1987, the KMT made little distinction between party and state business affairs. Party businesses profited from the boom generated by Taiwan's record $19 billion trade surplus in 1987 and subsequent surpluses afterwards. The party is still expanding its holdings, and the KMT is one of the wealthiest parties in the world with assets in companies to which it has granted favours. Sun Yat-sen who died poor and was an unusually incorrupt politician would have been appalled at the KMT's venality.

The New Party hoped to expose the KMT's financial transactions and money politics. It is another alternative party, besides the Democratic Progressive Party in local and national elections. Its demands for reform secured the 'Sunshine law' which was passed in 1993 despite the opposition of senior KMT officials. This law requires public officials to publicly declare financial assets and those of their immediate family members. However, it was not the New Party that caused the KMT to lose the presidential office. In March 2000 in Taiwan's second presidential election, the electorate rejected the Kuomintang's candidate and elected instead the Democratic Progressive Party's Chen Shui-bian, being tired of the KMT's 50 years in power and of its corruption.

In April 2000 the National Assembly voted to terminate itself. This was the work of the DPP and other political parties within it. The National Assembly had long been an unpopular body, wasting money and concerned, under Kuomintang domination, to prolong its life. It had not fulfilled the function that Sun Yat-sen designated for it of exercising the right of election, recall, referendum and initiative over the Five-Power government. It was responsible for electing or recalling the President and Vice-President but lost that power in 1996. It is now to be reconvened to vote on the Legislative Yuan's proposals to amend the Constitution, change the nation's territorial boundaries, or impeach the President or Vice-president. Its delegates will be elected by proportional representation based on the election of the Legislative Yuan.

The demise of the National Assembly does not mean that Sun's Five Power constitution would not work, as some Taiwanese have claimed,[53] since the National Assembly never performed the functions which Sun planned for it. Further, in his lectures on the Principle of Democracy he omitted it.

Before he was elected president, Chen Shui-bian advocated Taiwanese independence. Taiwan enjoys a standard of living that is fourth in East Asia after Japan, Singapore and Hong Kong. Some Taiwanese want to safeguard this and their democratic freedoms by establishing their independence. However, most Taiwanese do not. Chen Shui-bian received only 39 per cent of the votes, and after his election he vowed not to declare independence unless China attacks Taiwan. Mainland China and Taiwan have grown closer through trade. Taiwan is the second biggest outside investor in China behind Hong Kong which also acts as a channel for Taiwanese money. Mainland China is now Taiwan's third-largest export market. Political reunification may follow economic ties. Sun Yat-sen's ideas could be the ideology of reunification: his Principle of Nationalism realised.

Further, developing Sun's ideas on provincial government, Taiwan's constitution provides specifically for the safeguarding of Tibet's self-government. If all Sun's ideas on democracy were implemented in a united China, the issue of Tibet might be solved.

Sun's Three Principles are taught in Taiwan's high-schools, and most of its citizens are fully aware of them. Nevertheless, the Principle of Socialism has yet to be realised in Taiwan (although Sun's idea of land tax has been implemented and contributes to Taiwan's wealth). Until recently the Principle of Democracy was not even partly implemented at national level. However, there are signs that Taiwan is transforming into the multiparty democracy with highly-educated representatives that Sun would have wished.

15
Sun Yat-sen and Other Third World Countries: Indonesia, Vietnam and the Philippines

Sun Yat-sen's political ideas were an action-orientated system of belief also attractive to other Third World countries seeking to throw off imperial domination. They were particularly suitable because Sun Yat-sen's theory did not assume developed political and economic individualism, provided for lack of experience of democracy, and endeavoured to introduce a socialist system that was not Marxist/Leninist and would therefore have a wider appeal. Sun's economic theories faced the problem of modernising without totally Westernising. Three Third World countries whose revolutionary leaders were influenced by Sun Yat-sen were Indonesia, Vietnam and the Philippines.

Indonesia

In his famous Pantja Sila speech of 1945, President Sukarno of Indonesia explicitly acknowledges admiration for Sun Yat-sen. His very title 'Five Principles' (Pantja Sila) possibly shows the influence of Sun's 'Three Principles' which in turn slightly echoed Abraham Lincoln's definition of democracy and the French Revolution watchwords. In the Pantja Sila, Sukarno asserted that:

> If the whole Chinese considered Dr. Sun Yat-sen their preceptor, be sure that Bung Karno also, an Indonesian, with uttermost respect will feel grateful to Dr. Sun Yat-sen until he lies in the grave.[1]

Throughout the Pantja Sila, Sukarno referred with respect to Sun Yat-sen which could show he was deeply influenced by Sun's thought. However, it could be that Sukarno wanted to win support from the wealthy Chinese population in Indonesia, amongst which there was much admiration for Sun Yat-sen. At the beginning of the twentieth century the Chinese in the Indies had set up organisations, under the cover of reading clubs, supporting Sun's revolutionary movement to overthrow the Manchus.[2]

Undoubtedly Sukarno did admire Sun Yat-sen's teachings. However, despite Sukarno's claims, the latter's Five Principles did differ from Sun's Three Principles, a difference that was partly the result of different cultural, geographical and economical problems.

Sukarno's Five Principles were Nationalism, Internationalism, Democracy, Social Justice and Belief in God. Sukarno, a Moslem, emphasised the importance of religious belief which did not need to be of an Islamic nature. Sun Yat-sen was quiet on religious belief in China. This is unsurprising since China has never been an ecclesiastically organised society. As stated elsewhere, although a Christian himself, Sun Yat-sen belonged to a minority religion in China and he himself in any case was an unconventional Christian. Sukarno, on the other hand, believed that religious belief was necessary for the ethical life of the Indonesian people. Sun Yat-sen, however, coming from a different culture was aware that Confucian ethical teaching made a humanistic moral education possible. Thus Sun emphasised what he felt were the most important values in the Confucian tradition. Chiang Kai-shek elaborated on this in his New Life Movement which, however, had little influence on the moral fibre of the Chinese nation. Nevertheless, both leaders felt there was a need for moral teaching. Sukarno, in a society which was not essentially based on Confucian humanism, believed that Indonesian ethical life must be founded on monotheism, in which each religion should respect the other. In the Pantja Sila, Sukarno declared that his fifth principle was that Indonesian independence should be based on belief in the One Supreme God:

> Not only should the Indonesian people believe in God, but every Indonesian should believe in his own god... the Indonesian state shall be a state where every person can worship his god as he likes. The whole of the people should worship God in a cultured way, that is, without religious egoism and the state of Indonesia should be a state which has a belief in God.[3]

Sukarno was not only concerned with the ethical basis of Indonesia. By giving the Moslem majority equal status with Christians, Buddhists and Hindus, Sukarno was avoiding the problem of creating an Islamic state which Moslems wanted but which would offend the other religious groups. Sun Yat-sen did not have to face the problem of contending religious groups and, given the Confucian tradition of China, was able to be concerned with teaching values to the Chinese which were not religiously based.

Sukarno's Principle of Nationalism did have some features in common with Sun's. The Indonesian independence movement had first begun against Dutch imperialism, and then against the Japanese occupation in the Second World War. Likewise, by 1924 when Sun Yat-sen reformulated his Three Principles, the Kuomintang was aiming to overthrow Western imperialism. It had to contend with the Japanese occupation during the 1930s and 1940s until the American crushing of Japan in 1945. It was in this year that Sukarno gave his Pantja Sila speech as preparation for independence from the Dutch which was not finally achieved until 1949. Sukarno claimed that in 1918 he returned to nationalism from cosmopolitanism with which a socialist, Baars, had led him astray:

> In 1918, thanks be to God, there was another man who recalled me, and that was Dr Sun Yat-sen. In his work 'San Min Chu I' or 'The Three People's Principles' I found a lesson which exposed the cosmopolitanism taught by A Baars. Ever since then, nationalism has been implanted in my heart, through the influence of the Three People's Principles.[4]

However, Sukarno's claim of such indebtedness to Sun Yat-sen may be inaccurate. While it is likely that Sukarno had read press reports of Sun's teachings at this time (he later used a 1928 edition of The Three Principles printed in Shanghai), it is probable that in 1918 he was more influenced by the leader of Sarekat Islam, Abdul Muis, who pleaded, in 1917 that:

> Because our own conditions are now so miserable, they demand all our strength. They demand the efforts of nationalists, whose faults must not be dissipated. For the betterment of the whole world, we need not begin by turning into internationalists.[5]

Like Sun Yat-sen, Sukarno emphasised the idea of harmony in the Indonesian nationalist movement. In more lyrical evocative writings than Sun's, Sukarno used musical images to make his point:

> Only now Indonesian unity has its romanticism: what is the good of the 'gamelan' in the 'pendopo' if it is not played...the Indonesian 'gamelan' sounds Indonesian unity, at the full moon, full of the sense of fragrant flowers. Indonesia, the orphan, has found its mother again.[6]

Unlike Sun Yat-sen, Sukarno had more disparate people to weld together. There was no one major ethnic group, like the Han in China, on which to build unity. Perhaps because of this Sukarno drew on the ideas of Western thinkers to which Sun did not refer. Sukarno draws attention in his Pantja Sila speech to the fact that: 'According to Renan, the requirement for a nation is the desire to be united', and to Otto Bauer's idea that a nation is a unity of conduct which comes into being because of unity of destiny.[7] Sukarno felt that both these definitions were inadequate because they concentrated on the people and not on the place. He was, of course, aware that not all Indonesians shared the will for unity. He argued that Renan's and Bauer's argument should be complemented by a 'geo-political' notion of geographical unity:

> Indonesia is our country. Indonesia as a whole, neither Java alone, nor Sumatra alone, nor Borneo alone, nor Celebes alone, nor Ambon alone, nor the Moluccas alone, but the whole archipelago ordained by God Almighty to be a single unity between two continents and two oceans – that is our country...there is a relationship between people and place, between men and their lands.[8]

Because Sun Yat-sen was basically concerned with the Han people, while being aware of the question of national minorities, and because the Chinese were not scattered over many islands, Sun did not face the same problems as did Sukarno. Nevertheless, the latter claimed he owed a large debt to Sun Yat-sen's views on nationalism:

> I know there are many classical Chinese who do not like the basis of nationalism, because they embrace the idea of cosmopolitanism which says there is no nationalism, there is no nation. Formerly, many of the Chinese people were afflicted with the malady of cosmopolitanism, so that they said there was no Chinese nation, there

was no Japanese nation, there was no Indian nation, there was no Arab nation, but all were 'Humanity'...but Dr Sun Yat-sen arose with the lesson for the Chinese people, that there is Chinese nationalism.[9]

Like Sun Yat-sen, Sukarno also spoke of Pan-Asianism. In 1924 at Kobe, in Japan, Sun urged Asian peoples to unite to throw off the imperialist yoke. In such a movement Japan would play a leading part. Sukarno likewise spoke of 'Inter-Asianism' in which the Japanese would play an important role. However, like Sun Yat-sen, he was also aware of the problem of Japanese imperialism.[10]

One of Sukarno's Principles was internationalism which Sun Yat-sen did not expressly espouse. Sukarno differentiated internationalism from cosmopolitanism:

> When I say 'internationalism', I do not mean 'cosmopolitanism', which does not want the existence of nationalism, which says there is no Indonesia, there is no Japan, there is no Burma, there is no England, there is no America, and so on. Internationalism cannot flourish if it is not rooted in the soil of nationalism.[11]

Then in his typically flowery style: 'Nationalism cannot flourish if it does not grow in the flower garden of internationalism.'[12]

Although Sun did not expressly espouse the principle of internationalism as did Sukarno, his idea of universal brotherhood was similar. Like Sun Yat-sen, Sukarno did not believe in aggressive nationalism which would exalt his nation 'über Alles':

> Do not let us say that the Indonesian nation is the most perfect and the noblest whilst we belittle other people. We must proceed towards the unity of the world, the brotherhood of the world. We have not only to establish the State of Indonesian Merdeka, but we also have to proceed towards the familyhood of nations.[13]

This echoes Sun Yat-sen's idea:

> Let us today, before China's development begins, pledge ourselves to lift up the fallen and to aid the weak: then when we become strong and look back upon our own sufferings under the political and economic domination of the powers and see weaker and smaller peoples undergoing similar treatment, we will rise and smite that imperialism...unify the world upon the foundation of our ancient

morality and love of peace, and bring about a universal rule of equality and fraternity.[14]

Indeed, Sukarno's internationalism was similar to Sun's cosmopolitanism which was to grow out of nationalism and not be espoused before the nation was firmly established: 'We must understand that cosmopolitanism grows out of nationalism; if we want to extend cosmopolitanism we must first establish strongly our own nationalism.'[15]

Like Sun Yat-sen, Sukarno faced the problem of adapting Western political institutions to Asiatic needs. Sun combined the Western Executive, Legislative and Judicial powers with the Chinese ones of Examination and Control. Sukarno had no such similar tradition on which to draw. However, like Sun, Sukarno was sceptical about Western democracy:

> We have seen that in European states there are representative bodies, there is parliamentary democracy, but is it not precisely in Europe that the people are at the mercy of capitalism?...what is called democracy there is nothing but mere political democracy alone, there is no social justice and there is no economic democracy.[16]

Like Sun, Sukarno was a Republican:

> I am a Moslem, I am a Democrat because I am a Moslem...I ask that every Head of State should also be elected. Does not Islam say that Heads of State, both kalifs and emirs of the faithful, should be chosen by the people?[17]

Sukarno used Sun Yat-sen's teachings as well as those of Gandhi, Nehru and Jean Jaurès to support his argument that Western parliamentary democracy was a weapon used by the bourgeoisie to deny the proletariat political justice. Sukarno emphasised the importance of ideational struggle within the Indonesian representative body:

> God Almighty gave us minds so that in our social life from day to day we might constantly rub against each other, just like the pounding and husking of paddy to obtain rice, in turn to become the best Indonesian food.[18]

Sukarno believed, above all, in struggling together in mutual cooperation 'gotong-rojong'. This to a certain extent contradicted another idea he held, at times, that of class struggle. Sukarno's belief in mutual cooperation between classes can be found in Sun's Principle of Livelihood, where he argues that the Marxist analysis of society in terms of class struggle is false and that cooperation is possible and desirable. Sukarno argued for:

> The Principle of 'Gotong-rojong' between the rich and the poor, between the Moslem and the Christian, between the nonIndonesian and those of foreign descent who became Indonesians.[19]

He argued that 'Gotong-rojong' was a dynamic concept that meant: 'Toiling hard together, sweating hard together, a joint struggle to help one another.'[20]

In emphasising the importance of 'struggle', Sukarno in his Pantja Sila speech seemed to imply erroneously that the San Min Chu I had been realised: 'San Min Chu I could never have become a fact without the struggle of the Chinese people, friends, never.'[21] Sukarno's problem was, however, that the San Min Chu I had not been realised and he had no real model on which he could pattern his own society. Thus later he said in 1958:

> If you ask: 'Bung, I want an example', then I go back to what I have said already; all those matters I bring back to Indonesia's personality. Thus an exact example is not to be found overseas.[22]

Unlike Sun Yat-sen, Sukarno at first established a form of liberal democracy in which parties were allowed to rub off against each other. By 1956, however, he decided that this system had failed. He therefore introduced the idea of 'guided democracy' which partly resembled the idea of the Kuomintang's political tutelage.

In 1956 Sukarno argued against liberalism:

> This idea requires us to leave liberalism behind, liberalism which, by definition, is without leadership, and exchange it for a system which has leadership at its heart. Yes, leadership, the idea of which is: the notion of Indonesian socialism, a just and prosperous society with Indonesian traits.[23]

However, whereas Sun was to begin with a one-party state and end up with a liberal democracy that included political parties, Sukarno reversed the process.

In the 'Guided Democracy' of Indonesia, the 'golkar', or functional groups were to be the participants in the representative assembly. Sukarno had been advocating this system since the 1930s as had some of his fellow revolutionaries. Yamin, for example, said in 1945 that the People's Representative Body should consist of 'groups' (golongan). He did not clarify exactly what he meant but he cited the 1936 Russian Constitution and 'the Constitution of the San Min Chu I in China' as representative models.[24] Occupational groups were to be represented in the 1936 Constitution, while the National Convention of 1931 was composed of farmers and workers unions, merchant guilds and industrial associations, educational organisations, universities and professional associations in the Kuomintang. This Kuomintang form of representation may have served as a model for the Indonesian 'golkar' functional groups, in the 1950s and 1960s. However, if it did, it was not an accurate implementation of Sun's thought which expressly supported the party system.

It is, however, of interest that Guided Democracy had the elitist element which was later to lead the Kuomintang to abuse Sun's theory. For example, Abdulgani, the Vice Chairman of the National Council, said:

> It is clear that Guided Democracy is not an 'aristo-democracy' nor a 'demo~aristocracy'... when people take Guided Democracy to mean a compromise between Aristocracy and Democracy... they have, in the final analysis, accepted the opinion that there is a difference in the objectives of People and Leader. And this difference in objectives is not present at all in the true meaning of Guided Democracy.[25]

Sukarno did attribute his Principle of social justice to Sun Yat-sen:

> I said a while ago that the Principles of San Min Chu I are Mintsu, Minchuan, Minsheng: Nationalism, Democracy, Socialism. Then, our principles should be – do we want an independent Indonesia whose capitalists do their unscrupulous will, or will the entire people prosper, where every man has enough to eat, enough to wear, lives in comfort, feels cherished by his Motherland, which gives him sufficient... basic necessities. Which do we choose, Brothers and Sisters?[26]

However, Sukarno's socialism was not entirely like Sun Yat-sen's, for the latter was not so averse to capitalism as was the former. Sukarno sometimes referred to himself as a Marxist and spoke of class struggle; later he said it was not so much one's class as one's attitude that counts. If one adopts the attitude of the peasants and workers then one may be classed with them. Unlike Sun Yat-sen he saw the importance of the peasants early on in his career. It is not clear whether he invented the term 'Marhaen' (to mean the poor smallholders and smalltraders, those who own their means of production, but who are impoverished), but a speech that he gave using it in 1930 put the term into circulation. Sukarno argued:

> All the roots of the big indigenous enterprises have been pulled up and wiped out for a long time... by the old and modern imperialism ... now there only remains small trading, small shipping... small farming... added to this millions of workers will have no enterprise at all – now Indonesian society is a society typically of 'little men'. ... of Marhaen who have nothing that is not small.[27]

'Marhaen' was given by Sukarno a wider sense than that of 'proletariat'. He felt this was developing Marxism which could be combined with Nationalism to form 'socio-nationalism' against imperialism. In contrast, Sun Yat-sen's thought distinguishes Nationalism and Livelihood from International Marxism.

In the 1950s, Sukarno was much influenced by the Yugoslav model of workers' councils, which he wanted to introduce into Indonesia in the form of enterprise councils. He believed, too, in the 'social function' of land under the authority of the collectivity. Sukarno's Principle of Socialism then was more anti-capitalist than Sun's, probably because of the different socio-economic conditions pertaining in Indonesia.

Whatever the differences in their theories, certainly Sun Yat-sen was an acknowledged influence on Sukarno. It is a credit to his idealism that the latter wanted to acknowledge him. Perhaps the most far-flung echoes of Sun Yat-sen's gong was to be found in the Five Principles which became the Bandung Declaration. According to Dick Wilson in *Asia Awakes*, in 1954:

> The Indonesian Prime Minister had visited New Delhi and referred in a speech to the Five Principles (Pantja Sila) propounded by Sukarno in 1945 as the philosophical basis of the State of Indonesia, namely Nationalism, Humanism, Freedom, Social Justice and Faith in God. This had struck a chord among his Indian hearers, to whom the phrase 'Panchsheel' recalled the first five commandments of Buddha 2,500 years ago. Nehru had immediately given the name Panchsheel to the Five Principles of peaceful coexistence launched by himself and Chou En-lai and they in turn became the basis for the Bandung Declaration.[28]

Vietnam

The second Third World country that was influenced by Sun Yat-sen was Vietnam. This was not surprising since Vietnam had a Confucian history, Chinese-based language and, like China, was struggling to free herself from Western imperialism. Moreover, Sun Yat-sen often visited his Chinese supporters in Vietnam, while Vietnamese scholars were able to understand his revolutionary writings. By 1900, Sun Yat-sen was a well-known figure in Vietnam. Like Sun Yat-sen and other Chinese revolutionaries, moreover, Vietnamese insurgents took refuge in Japan until that country succumbed to French pressure and expelled them.

The greatest Vietnamese revolutionary, Ho Chi Minh, was more influenced by Marxism than Sun Yat-sen, although the latter did have some effect on him as will be shown later. Ho Chi Minh saw the road to nationalism as being Marxist/Leninist, while Sun distinguished between socialism, nationalism and international Marxism. However, one of Ho Chi Minh's predecessors, Phan-boi Chau, who dominated the Vietnamese revolutionary movement until his arrest by French colonial police in 1925, was clearly influenced by Sun Yat-sen. Until about 1908, Phan worked for Vietnamese independence under Sun's leadership.[29] He supported Sun's principles and then Sun's idea of a democratic republic for Vietnam until 1920. After that point Phan-boi Chau showed greater sympathy for Marxism, having established links with the Russians in Peking.

When Sun's Three Principles were first formulated in Tokyo in 1905, they were published in Sun's party newspaper to which Phan-boi Chau would have had access. In 1908, Phan-boi Chau began to work closely with Sun. His ultimate aim was a Far Eastern Alliance of Asiatic peoples against imperialism and feudalism. In 1909, Phan put his Vietnamese soldiers at Sun's disposal and sent 500 rifles to him via Sun's brother.[30] In 1912, the Party for the Restoration of Vietnam was established under Phan-boi Chau's leadership in Canton; its goals were similar to Sun's. In 1914, Phan-boi Chau organised another committee for 'The Activation of China and the Resurgence of Asia'. Its President was a Sun Yat-sen supporter and Phan-boi Chau was its Vice-Chairman. Its objective was the liberation of China, Vietnam, India, Burma and Korea.[31]

In 1913, Phan-boi Chau was imprisoned in Canton by Sun's enemies; in 1916 after Sun's return he was freed. Like Sun Yat-sen, Phan-boi Chau believed in the Confucian Great Community, but Phan was more sympathetic to a Marxist analysis of society than was Sun Yat-sen; he was also more concerned with the peasants and workers than was Sun. Moreover, the latter had experience of Western liberal democracies which Phan-boi Chau lacked. Nevertheless, the early Vietnamese revolutionary was influenced by Sun Yat-sen. The similarities of the cultures made a revolution in Vietnam possible on the lines of the Three Principles.

However, the model would have had to be that formulated by Sun Yat-sen in 1924, when he was moving towards a greater concern with the peasants' and workers' movement. Phan-boi Chau's revolution was not to be funded by merchants and businessmen as was Sun's, neither could he have hoped for such international support. His lack of experience of Western liberal democracy made it less likely that he would have upheld this as an ideal as strongly as Sun Yat-sen. Nevertheless, influenced by Sun, Phan-boi Chau did attempt to form a common Asiatic anti-imperialist movement that was initially not Marxist/Leninist.

Phan-boi Chau's revolutionary movement was replaced in the 1920s by the more militant and Marxist Thanh Nien (Association of Revolutionary Annamite Youth) led by Ho Chi Minh. Ho, a Communist, was sent by the Comintern to be Borodin's advisor and interpreter in Canton since Ho could speak Cantonese. Ho was given the Comintern's permission to set up a training centre for young Annamese rebels. At this training centre, Ho, under the name of Vuong, gave instructions in Marxist/Leninism and in Sun Yat-sen's teachings.[32] Ho invariably wore a Sun Yat-sen suit which might indicate the respect he felt for him. At the political training centre were not only portraits of Marx and Engels, but also of Sun Yat-sen.[33] Ho Chi Minh was initially inspired by Sun Yat-sen's revolutionary success in 1911, feeling, like him, that he should arouse sympathy from abroad for his revolutionary course. (Possibly the fact that Sun returned to China to head the new Republic accompanied by Phan-boi Chau intensified Ho Chi Minh's interest in the 1911 Chinese Revolution.) However, he decided against joining Phan-boi Chau's party and to follow Sun Yat-sen's example by searching for support abroad.[34]

Hoai Thanh in *Days with Ho Chi Minh* relates how Ho Chi Minh (also known as 'Thanh'):

> had been at the school for eight months when one Monday morning in October 1911, there was news that teacher Thanh has left the school without warning... He felt more and more then need for

going abroad...Just at that time the Chinese nationalist revolution (1911) was successful and had a great repercussion in our country.[35]

Ho therefore left for Saigon to attend a school that taught cooking and baking, and with these skills he left for Europe in 1914. He eventually ended up working in London's 'Carlton Hotel', first as a dish-washer and then as a pastry cook (under the supervision of the famous chef Escoffier). He was saddened by the great gulf between the luxurious lives of the hotel guests and the poverty of those that had to serve them.[36] It is possible that partly because of his experiences as a hotel kitchen-worker in London that his socialism developed into a more extreme variety than that of Sun Yat-sen who, in the city during 1896–97, had obviously different experiences and contacts. Undoubtedly Ho Chi Minh did not agree with Sun's rejection of the idea of class struggle.

However, there is evidence that during the years 1925–26 when Ho Chi Minh stayed in Canton where Sun Yat-sen was still greatly revered, Ho was deeply influenced by certainly one aspect of Sun Yat-sen's thought. Sun admired Abraham Lincoln greatly, which may well have nurtured Ho Chi Minh's own 'Lincolnism'.[37] Ho retained an oscillating respect for liberalism, particularly the anti-racist aspect in the USA and this may have encouraged the initial cooperation between the Americans and Vietnamese to subjugate the Japanese and prevent the French from returning in 1945. However, the subsequent American intervention in Vietnam created hatred of the United States by Ho Chi Minh's supporters. At the same time, the admiration for 'Lincolnism' could not have been eradicated and might be the basis for future understanding and cooperation with the USA.

Sun Yat-sen and the Philippines

Sun Yat-sen supported the Philippines' Independence Movement between 1898 and 1903.[38] In 1896, the Filipinos had revolted against Spain and declared the independence of the Philippines in June 1898. At this point the Philippines were ceded by Spain to the United States under the treaty of Paris in December 1898 which concluded the Spanish–American war. The Philippine Republic collapsed soon afterwards as a result of the Filipino–American war.

The Philippine movement for independence against the Spanish at the end of the nineteenth century was led by Dr Jose Rizal, who is known as the Founding Father of the Philippines. Rizal was partly of Chinese descent and had ideals and a background similar to that of Sun Yat-sen.

Born in 1861, Rizal was of the same generation as Sun Yat-sen, and both revolutionaries were doctors of medicine who believed their societies needed curing from their ills. Like Sun, Rizal was concerned to relieve his country from imperialist exploitation, this time from the Spanish. Rizal received a Western education and, like Sun, was influenced by Western political ideas. Rizal's approach to awakening the Philippine people to awareness of their socio-economic and political degradation was by writing novels. Rizal received a doctoral degree for literature in Europe as well as medicine. In 1887 and 1891 he published two novels entitled *El Filibusterismo* and *Noli me Tangere*, and a series of articles, *The Philippines a Century Hence*, to awaken the Filipinos to the ideas of freedom and equality. He became known as the Rousseau of the Philippines.[39] Rizal's approach to awaken the Philippine people to their plight through novels was therefore slightly different from Sun Yat-sen's, but Rizal, like Sun, believed in the moderate approach to the Revolution. Sun said in 1923:

> Because I have claimed that I am a revolutionary, suspicion arises in the community. Actually, a Chinese revolutionary is moderate, not radical. What he seeks is a good and stable government.

Likewise Rizal believed in: 'love being the motivating force of the revolution'.[40]

In 1891, Rizal opened a medical clinic in Hong Kong partly as a cover for his revolutionary activities, and he began learning Chinese.[41] Sun Yat-sen was studying medicine at the College of Medicine for Chinese in Hong Kong at this time. Although there is no record that the two men actually met, one of Rizal's closest friends was Dr Sun's teacher. Mariano Ponce records:

> Sun Yat-sen was familiar with Philippine events, following, step by step, their course and development with the keenest interest. He had studied with special zeal the history and personality of our greatest men, like Rizal and Del Pilar, whose activities in the political development of our country he had more than once expounded to his audience in speech and writing.[42]

Likewise, Rizal must have known that Sun had organised the Hsing Chung Hui in November 1894 at Honolulu and had instigated the revolutionary uprising in China in October 1895. In 1892, Rizal returned to the Philippines and in December 1896 was sentenced to death for his revolutionary activities. At this time Sun Yat-sen had just been released from the Manchu Legation in London.

The martyred Rizal was succeeded as leader of the Filipino independence movement by Emilio Aguinaldo whose personal representative as head of the Philippine revolutionary committee in Hong Kong was Mariano Ponce. In 1896, when the latter was still in Barcelona, he read of Sun's kidnapping in London.[43] With this story Mariano Ponce began his book, *Sun Yat-sen – El Fundador de la Republica de China*, which was published in 1912, the year in which Sun was elected President of the Republic of China.

The publication of the book undoubtedly did much to bring Sun Yat-sen and his ideas to the attention of the Filipinos. In his foreword to the book, Teodoro N. Kalaw (a Filipino scholar) writes:

> The book is worthy of the interest and the importance which the Far East now demands as well as of the remarkable personality of the subject written about... Manila received with great surprise the news of the rebellion of October 1911 against the Manchu dynasty and for the establishment of a Chinese Republic. Lovers of freedom which Filipinos all are, sympathized with this great movement, and, though doubting its happy success, they all hoped for it the best of results.
>
> What is China doing now? What has it achieved, this great Chinese nation, but a work also essentially constitutional in nature? A fight through democratic means against despotism and tyranny on its institutions of government?[44]

Kalaw goes on to suggest that Japan, the Philippines and China were all inspiring each other with their revolutions.[45] The Chinese experiment was a study model for the Philippine people.[46] Thus Kalaw, like Sun Yat-sen, believed that the government should be more concerned with the stability, rather than the freedom of individuals.

The publication of Ponce's book would have publicised Sun Yat-sen in the Philippines as a man of humane ideas. Ponce, for example, recorded that: 'I had heard Sun Yat-sen on various occasions tell young Orientals: "Let us get to know one another and we will love each other more."'[47] For that reason, Sun had been one of the most enthusiastic sponsors of the Association of Oriental Youth, which students from different countries had formed in Tokyo. This association included Koreans, Chinese, Japanese, Indians, Siamese and Filipinos and gained the patronage of prominent Japanese politicians. Ponce believed that:

The name of Sun Yat-sen will figure among those of the great benefactors and will exemplify a dedicated patriotism worthy of emulation. The labour he performed was colossal; and his selflessness, his disinterested renunciation of the benefits that circumstances offered him, as just reward for his efforts, enhance the value of his merits a hundredfold. The essence of his great personality was modest simplicity, austerity in his private life.[48]

Mariano Ponce had first-hand experience of Sun Yat-sen as he became one of his personal friends. Ponce records how he met Sun Yat-sen:

> One cold winter night of 1899, in Tokyo, I was invited to dine at the house of a prominent Japanese politician, the Hon. Inukai Ki, member of the Imperial Diet... leader of the Shinpoto (Democratic Party) in Parliament. I was presented to the other guests whom I had not met, most of them Japanese politicians and scientists. Among the guests was Sun Yat-sen. His name aroused a recollection of what I had read in Barcelona about the kidnapping in London. From that night dates my personal knowledge of him. Both of us lived in Yokohama and that night we went home together. Because we lived in the same city we saw each other often. Both of us, each in his own way, pursued the same goal, the happiness of our respective countries – and this united us in mutual sympathy.[49]

Ponce asked Sun Yat-sen to help him procure Japanese weapons for the Philippines. Ponce knew that the Japanese were adverse to offending the Americans by supporting the Filipino revolutionaries. Sun agreed to help the Filipino revolutionaries and discussed the matter with his friend Miyazaki Torazo who in turn discussed the matter with Inukai Ki. He in turn suggested that a Japanese politician, Nakamura Haizu, could be responsible for shipping arms and munitions to the Philippines. Unfortunately Nakamura proved untrustworthy and purchased worthless munitions and embezzled part of the money with which he had been entrusted. This led to the failure of the Philippine Independence Movement and the Chinese revolutionary uprising at Huichow for which the weapons were also intended. Sun Yat-sen tried to retrieve the money from Nakamura but refused to exact any further compensation from him. Sun was pressured by a Japanese supporter to take Nakamura's house, but refused, stating: 'Nakamura has been expelled from the party and his political reputation is gone. How could I endure seeing him lose his home.'[50]

186 *The Political Thought of Sun Yat-sen*

Sun Yat-sen's demonstration of benevolence won him supporters. Through his idealism and kindness he inspired Mariano Ponce's book about him which undoubtedly was a source of inspiration for the Filippino revolutionaries, although the actual extent of this influence is not evidentially determined.

Besides the Filipino revolutionary movement, there was also in the Philippines another group who became greatly influenced by Sun Yat-sen: the 'hua-ch'iao', who had settled in the Philippines over the centuries and had come mainly from the south-eastern provinces of Fukien and Kwangtung.[51] At the end of the nineteenth century, in fact, they had been more inclined to support the reformist and constitutional monarchy movements of K'ang Yu-wei and his disciple Liang Ch'i-ch'ao, rather than the more radical revolutionary party of Sun Yat-sen.[52] In 1899 a branch of the Protect the Emperor Society was organised in Manilas. Many Chinese in the Philippines feared that Sun would either plunge China into another Taiping Rebellion or else, if they did support him, their relatives in mainland China would suffer.[53] However, the death of the Kuang Hsu emperor in 1908 was a blow to the monarchist reformers, and the overseas Chinese then gave more support to Sun Yat-sen's revolutionary movement whose supporters were organised from the Manila Reading Club. The Revolution of 1911 resulted in the overseas Chinese in the Philippines contributing their wealth and blood to Sun Yat-sen's revolution. From the Philippines, too, Sun won one of his most articulate supporters, an American judge Paul Linebarger, who heard of the revolution from his cook's experiences. Linebarger published his book *The Gospel of Sun Chung Shan* in 1932 in Paris, and did much to arouse Western admiration for Sun Yat-sen's teachings.[54]

In 1928, in the year when Sun Yat-sen's Three Principles were adopted as the foundation of Chinese education, Teodoro Kalaw urged that every Filipino should read Sun's Principles (which had been translated into English).[55] It is impossible to gauge precisely how Sun Yat-sen's ideas did influence Filipino political thinking, as Filipino revolutionaries did not express their political thinking as being clearly patterned on Sun Yat-sen's. Nevertheless, his idealism and constitutional experiment was a source of inspiration for their own: a source which may have helped reduce ethnic tensions between Filipinos and overseas Chinese.

Sun Yat-sen's Three Principles may therefore have had a potential value for Third World countries. However, because of the former Soviet interest in Southeast Asia and the Communist superiority in revolutionary techniques, beside the need to tailor Sun Yat-senism to national needs while gaining foreign financial support, his ideas did not bear the Pan-Asiatic fruit he had once hoped for.

A fourth country that, it will be argued for the first time, was influenced by Sun's political thought is Gaddafi's Libya. This will be examined in the next chapter.

16
Sun Yat-sen's Influence on Muammar Gaddafi

In Asia, in the Arab countries and in Latin America, many esteemed patriots and far-sighted statesmen who sympathise with the ideas of Dr. Sun and the cause he espoused are doing their utmost to preserve the national independence of their own countries, to fight against colonial rule and clear their lands of the aggressive forces of imperialism.[1]

Indeed it will be argued that at least one Arab revolutionary has been profoundly influenced by Sun Yat-sen's thought: Muammar Gaddafi. In fact the latter's admiration for the former has been so great that Gaddafi once likened Abu Nidal to Sun Yat-sen, probably in order to give Nidal a more heroic image.[2] Moreover, it will later be argued that Gaddafi's theory of Socialism in particular cannot be understood without illuminating the background of Sun's influence.

Over fifty years separates the revolutions of Sun Yat-sen and Muammar Gaddafi, yet certain similarities can be detected in their revolutionary thinking and methods, probably due to Sun's influence on Gaddafi who studied the former's revolution. It is also possible to see their common personality traits. Sun Yat-sen and Gaddafi were presented with similar problems. Firstly, the overthrow of a corrupt monarchical system and the ousting of Western imperialism; secondly, the introduction of a democratic system to a people largely illiterate and unused to any form of democracy; thirdly, the implementation of a radical programme of socialist reforms to benefit the impoverished; and fourthly, a welding together of their people in national pride and a common identity based partly on blood relationships and on ancient civilised greatness.

Both Sun Yat-sen and Gaddafi have suffered from unsympathetic press reportage. Sun Yat-sen was regarded as a hare-brained revolutionary of unsound ideas and of no consequence. Gaddafi has suffered from the anti-Islamic bias that pervades much of the Western press which even took seriously his joke that Shakespeare was an Arab (a pun on 'sheikh').[3] Moreover, the West has never forgiven the 27-year-old soldier for ousting its military and commercial presence from Libya without compensation in 1969, after Gaddafi had overthrown King Idris in a bloodless coup. As a result, Gaddafi has been portrayed unsympathetically and with derision. His Bedouin Arab clothes are seen as an eccentricity by Westerners who adore their own traditional costumes. Just as Gaddafi has his own distinctive style, so did Sun Yat-sen, both expressing their individuality.

As a result of prejudice Gaddafi has received little Western acknowledgement of his tremendous reforms in Libya, a revolution that may, to some extent, have been inspired by Sun Yat-sen. Gaddafi has transformed the feudal kingdom of King Idris into an Islamic social welfare state, by using Libya's oil revenues that Gaddafi's hard-line tactics had quadrupled during his first five years in power. Indeed, he may have done more for the impoverished of his country than the Western leaders have done for theirs. In the words of the distinguished African historian, Ali A. Mazrui in *Nationalism and New States in Africa*:

> The transformation in Libya's social services is astonishing. Medicine is free and tuberculosis cases have dropped by more than 80 per cent since 1971. Education is free and compulsory. Between 1969 and 1976 the number of school children doubled and that of university students quadrupled. Vast construction programmes have rehoused shanty-dwellers in practically free accommodation. There is full employment and comprehensive social security.[4]

Above all, neither Sun Yat-sen nor Gaddafi have been given the credit they deserved for endeavouring to carry out revolutions with the minimum of bloodshed. Gaddafi's coup in 1969 was bloodless (although later he did authorise the assassination of some people perceived as threats to the regime). Sun Yat-sen has been called the kindest of all revolutionaries;[5] he relinquished the presidency of the Republic of China in 1912 to Yüan Shih-k'ai to avoid further bloodshed. He emphasised the harmony of interests between the working and entrepreneurial classes and deplored the Marxist concept of class struggle and concomitant acceptance of the inevitability of violence which would 'cut the tangled hemp with a sharp knife'.[6] Sun was not given to vindictive killings; he believed in the Royal Way of non-violence. He quoted an ancient saying: 'He who delights in not killing a man can unify a nation.'[7]

Gaddafi likewise did not speak approvingly of violence: 'violence and change by force are themselves undemocratic, although they take place as a result of the existence of a previous undemocratic situation.'[8]

Gaddafi's *Green Book* was published in three parts: the first in 1976, the second in 1978 and the third in 1979. It is designed to promote a cultural revolution as did Mao's *Red Book*, of which Gaddafi was aware (green is the colour of Islam), but its format and content resembles Sun Yat-sen's Three Principles far more than that of Mao's *Red Book*. Gaddafi's *Green Book* is concerned with democracy (part I), socialism (part II) and nationalism (part III).

In her penetrating interview with Gaddafi in *Gaddafi: Voice from the Desert*, Mirella Bianco elicits the fact that he was not influenced by such great Islamic thinkers as Jamal al-Din al-Afghani and Mohammed Abdou whose works he had never read.[9] This perhaps casts doubt on the general assumption, voiced by such commentators as Jonathan Bearman that Gaddafi's thought was 'rooted within the tradition of the Arab [sic] philosopher Jamal al-Din al-Afghani, and his disciple, the Egyptian national Mohammed Abdou'.[10] (Although it is possible to write in a tradition, the thinkers of which one has never read.) Gaddafi did study *The Philosophy of the Revolution* by Gamal Abdul Nasser whom he admired greatly. However, neither in format nor in content does Nasser's work resemble the *Green Book*. Neither, indeed, does the Egyptian National Charter of 1962. Gaddafi also studied the revolutions of Castro, and perhaps rather surprisingly of Sun Yat-sen:

> Take these books about Cuba; I read them when I was still a civilian, and when I thought our revolution might perhaps be a popular revolution... From this viewpoint any revolutionary experience could be useful to us and would be worth studying. It wasn't basically the ideological content which interested us, it was the method by which the revolution had been achieved, the practical side of things, the techniques in fact. That is *why I studied, among others, the Chinese revolution of Sun Yat-sen, the father of modern China*. Here again we are looking the means and not the ideas, we were looking for a method which we could use in our turn. We were not looking for a doctrine.[11] (My italics)

Although Gaddafi denies he was looking for a doctrine, it is most unlikely that he could have studied Sun Yat-sen's revolution without being aware of Sun's Three Principles whose format closely resembles that of Gaddafi's *Green Book*. Moreover, Gaddafi did not use Sun's methods of revolution which involved overseas Chinese support because no similar base of disaffected Libyans existed. Neither did Gaddafi, unlike Sun Yat-sen, look for foreign support for his revolution which he wanted to be purely Libyan.[12] Gaddafi's bloodless coup resembled Sun Yat-sen's revolution more in its humaneness than in any other method. It is, however, possible that Gaddafi was more influenced by Sun Yat-sen's Three Principles than he realised. Like Sun Yat-sen, he wrote his 'Third Universal Theory' in a simple style for easy comprehension in order to galvanise his people to action. Like Sun Yat-sen his theory was meant to be an alternative to the existing ideologies in the political world. Both Sun Yat-sen and Gaddafi were inspired by messianic spiritual beliefs; Sun Yat-sen believed that God had sent him on a mission to save China and had saved him when he had been kidnapped in London;[13] and Gaddafi is a devout Muslim and at times also believed he had been saved by God for his mission: '... it was God himself who saved us'[14] from probable arrest just before his coup in 1969. Gaddafi may have studied Sun's ideas when he entered Benghazi University to read history before entering the Military Academy. It is most unlikely that he read Sun Yat-sen's works when he came to England for a three-month military training course in Bovington, Dorset, since they were not available there.

Like Sun Yat-sen, Gaddafi carried out his revolution before fully enunciating his ideas. Unlike Sun, he was successful in retaining power and was able to oversee the implementation of his ideas. Gaddafi's *Green Book* deals first with democracy, then socialism and then nationalism. It is possible that Gaddafi placed nationalism last because, by the time he put pen to paper, his revolution had taken place and the imperialist power had been overthrown. Likewise Sun Yat-sen dropped the idea of nationalism from his programme after the 1911 Revolution had overthrown the Manchu dynasty and he had thought the goal of nationalism had been achieved. He later reintroduced the idea appreciating that the ousting of the Western imperialist powers must be a priority for the Kuomintang.

Democracy

Like Sun Yat-sen, Gaddafi is more concerned with implementing 'true' democracy rather than liberty to which he refers more in his discussion of socialism rather than democracy.

Both Gaddafi and Sun Yat-sen are strongly critical of Western representative democracy which they regard as only an outdated stage in the development of democracy. Sun believed that: 'the West has not yet found any proper method of carrying out democracy and that the truths of democracy have not yet been fully manifested.'[15] Sun thought that the reason was that the West had not developed political machinery commensurate with their technological achievements. The people were reluctant to develop a powerful governmental machine that they could not control:

> The people are naturally the motive power in a democracy, but the people must also be able at any time to recall the power they set loose. Therefore the people will use only a low powered government, for they cannot control a government of several hundred thousand horse power and will not dare to use it.[16]

Sun believed that just as China once led the world in technological achievements, so it might set it an example with progressive political machinery.

Gaddafi similarly believes that he has solved the problem of the instrument of government, denouncing Western liberal democracy as false democracy; representative government is not truly representative of the people. Unlike Sun Yat-sen he is also strongly critical of the party system and plebiscites, perhaps because he wrote with twentieth-century hindsight of these methods of democracy. The party system encourages parties to spend more time criticising each other rather than considering the national interests. Government represents at best its own party or only a part of it, and governments can come to power even if most of the electorate has not voted for them. As for plebiscites, these do not allow the people to express their reasons for voting as they do:

> The people...have been allowed to utter only one word; either 'yes' or 'no'...Everyone should make clear what he wants and the reasons for his approval or rejection.[17]

To Gaddafi:

> Representation is fraud...it is a demagogic system in the real sense of the word...After the successful establishment of the era of the republics and the beginning of the era of the masses, it is unreasonable that democracy should mean the electing of only a few representatives to act on behalf of great masses. This is an absolute theory and an outdated experience. The whole authority must be the people's.[18]

Both Sun Yat-sen and Gaddafi wish to implement direct democracy but appreciate that national size presents a problem. Wrote Sun:

> The fact that only the small state of Switzerland has tried a partial form of direct sovereignty makes many people question whether it is applicable to large states also.[19]

According to Gaddafi:

> Direct democracy is the ideal method which, if realised in practice, is indisputable and non-controversial. The nations departed from direct democracy because however small a people might be, it was impossible to gather them together at one time in order to discuss, study and decide on their policy.[20]

It has been argued that Gaddafi was influenced by Rousseau in his thinking on direct democracy.[21] So also was Sun who asserted that: 'Rousseau's advocacy of the original idea of democracy was one of the greatest contributions to government in all history'.[22]

Both Gaddafi and Sun are concerned with introducing democracy at a local level. Sun would give his people the four rights of election, initiation, referendum and recall, while Gaddafi introduced basic people's congresses to which every citizen belonged and in which national issues could be debated. This is the basis of his Jamahiriya state. Gaddafi however, in theory, was not as elitist as was Sun and did not distinguish between the people's sovereignty and their ability. Sun introduced his five-power constitution which would allow those with ability to govern and yet be a political machine in theory but not in practice, controlled by the people.

Gaddafi's political machine was in theory to be different:

> First, the people are divided into basic popular congresses. Each basic popular congress chooses its secretariat. The secretariats together form popular congresses which are other than the basic ones. Then the masses of those basic popular congresses choose administrative people's committees to replace government administration. Thus all public utilities are run by people's committees which will be responsible to the basic popular congresses and these dictate the policies to be followed by the people's committees and supervise its execution.[23]

Thus Gaddafi describes his republic of the masses. However, the choice of people for the secretariat was likely to be those who were qualified: with perceived ability.

In March 2000, Gaddafi abolished 12 ministries, devolving their powers to provincial and local level. However, key ministries such as foreign policy, security and information, as well as the oil industry, remain under central control. Rather than developing direct democracy, Gaddafi is probably more concerned with breaking up power bases and asserting his personal control. He believed oil revenues had been misused.[24]

Gaddafi added a syndicalist aspect to his Jamahiriya:

> All citizens who are members of those popular congresses belong, professionally and functionally to categories. They have, therefore, to establish their own unions and syndicates in addition to being, as citizens, members of the basic popular congresses or the people's committees. Subjects discussed by basic popular congresses or the people's committees, syndicates and unions, will take their final shape in the General People's Congress, where the secretariats of popular congresses, syndicates and unions meet. What is drafted by the General People's Congress, which meets annually or periodically will, in turn, be submitted to popular congresses, people's committees, syndicates and unions. The people's committees, responsible to the basic popular congresses will, then, start executive action. The General People's Congress is not a gathering of members or ordinary persons as is the case with parliaments. It is a gathering of the basic popular congresses, the people's committees, the unions, the syndicates and all professional associations.[25]

In this Gaddafi, like Sun, thought he had solved the problem of the instrument of governing. However, like Sun, his solution was open to dictatorial abuse, and the representative committees have been alleged to have crushed opposition to Gaddafi. His syndicalism may well have been influenced by Mussolini's Fascist occupation of Libya. Ironically, although Sun laid out a different constitutional structure, his theory was also developed by the Kuomintang so that it resembled aspects of Mussolini's policy. In his Manifesto on a People's Conference of 11 November 1924, Sun suggested that the preliminary conference that was called before the convening of the People's Conference to devise the means of reconstructing China should include delegates from industrial organisations, Chambers of Commerce, educational associations, universities, student unions, labour organisations, peasant organisations, loyal armies and political parties.

The National Convention in 1931 in China was composed of functional groups. As mentioned previously the Kuomintang form of representation may have served as a model for the Indonesian 'golkar' functional groups in the 1950s and 1960s. In so far as Sun Yat-sen allowed one-party tutelage for an indefinite period, the end product of his thought with its dictatorial and syndicalist aspects under Chiang Kai-shek did bear some resemblance to Gaddafi's both in its expressed ideals and in their realisation.

Obviously, there were many influences on Gaddafi's thinking. It has been suggested, for example, that the tribal system of Libya influenced his chance of basic congresses for his system of government. Nevertheless, I argue that as Gaddafi expressly stated that he had studied Sun Yat-sen's revolution, and as his thinking on democracy bears some similarity to Gaddafi's, the latter may have unconsciously absorbed some ideas from Sun Yat-sen.

Socialism

Perhaps, however, it is in his theory of socialism that Gaddafi's thinking most resembles Sun Yat-sen's. To the latter the state had an obligation to see that what he perceived as man's four basic needs were cheaply supplied:

> Economists have always spoken of three necessities of life – food, clothing and shelter. My study leads me to add a fourth necessity, an extremely important one – the means of travel.[26]

Gaddafi similarly argues for the provision of these needs which he places in the same order:

> The material needs of man that are basic, necessary and personal, start with food, housing, clothing and transport ... These must be within his private and sacred ownership.[27]

Sun expressly argues against certain tenets of Marxism such as that of surplus value. Gaddafi does not refer to Marx by name, but nevertheless uses arguments similar to Sun's that reject Marx's theory and stress that the worker's labour is only a factor in production. Sun argued: 'Marx gave all the credit for production to the labour of the industrial worker and overlooked the labour of other useful factors.'[28] These he believed were the raw materials and the agriculturalists involved in their production, machines and the people who invented and produced them, as well as the workers in the factory. Thus the latter could not claim their labour was the sole agent of production. In this argument Sun was heavily influenced by an American scholar, Maurice William.[29]

Gaddafi similarly argues:

> The industrial establishment is based on raw materials, machines and workers. Production is the outcome of the worker's use of the machines in the factory to manufacture raw materials... The three factors are equally essential in the process of production. Without these three factors there will be no production. Any one factor cannot carry out this process by itself.[30]

Therefore, argues Gaddafi, all three factors should be regarded as equally important.

Some commentators have been very dismissive of Gaddafi's theory of socialism. David Blundy and Andrew Lycett describe the second volume of the *Green Book* as being 'the most full of waffle'.[31] If, however, it is understood that Gaddafi was arguing a possibly rehashed version of Sun's ideas, against the Marxian concept of surplus value, then his argument can be seen in a more meaningful light. Gaddafi might also have been half-remembering Sun Yat-sen's argument that capitalism and workers should be regarded as consumers who have harmonious interests rather that producers in conflict when he asserted that: 'It is not only the factory which is important, but also those who consume its production.'[32]

Gaddafi's ideas of an ideal primitive communism are similar to those of Sun who believed: 'The first society formed by man was a communist society and the primitive age was a communist age.'[33] Likewise, Gaddafi argued that:

> Natural law has led to natural socialism based on an equality among the economic factors of production and has almost brought about, among individuals, consumption equal to nature's production. But the exploitation of man by man and the possession by some individuals of more of the general wealth than they need is a manifest departure from natural law and the beginning of distortion and corruption in the life of the human community. It is the beginning of the emergence of the society of exploitation.[34]

In some ways Gaddafi's theory of socialism does resemble Sun's Principle of Livelihood. However, Sun argues against Marxist theory and methods but for its goals, although intending only to regulate capital immediately. Gaddafi rejects atheistic communism and has imprisoned communists; nevertheless, his socialism abolishes capitalism together with the idea of profit and his method of land reform is more far-reaching than Sun's. That Gaddafi has been influenced by Marx's ideas is shown by his references to the dialectic as in his assertion that:

> The overturning of contemporary societies, to change them from being societies of wage-workers to societies of partners is inevitable as a dialectic result of the contradictory economic theses prevailing in the world today and in the inevitable dialectical result of the injustice to relations based on the wage system, which have not been solved.[35]

Gaddafi's ideas on land reform were not those of Sun Yat-sen. Gaddafi believed that land is: 'no one's property. But everyone has the right to use it, to benefit from it by working, farming or pasturing.'[36]

Sun Yat-sen, however, believed in the 'equalisation of land ownership' and that ultimately 'each tiller of the soil will possess his own fields'.[37] Nevertheless, Sun's idea that ultimately 'the people will not only have a communistic share in state production but they will have a share in everything' is not dissimilar to the ideas of Gaddafi who in fact modified his views on land ownership after his revolution. Sun spent much time on discussing how agricultural methods should be improved. It is possible that, indirectly, Gaddafi's country benefited from Sun's stressing the need for progress in the agricultural sciences. In 1962 Libya received an agricultural mission from Taiwan which remained in Libya until 1969 when the project was completed.

Nationalism

Gaddafi's third book on nationalism also bears resemblance to Sun's Principle of Nationalism. He sees nationalism as being based on blood ties beginning with the family, extending to the tribe and then to the nation. Sun also emphasised that Chinese nationalism is based on blood links from the family to the clan and then to the nation. Both revolutionaries, however, admit of other factors in creating nationalism

(Gaddafi has been accused of Fascism in his emphasis on blood link).[38] Like Sun, Gaddafi believed nationalism to be an essential cohesive force:

> Nationalism in the world of man and group instinct in the animal kingdom are like gravity in the domain of mineral and celestial bodies. If the mass of the sun were smashed so that it lost its gravity, the gases would blow away and its unity would no longer exist. Accordingly, the unity is the basis for its survival ... For this reason a group struggles for its own natural unity, because its survival lies on that.[39]

Gaddafi was well-aware of the influence of religion in bonding together a nation and aware that national and religious loyalties could conflict. He was conscious of the problem of the Christians in the Lebanon for example, and consequently he argued that each nation should have one religion only:

> There is no other solution but to be in harmony with the natural rule that each nation has one religion. When the social factor is compatible with the religious factor, harmony is achieved and the life of groups become stable and strong and develop soundly.[40]

It might be thought that because the Chinese cultural background was different Sun did not put forward a similar argument: yet he did. In his first lecture on nationalism he argued that religion was a very powerful factor in the development of races. He cited the cases of Jews and Arabs being held together by their common religions. More appropriately for the Chinese he said that people who worship the same gods or the same ancestors tend to form one race. Moreover, Sun's emphasis on Confucian values can perhaps be seen as an awareness that a nation should have the same values ethically if not spiritually.[41]

Gaddafi's *Green Book* has been undoubtedly influenced by his Islamic beliefs, his Bedouin background of poverty and austerity, his admiration for Nasser, his awareness of the social experiments in Yugoslavia and Algeria and the ideas of such Western thinkers as Rousseau. However, as I have argued here, he was also influenced to some extent by the ideas of Sun Yat-sen – in so far as Gaddafi wished to transform the whole of the Arab world with his Third Universal Theory, the influence of the Father of Modern China on this Arab leader is of no small significance.

Conclusion

This book has attempted to demonstrate that Sun Yat-sen's political thought was a courageously unique synthesis of Eastern and Western ideas which has influenced Chinese revolutionary leaders and Third World countries. While absolute originality seems impossible in political thinking, a synthesis of different political systems might be regarded as a distinctive contribution to the realm of political ideas. Sun Yat-sen's political thought was in this category. As such it showed the problems of originality: not all the ideas were practicable and undoubtedly Sun's programme, if put into effect, would have needed to be altered as faults were revealed in its practicability. Had Sun Yat-sen's ideas been implemented in China, albeit in a modified form, the impact of his political thought would have been greater than it is today.

Sun's inability to implement his programme was partly the result of the foreign powers' failure to discern in him the investment that he was. Sun's poor health and the excessive demands on his time and energy by political events, together with his failure to see early on that his revolution should be based on the labouring masses as well as foreign capital, also contributed to his failure to implement his ideas. Had Sun been succeeded by a leader who was determined to implement his Three Principles the history of his political programme and that of China would have been different and probably more liberal. It was Sun's achievement to attempt to introduce a programme that, while being revolutionary, did demonstrate a continuity with China's past. This was important to a country not given to excessive approval of individualist thinking and which needed to retain its ethnic identity intrinsically entwined with its Confucian heritage.

It is arguable, however, that despite the distinctive Chinese aspect of Sun's ideas, they do have significance for those who search for alternative political systems to communist authoritarian regimes, liberal democracy and right-wing dictatorships. Sun's political programme can be classified in none of these categories and, as such, particularly as Sun was clearly concerned for its practical implementation and not mere academic discourse, his thought should not be dismissed lightly. The morphological problems that usually accompany intellectual creativity were exacerbated by the circumstances in which Sun produced his work. Sun's lack of polished presentation may have counted against his acceptability. The political scientists who show contempt for Sun's ideas demonstrate the equivalent short-sightedness of Western politicians to Sun at the beginning of the twentieth century. Rather than being dismissed as unsound, Sun's ideas should be regarded as a courageous contribution to political debate.

This book has attempted to trace the development of Sun's thought. After his petition to Li Hung-chang was rejected, Sun organised the Hsing Chung Hui and began thinking in terms of a republic for China. By 1895 he regarded himself as a revolutionary but had no clear ideas as to a social revolution in China. He expressed these as his Three Principles in 1905, stating that they had been long developing in his mind as their genesis was his sojourn in London during 1896–97. I have argued that Sun's claim was largely correct. However, he wanted the support of the British government (not only its benevolent neutrality, but also financial and military assistance) for his revolution and for asylum in Hong Kong. He therefore kept silent on his observation of the suffering and rising discontent of the working classes and his probable contacts with socialist leaders. His subsequent stay in Japan reinforced his ideas with the possible additional introduction of the thinking of Bluntschli at this time. His Three Principles had changed, however, by 1924 again partly because of the demands of his foreign policy: this time the need for Russian support.

Sun's political thought has implications for countries other than China. He faced the problem that liberal democracies often propel into power politicians of low calibre who can be best marketed, rather than the best statesmen. Further, liberal democracy is no guarantee against improbity. Sun's idea of the Five-Power government which comprised the Executive, Legislature, Judiciary, Control and Examination was meant to solve this. Corruption is endemic in most Third World countries and can often be evidenced in the West. Sun's concept of the Control, empowered to initiate impeachment proceedings, could do much to tackle this recurring problem provided the Control were staffed by civil servants independent of political loyalties. However, in developing countries a politically neutral civil service is still difficult to establish. In the West the Control could replace the committees and independent counsels that are brought in to deal with improbity and are often seen as biased.

Sun's idea of the Examination power to investigate the abilities of politicians is more difficult since many academic qualifications are of questionable use in politics. No university course in politics has yet been designed to produce politicians of high calibre, but the possibility of this being done cannot be ruled out. Sun's theories do show an elitist outlook which was unfortunately abused by Chiang Kai-shek. However, it is clear that for some unascertainable reasons some people do have unusual qualities of leadership and political far-sightedness though no political system at the moment facilitates such people achieving political power. There is a dearth of outstanding political leaders; the problems posed by Plato's Republic remain. While Sun did not solve them, his attempts might well have been a step towards a solution had they been implemented.

Sun tackled the problem that the electorate in liberal democracies are usually powerless except during elections. His suggestion of direct democracy is worthy of consideration.

Sun Yat-sen's political thought shows the problems of endeavouring to graft a new flexible political programme onto a previously oppressive one. His programme for revolution and reconstruction may serve, with modifications, as a model for nations endeavouring to throw off foreign or domestic oppressive regimes. Sun's nationalism was naturally suited to China's particular historical legacy yet, at the same time, he demonstrated the value of attaining national cohesion and independence before involvement in internationalism. Newly independent nations need ideas other than those offered by Western or Communist governments. Sun's emphasis on approaching the problem of a new nation's democratic education through granting citizens extensive rights first to participate in local government, would seem a highly practicable one. Local democracy in which peasants can vote on issues that immediately interest and affect them is an effective way for them to learn the democratic process. China has already introduced this. Sun's idea that it should lead upwards, gradually to democracy at national level under a strong government to prevent instability, is surely the best way for China to democratise. Sun's Principle of Livelihood presents a less extremist approach to social reform than does Marxism and, tailored to suit national needs, might be more attractive than violent movements for land reform such as that of the Maoist guerrillas now fighting in Nepal, or those that might develop in the Indian subcontinent or Latin America.

Sun's thought solves the problem of how to achieve democratic and socialist revolutions at the same time. Usually a Third World country either achieves political reform but deprives its citizens of freedom in doing so, or it develops liberal democracy and leaves much of its population suffering such economic and social deprivation that it cannot enjoy its political liberties. Sun's political theory is unique in that it develops democratic and socio-economic reforms together.

Whatever may be asserted about 'the end of ideology', it can be argued that liberal democracy without socialism is unsuitable for most Third World countries: Sun's synthesis of Western and Oriental ideas provides a more appropriate ideology for the developing world.

While Sun Yat-sen should have earlier paid more attention to the needs and support of the Chinese peasantry, convincing the business and landed classes it was in their interest to accept social reform, Sun rightly looked for foreign capitalist support. Although at the time he often received nothing but ridicule, Sun's ideas of international investment in China do not seem so unrealistic in view of the international business interest in mainland China today.

Sun's Confucianism which illuminated his thinking was untraditional, derived partly but not uncritically from the influence of K'ang Yu-wei and Liang Ch'i-ch'ao. Sun's theory of socialism influenced by the Confucian virtue of harmony (as well as Fabianism) resulted in a far less destructive theory than the Marxist emphasis on class antagonism.

Sun's Christianity was also unconventional. It has been suggested in this thesis that he was a Taiping Christian before being baptised an ecclesiastically acceptable one. Sun's Christianity may have aided his unusual approach to social organisation and thus helped inspire his synthesis of Western and Chinese ideas. Certainly it gave a messianic drive to his political action which aimed at China's salvation. Sun's Christianity might possibly be a source of inspiration for revolutionary Christians in the Third World.

Few political theorists have organised a revolution to implement their ideas. Few revolutionaries have devised their own original political theory. Sun Yat-sen did both. He wanted to give the Chinese 'full happiness' through his national, democratic and socio-economic reforms, and with Western backing he could have implemented his political thought. After Sun's revolution overthrew the Manchu dynasty, he resisted the desire for power which could have caused civil war, relinquishing the presidency of China to Yüan Shih-k'ai. Also, Sun did not succumb to the temptation of financial corruption; he died a poor man. But ethically his life was successful.

Sun Yat-sen did more than bring down an empire. He gave the Chinese a lasting inspiration so that both mainland and Taiwanese leaders claim to have taken up his mantle. If Taiwan as well as Hong Kong become part of China, Sun's name and ideals may possibly be a unifying influence. Respected by Mao Tse-tung, Chou En-lai as well as by Chiang Kai-shek, Sun Yat-sen was also admired by revolutionary leaders in other Third World countries, such as Indonesia, Vietnam, the

Philippines and even Gaddafi's Libya. This is probably partly because like Gandhi's, Sun Yat-sen's name has a particular moral and humanistic resonance.

Sun Yat-sen now lies in a mausoleum on a hill above Nanking where he declared the Republic of China in 1912. Thousands still make pilgrimages there. Sun is honoured not only for his actions, but also for his ideals. The respect paid to him as the 'Father of Modern China' may well increase as the ideas of successive revolutionaries are discarded. In the next century he may well be a focal point of loyalty for a united China. His unique position in the history of China is unlikely to be diminished.

Notes

Introduction

1 *Sun Zhong Shan Xuanji* (Beijing, 1981), p. 712.
2 Donald W. Treadgold, *The West in Russia and China* Vol. 2 (Cambridge, 1973), p. 95.
3 Preface to Tai Chi-t'ao, *Die Geistigen Grundlagen des Sun Yat-senismus* trans by Richard Wilhelm (Berlin, 1931), p. 8.
4 C. Snyder, *Far Eastern Economic Review*, no. 10, 6 March 1971.
5 Sukarno, 'Pantja Sila', in *The Indonesian Revolution: Basic Documents* (Jakarta, 1960), p. 42.
6 Simon Leys, *The Chairman's New Clothes* (London, 1977), p. 233.
7 Marie-Claire Bergère, *Sun Yat-sen* (Paris, 1994) (trans Stanford, 1998), p. 391.

1 The Early Evolution of Sun Yat-sen's Political Thought

1 Information on Sun's early life has been drawn from Lo Chia-lun *Kuo-fu nien-pu* (Chronological Biography of Sun Yat-sen) Vol. I (Taipei, 1969). Sun's own autobiography in *Memoirs of a Chinese Revolutionary* by Sun Yat-sen (Taipei, 1953), *Sun Zhong Shan Xuanji* (Selected Works of Sun Yat-sen) (Beijing, 1981), pp. 191–6.
2 *Sun Chung-shan ch'üan-chi* (Complete Collected Works of Sun Yat-sen) (Beijing, 1981) Vol. 3, p. 329.
3 Franz Michael and Chang Chung-li, *The Taiping Rebellion: History and Documents*, 3 vols (Seattle, 1966–71) Vol. 2, p. 314.
4 *Sun Chung-shan ch'üan-chi* Vol. I, pp. 46–8.
5 Sidney H. Chang and Leonard H. D. Gordon, *All Under Heaven: Sun Yat-sen and His Revolutionary Thought* (Stanford, California, 1991), p. 14.
6 *Ibid.*, p. 13.
7 *Sun Zhong Shan Xuanji*, p. 192.
8 Chang and Gordon, *op. cit.*, p. 14.
9 *Sun Zhong Shan Xuanji* pp. 1–13. English translation in *China's Response to the West* (Ssu-yu Teng and John K. Fairbank) (New York, 1975), pp. 224–5.
10 *Sun Zhong Shan Xuanji*, p. 12.
11 Hsu Leonard, *Sun Yat-sen, His Political and Social Ideals* (Los Angeles, 1933), p. 4, Fn 5.
12 *Ibid.*, p. 6.
13 Milton J. T. Shieh, *The Kuomintang, Selected Historical Documents, 1894–1969* (New York, 1970), p. 2.
14 Harold Z. Schiffrin, *Sun Yat-sen and the Origins of the Chinese Revolution* (Los Angeles, 1970), p. 42.
15 *Ibid.*, p. 42.
16 Chang and Gordon, *op. cit.*, p. 17.
17 Marie-Claire Bergère, *Sun Yat-sen* (Stanford, 1998), p. 50.

18 *Sun Chung-shan ch'üan-chi*, Vol. 1, p. 20.
19 Wu Yuzhang, *Recollections of the Revolution of 1911* (Beijing, 1962), p. 16.
20 Schiffrin, *op. cit.*, p. 43.
21 Hsu, *op. cit.*, p. 12.
22 *Sun Chung-shan ch'üan-chi* Vol. 1, pp. 21–2. Translation Milton Shieh *op. cit.*, pp. 3–7.
23 The following information has been drawn from Lo Chia-lun, *op. cit.*, p. 19. Schiffrin, *op. cit.*, pp. 85–8. *Sun Zhong Shan Xuanji*, pp. 193–6
24 See Marie-Claire Bergère, *op. cit.*, pp. 49, 80, for details of Sun's relations with secret societies.
25 Joseph R. Levenson, *Confucian China and its Modern Fate* (Los Angeles 1965), Vol. II, p. 121.

2 The Development of Sun Yat-sen's Political Ideas in England 1896–97

1 *Sun Zhong Shan Xuanji* (Selected Works of Sun Yat-sen) (Beijing, 1981), p. 31.
2 Sun Wen, *Kuo-fu ch'üan-chi* (Taipei, 1957), Vol. 2, p. 84 (Complete Works of the Founding Father of the Nation).
3 Harold Z. Schiffrin, *Sun Yat-sen and the Origins of the Chinese Revolution* (Los Angeles, London, 1970), p. 137.
4 Sun Yat-sen, 'My Reminiscences' *The Strand Magazine* (1912), p. 304.
5 James Cantlie and C. Sheridan Jones, *Sun Yat-sen and the Awakening of China* (London, 1912), p. 56.
6 T'ang Liang Li, *The Inner History of the Chinese Revolution* (London, 1930), p. 25.
7 Jean Longuet, *Le Mouvement Socialist International* (Paris, 1913), p. 526.
8 Schiffrin, *op. cit.*, p. 135.
9 *Ibid.*, p. 128.
10 J. Y. Wong, *The Origins of a Heroic Image* (Hong Kong, 1986), p. 283.
11 *Ibid.*, p. 18.
12 Timothy Richard, *Forty-Five Years in China* (New York, 1916), p. 350.
13 Wong, *op. cit.*, p. 227.
14 Edwin Collins' preface to *Britain's Greatness Foretold* by Marie Trevelyan (London, 1900) p. 1xiii.
15 Wong, *op. cit.*, p. 273.
16 James Cantlie and C. Sheridan Jones, *Sun Yat-sen and the Awakening of China* (London, 1912), p. 249.
17 Y. Yamakawa, *The Independent*, 11 January 1912, p. 76.
18 Chun-tu Hsüeh, *The Chinese Revolution of 1911 New Perspectives* (Hong Kong, 1986), p. 34.
19 Sun Yat-sen and Edwin Collins, 'China's Present and Future' in *Fortnightly Review*, 1 March 1897, p. 424.
20 Sun Yat-sen and Edwin Collins, 'Judicial Reform in China' in *East Asia*, July 1897, p. 3.
21 i.e. Professor Wong's.
22 Wong, *op. cit.*, p. 241.
23 *The London and China Express* 12 March 1897 Supplement p. 2 for review of Sun's 'China's Present and Future'.
    Ibid., 9 July 1897. Supplement p. 1 for review of his 'Judicial Reform in China'.

24 *Ibid.*, 12 March 1897 (p. 232 of 1897 volume).
25 *The New York Times*, 23 March 1897, p. 6.
26 *Fortnightly Review*, p. 424.
27 *Ibid.*, p. 425.
28 *Ibid.*, p. 438.
29 *Ibid.*, p. 440.
30 *Le Temps (Le petit Temps)* 11 March 1897, p. 34.
31 'L', 'The Future of China', in *Fortnightly Review* 1 August 1896, p. 163.
32 *Ibid.*, p. 165.
33 *Ibid.*, p. 166.
34 *Ibid.*, p. 177.
35 Wong, *op. cit.*, p. 244 quoting Wu Xiang xiang Sun Yizian zhuan Vol. I, p. 194.
36 For further discussion of 'L's identity see my PhD thesis, A C Wells *The Political Thought of Sun Yat-sen* (London, 1994).
37 Timothy Richard, *Conversion by the Million* (Shanghai, 1907) Vol. II, p. 225.
38 *East Asia op. cit.*, p. 13.
39 Sun Wen, *Kuo-fu ch'üan-chi* (Taipei 1957) Vol. II, p. 84.
40 Sun Wen, *Kuo-fu ch'üan-chi* (Taipei, 1957) Vol. II, p. 80.
41 *Sun Zhong Shan Xuanji* (Beijing, 1981), p. 621.
42 'L', *The Future of China*, p. 165.
43 *Sun Zhong Shan Xuanji*, p. 621.
44 Sun Yat-sen, *Kidnapped in London* (Bristol, 1897), p. 16.
45 Wong, *op. cit.*, p. 132.
46 *Ibid.*, p. 261.
47 *Ibid.*, p. 260.
48 *Free Russia*, May 1897, p. 1.
49 Sun Yat-sen, *Kidnapped in London*, p. 134.
50 Sun Yat-sen and Edwin Collins, 'China's Past and Present', in *Fortnightly Review* (1897), p. 424.
51 'L', 'The Future of China', in *Fortnightly Review* (1896), p. 17.
52 *Ibid.*, p. 174.
53 *Sun Zhong Shan Xuanji*, p. 87.
54 *Ibid.*, p. 737.
55 *Ibid.*, p. 753.
56 Sun Wen, *Kuo-fu ch'üan-chi* (Taipei, 1957) Vol. II, p. 84.
57 Sun Yat-sen, *Kidnapped in London*, p. 30.
58 J. Y. Wong (ed.), *Sun Yat-sen. His International Ideas and International Connections* (Sydney, 1987), p. 152.
59 Schiffrin, *op. cit.*, p. 560.
60 'L', *op. cit.*, p. 173.
61 Sun Yat-sen, 'China's Next Step', in *The Independent* vol. XXII (1912), p. 1316.

3 Sun's Western influences in the Japanese Crucible

1 *Justice*, 26 June 1897.
2 Jean Longuet, *Le Mouvement Socialiste International* (Paris, 1913), p. 520.
3 Martin Bernal in *Modern China's Search for Reform* (ed. Jack Gray, London, 1969), p. 68.
4 'Early Socialist Currents in the Chinese Revolutionary Movement', Robert A. Scalapino and Harold Schiffrin, *Journal of Asian Studies* (May, 1959), p. 336.

5 Bernal, *op. cit.*, p. 69.
6 Longuet, *op. cit.*, p. 531.
7 Bernal, *op. cit.*, p. 72.
8 *Ibid.*, p. 72.
9 Li Yu-ning, *The Introduction of Socialism into China* (New York, 1971), p. 23.
10 *Ibid.*, p. 24.
11 Wu Yu Zhang, *Recollections of the Revolution of 1911* (Beijing, 1981), p. 72.
12 Bernal, *op. cit.*, p. 76.
13 Philip Huang, *Liang Ch'i-ch'ao and Modern Chinese Liberalism* (Seattle, 1972), p. 63.
14 *Ibid.*, p. 84.
15 *Sun Zhong Shan Xuanji* (Selected Works of Sun Yat-sen) (Beijing, 1981), p. 765.
16 Liu Yeou-hwa, *A Comparative Study of Dr Sun Yat-sen's and Montesquieu's Theory of Separation of Powers* (PhD thesis 1983, Claremont College USA), p. 81.
17 Johan Kaspar Bluntschli, *The Theory of the State* (Oxford, 1885), p. 453.
18 *Ibid.*, p. 450.
19 *Ibid.*, p. 458.
20 Harold Z. Schiffrin, *Sun Yat-sen and the Origins of the Chinese Revolution* (Los Angeles, 1970), p. 212.
21 *Ibid.*, p. 26.
22 *Sun Zhong Shan Xuanji*, p. 692.
   Sun Yat-sen, *op. cit.*, p. 151.
23 Bluntshli, *op. cit.*, p. 497.
24 Schiffrin, *op. cit.*, p. 142.
25 *Sun Zhong Shan Xuanji*, p. 718.
26 Paul M. Linebarger, *The Political Doctrines of Sun Yat-sen* (Baltimore, 1937), p. 98.
27 *Sun Zhong Shan Xuanji*, p. 201.
28 *Sun Zhong Shan Xuanji*, p. 844.
29 Martin Bernal, *Chinese Socialism to 1907* (Ithaca, 1976), p. 50.
30 Paraphrased from *Sun Zhong Shan Xuanji*, pp. 80–9.
31 *The Globe*, 17 February 1912, p. 6.
32 Sun Wen *Kuo-fu ch'üan-chi* (Taipei, 1957), p. 84.

4 Sun's Thought between 1905/6 and 1919: Populism and Elitism

1 Bernard Martin, *Strange Vigour* (London, 1984), p. 230
2 *Sun Zhong-shan ch'üan-chi* (Complete Collected Works of Sun Yat-sen) (Beijing, 1981) Vol. 3, p. 325.
3 *Ibid.*, p. 327.
4 Jude Howell, 'A Silent Revolution', in *China Review* (Summer, 2000), p. 11.
5 Corinna Hana in G. K. Kindermann, *Sun Yat-sen: Founder and Symbol of China's Revolutionary Nation Building* (Munich, 1982), p. 139.
6 Chatterji, K., *National Movement in Modern China* (Calcutta, 1958), pp. 95, 97.
7 FO/371/6614 (FO84/81/10) C. W. Campell's Minute (13 January 1921).
8 Letter from William Redfield, Secretary, Department of Commerce, Washington USA in *Sun Yat-sen, The International Development of China* (New York and London, 1922), p. 257.
9 Sun Yat-sen, *Ibid.*, p. 237.

10 Ibid., p. 11.
11 Ibid., p. 11.
12 Ibid., p. 74.
13 Ibid., p. 217.
14 N. Gangulee, *The Teachings of Sun Yat-sen* (London, 1945), p. xxxviii.
15 See Josef Fass, *Sun Yat-sen and the May 4th Movement*, Archiv Orientalni 38, 1968, pp. 577–84 for full discussion of Sun's role.
16 *Sun Zhong Shan Xuanji* (Selected Works of Sun Yat-sen) (Beijing, 1981), p. 82.
17 Sun Yat-sen, *Memoirs of a Chinese Revolutionary* (London, 1927), p. 60.
18 Michael Oakeshott, *Rationalism in Politics* (London, 1962), p. 122.
19 Sun Yat-sen, *Memoirs of a Chinese Revolutionary* (London, 1927), p. 5. *Sun Zhong Shan Xuanji* (Beijing, 1981), p. 116.
20 Ibid., p. 100.
    Ibid., p. 157.
21 Ibid., p. 102.
    Ibid., p. 159
22 Ibid., p. 104. Ibid., p. 159 (*Kuo fu chuan chi*, Vol. 2 (Taipei, 1957), p. 47).
23 Donald Treadgold, *The West in Russia and China*, Vol. 2 (Cambridge, 1973), p. 87.
24 Ibid., p. 218.
25 J. Y. Wong, *The Origins of a Heroic Image* (Hong Kong, 1986), p. 261.
26 *Sun Zhong Shan Xuanji*, p. 146.
27 Hu Shih and Lin Yu-Fang, *China's Own Critics* (with commentary by Wang Ching-wei) (Peiping, 1931), p. 48.
28 Ibid., p. 53.
29 *Sun Zhong Shan Xuanji*, p. 762. Sun Yat-sen, *San Min Chu-I*, trans Frank Price (Shanghai, 1927), p. 288.
30 Sun Yat-sen, *Memoirs of a Chinese Revolutionary* (London, 1927), p. 117. *Sun Zhong Shan Xuanji*, p. 164.

5 Sun's Political Thought between 1919 and 1924

1 Sidney H. Chang and Leonard H. D. Gordon, *All Under Heaven: Sun Yat-sen and His Revolutionary Thought* (Stanford, 1991), pp. 61, 69.
2 F.O. 371/6614 p. 193.
3 Ibid., p. 187.
4 Sun Yat-sen, *Fundamentals of National Reconstruction* (Taipei, 1953), p. 10.
5 Ibid., p. 13.
6 Ibid., p. 10.
7 Ibid., p. 11.
8 Ibid., p. 12.
9 Ibid., p. 13.
10 Ibid., p. 13.
11 Ibid., p. 14.
12 Sun Yat-sen *op. cit.*, p. 120. Sun accepted federation in 1911 but then gradually changed his mind. See Paul M. A. Linebarger, *The Doctrines of Sun Yat-sen* (Baltimore, 1937), pp. 228–9. For an interesting discussion of Sun's rejection of federalism see Marie-Claire Bergère, *Sun Yat-sen* (Stanford, 1998), pp. 380–1.
13 Sun Yat-sen, *op. cit.*, p. 15.

14 *Ibid.*, p. 15.
15 *Ibid.*, p. 16.
16 Sir Charles Petrie, *The History of Government* (London, 1929), p. 204.
17 Roger Thompson, 'China's First Local Elections', *History Today*, July 1997, p. 51.
18 Carole Pateman, *Participation and Democratic Theory* (Cambridge, 1970), p. 33.
19 *Ibid.*, p. 58.
20 Sun Yat-sen, *op. cit.*, p. 161.

6 The Principle of Nationalism

1 Charles Drage, *Two-Gun Cohen* (London, 1934), p. 130.
2 *Ibid.*, p. 137.
3 *Sun Zhong Shan Xuanji* (Beijing, 1981), p. 616. Sun Yat-sen, *San Min Chu-I* trans by Frank Price (Shanghai, 1927), p. xii.
4 *Sun Zhong Shan Xuanji*, pp. 616–879. Sun Yat-sen, *op. cit.*, pp. 3–148.
5 *Sun Zhong Shan Xuanji*, p. 621. Sun Yat-sen, *op. cit.*, p. 12.
6 *Sun Zhong Shan Xuanji*, p. 677. Sun Yat-sen, *op. cit.*, p. 120.
7 *Sun Zhong Shan Xuanji*, p. 627. Sun Yat-sen, *op. cit.*, p. 23.
8 S. Chang and L. Gordon, *All Under Heaven: Sun Yat-sen and his Revolutionary Thought* (Stanford, 1991), p. 23.
9 *Sun Zhong Shan Xuanji*, p. 629. Sun Yat-sen, *op. cit.*, p. 27.
10 *Sun Zhong Shan Xuanji*, p. 650. Sun Yat-sen, *op. cit.*, p. 68.
11 *Sun Zhong Shan Xuanji*, p. 661. Sun Yat-sen, *op. cit.*, p. 88.
12 *Sun Zhong Shan Xuanji*, pp. 674–5. Sun Yat-sen, *op. cit.*, p. 115.
13 *Sun Zhong Shan Xuanji*, p. 617. Sun Yat-sen, *op. cit.*, p. 5.
14 *Sun Zhong Shan Xuanji*, p. 680. Sun Yat-sen, *op. cit.*, p. 126.
15 *Sun Zhong Shan Xuanji*, p. 654. Sun Yat-sen, *op. cit.*, p. 75.
16 *Sun Zhong Shan Xuanji*, pp. 629–630. Sun Yat-sen, *op. cit.*, p. 27.
17 *Sun Zhong Shan Xuanji*, p. 689. Sun Yat-sen, *op. cit.*, p. 142.
18 *Sun Zhong Shan Xuanji*, p. 192.
19 *Sun Zhong Shan Xuanji*, p. 621. Sun Yat-sen, *op. cit.*, p. 12.
20 Elie Kedourie, *Nationalism* (London, 1966), p. 9.
21 *Sun Zhong Shan Xuanji*, p. 622. Sun Yat-sen, *op. cit.*, p. 14.
22 *Sun Zhong Shan Xuanji*, p. 699. Sun Yat-sen, *op. cit.*, p. 105.
23 *Sun Zhong Shan Xuanji*, p. 648. Sun Yat-sen, *op. cit.*, p. 64.
24 J. B. Levenson, *Confucian China and its Modern Fate* (Los Angeles, 1965), p. 103.
25 *Ibid.*, p. 114.
26 *Sun Zhong Shan Xuanji*, p. 660. Sun Yat-sen, *op. cit.*, p. 86.
27 Sun Yat-sen, *op. cit.*, pp. 10, 11, 66. Zhou Xun, *Chinese Perceptions of the 'Jews' and Judaism'* (Richmond, Surrey 2001) pp. 56–57.

7 The Principle of Democracy

1 *Sun Zhong Shan Xuanji* (Beijing, 1981), p. 701. Sun Yat-sen, *San Min Chu-I*, trans Frank Price (Shanghai, 1927), p. 169.
2 *Ibid.*, p. 701. Sun Yat-sen, *op. cit.*, p. 170.
3 *Sun Zhong Shan Xuanji*, p. 712. Sun Yat-sen, *op. cit.*, p. 191.
4 *Sun Zhong Shan Xuanji*, p. 724. Sun Yat-sen, *op. cit.*, p. 214.
5 'huai' has been translated by Frank Price as 'locus'.

210 Notes

6 Sun Yat-sen, 'Five Power Constitution' (1921) in Sun Yat-sen, *Fundamentals of National Reconstruction* (Taipei, 1953), pp. 48–9.
7 *Sun Zhong Shan Xuanji*, p. 787. Sun Yat-sen, *op. cit.*, p. 334.
8 *Sun Zhong Shan Xuanji*, p. 712. Sun Yat-sen, *op. cit.*, p. 188.
9 Chen Yuan-chyuan in G. K. Kindermann, *Sun Yat-sen: Founder and Symbol of China's Revolutionary Nation Building* (Munich, 1982), p. 145.
10 *Sun Zhong Shan Xuanji*, p. 87. ('Speech on the anniversary of the founding of Min Bao', untranslated).
11 *Sun Zhong Shan Xuanji*, p. 766. Sun Yat-sen, *op. cit.*, p. 296.
12 *Sun Zhong Shan Xuanji*, p. 794. Sun Yat-sen, *op. cit.*, p. 346.
13 *Sun Zhong Shan Xuanji*, p. 793. Sun Yat-sen, *op. cit.*, p. 345.
14 *Sun Zhong Shan Xuanji*, p. 712. Sun Yat-sen, *op. cit.*, p. 192.
15 *Sun Zhong Shan Xuanji*, p. 711. Sun Yat-sen, *op. cit.*, p. 189.
16 *Sun Zhong Shan Xuanji*, p. 749. Sun Yat-sen, *op. cit.*, p. 263.
17 Sun Yat-sen, 'Problems of the Revolutionary Reorganisation of China', in *Memoirs of a Chinese Revolutionary* (London, 1927), p. 121.
18 Chen Yuan-chyuan, *op. cit.*, p. 147.
19 Sun Yat-sen, *op. cit.*, p. 121.
20 *Sun Zhong Shan Xuanji*, p. 89.
21 *Sun Zhong Shan Xuanji*, p. 740. Sun Yat-sen, *San Min Chu-I*, p. 245.
22 *Sun Zhong Shan Xuanji*, p. 740. Sun Yat-sen, *op. cit.*, p. 244.
23 *Sun Zhong Shan Xuanji*, p. 798. Sun Yat-sen, *op. cit.*, p. 354.
24 Sun Yat-sen, *Fundamentals of National Reconstruction*, p. 11.
25 *Sun Zhong Shan Xuanji*, p. 798. Sun Yat-sen, *op. cit.*, p. 354.
26 Sun Yat-sen, *Fundamentals of National Reconstruction*, p. 16.
27 Chester C. Tan, *Chinese Political Thought in the Twentieth Century* (Newton Abbot, 1972), p. 133.
28 Manifesto of the First National Congress, 30 January 1924, quoted in the *Teachings of Sun Yat-sen* (ed.) N. Gangulee (London, 1945), p. 100.
29 *Ibid.*, p. 98.
30 See Chapter 4.
31 Corinna Hana in G. K. Kindermann, *East/West Synthesis – Sun Yat-sen: Founder and Symbol of China's Revolutionary Nation Building* (Munich, 1982), p. 137.
32 *Sun Zhong Shan Xuanji*, p. 795. Sun Yat-sen, *San Min Chu-I*, p. 349.
33 Sun Yat-sen, *Fundamentals of National Reconstruction*, p. 7.
34 *Sun Zhong Shan Xuanji*, p. 762. Sun Yat-sen, *San Min Chu-I*, p. 288.
35 Sun Yat-sen, *Fundamentals of National Reconstruction*, p. 48.
36 *Ibid.*, pp. 22, 38.
37 *Ibid.*, p. 22.
38 *Ibid.*, p. 40.
39 Chen Yuan-chyuan, *op. cit.*, p. 158.
40 Liu Yeou Hwa, *A Comparative Study of Dr. Sun Yat-sen's and Montesquieu's Theory of the Separation of Powers* (PhD 1983, Claremont College, USA), p. 127.
41 *Sun Zhong Shan Xuanji*, p. 712. Sun Yat-sen, *op. cit.*, p. 191.
42 Donald W. Treadgold, *The West in Russia and China* Vol. 2 (Cambridge, 1973), p. 130.
43 Chester Tan, *Chinese Political Thought in the Twentieth Century* (Newton Abbot, 1972), p. 229.

44 *Sun Zhong Shan Xuanji*, p. 862. Sun Yat-sen, *op. cit.*, p. 481.
45 *Sun Zhong Shan Xuanji*, p. 753. Sun Yat-sen, *op. cit.*, p. 270.
46 See Chapter 2.
47 See F. Hayek's argument in *The Road to Serfdom*, (London, 1986).

8 The Principle of Livelihood

1 T'ang Liang Li, *The Inner History of the Chinese Revolution* (London, 1930), p. 127.
2 Corinna Hana in G. K. Kindermann, *Sun Yat-sen: Founder and Symbol of China's Revolutionary Nation Building* (Munich, 1982), p. 138.
3 T'ang Liang Li, *op. cit.*, p. 172.
4 Cui Dan, *The Cultural Contribution of British Protestant Missionaries and British American Cooperation to China's National Development During the 1920's* (Maryland, 1998), p. 274.
5 C. Martin Wilbur in *Cambridge History of China* (Cambridge, 1983) Vol. 12, p. 535.
6 *Sun Zhong Shan Xuanji* (Beijing, 1981), p. 850. Sun Yat-sen, *San Min Chu-I*, trans Frank Price (Shanghai, 1927), p. 457.
7 A. C. Wells, *The Political Thought of Sun Yat-sen* PhD thesis (London, 1994), pp. 203–6.
8 *Sun Zhong Shan Xuanji op. cit.*, p. 844. Sun Yat-sen, *op. cit.*, p. 444.
9 FO/371/6614 (FO 84/81/10) C. W. Campbell's minute (13 January 1921) (This seems never to have been quoted before).
10 *Sun Zhong Shan Xuanji op. cit.*, p. 812. Sun Yat-sen, *op. cit.*, p. 382.
11 *Sun Zhong Shan Xuanji op. cit.*, p. 817. Sun Yat-sen, *op. cit.*, p. 391.
12 Maurice William, *The Social Interpretation of History* (New York, 1921), p. 80.
13 *Sun Zhong Shan Xuanji op. cit.*, p. 806. Sun Yat-sen, *op. cit.*, p. 371.
14 William, *op. cit.*, p. xxv.
15 *Ibid.*, p. 103.
16 *Sun Zhong Shan Xuanji op. cit.*, p. 817. Sun Yat-sen, *op. cit.*, p. 391.
17 Harold Z. Schiffrin, *Sun Yat-sen: Reluctant Revolutionary* (Toronto, 1986), p. 256.
18 Maurice Zolotow, *Maurice William and Sun Yat-sen* (London, 1948), p. 107.
19 William, *op. cit.*, p. 239.
20 *Ibid.*, p. 168.
21 *Sun Zhong Shan Xuanji op. cit.*, p. 844. Sun Yat-sen, *op. cit.*, p. 444.

9 The Influence of Christianity on Sun Yat-sen

1 Donald W. Treadgold, *The West in Russia and China* Vol. 2 (Cambridge, 1973), p. 91.
2 *Ibid.*, p. 93.
3 *Ibid.*, p. 91.
4 Lyon Sharman, *Sun Yat-sen: His Life and Its Meaning* (New York, 1934), p. 310.
5 Gottfried Karl Kindermann, *Sun Yat-sen: Founder and Symbol of China's Revolutionary Nation Building* (Munich, 1982), p. 72.
6 Richard Wilhelm's preface to Tai Chi-t'ao's, *Die Geistigen Grundlagen des Sun Yat-senismus* (Berlin, 1931), p. 8.
7 C. R. Hensman, *Sun Yat-sen* (London, 1971), p. 68.
8 Treadgold, *op. cit.*, p. 80.

9 Ibid., p. 81.
10 Ibid., p. 88.
11 Ibid., p. 92.
12 Ibid., p. 97.
13 N. Gangulee, *The Teachings of Sun Yat-sen* (London, 1945), p. 37.
14 Wu Yuzhang, *Recollections of the Revolution of 1911* (Beijing, 1981), p. 45.
15 Harold Z. Schiffrin, *Sun Yat-sen: Reluctant Revolutionary* (Toronto, 1980), p. 25.
16 Harold Z. Schiffrin, *Sun Yat-sen and the Origins of the Chinese Revolution* (Los Angeles, 1970), p. 15.
17 Ibid., p. 16.
18 Treadgold, *op. cit.*, p. 96.
19 Ibid., p. 78.
20 Ibid., p. 91.
21 Schiffrin, *Sun Yat-sen and the Origins of the Chinese Revolution*, p. 118.
22 Marius B. Jansen, *The Japanese and Sun Yat-sen* (California, 1954), p. 240.
23 Ibid., p. 240.
24 Ibid., p. 240.
25 Ibid., p. 240.
26 T'ang Liang-li, *Inner History of the Chinese Revolution* (London, 1930), p. 16.
27 Treadgold, *op. cit.*, p. 80.
28 Schiffrin, *Sun Yat-sen and the Origins of the Chinese Revolution*, p. 15.
29 T'ang, *op. cit.*, p. 18.
30 Treadgold, *op. cit.* p. 80.
31 Ibid., p. 93.
32 Ibid., p. 52.
33 *Sun Zhong Shan Xuanji*, p. 7.
34 Schiffrin, *Origins*, p. 90.
35 Ibid., p. 90.
36 *Sun Zhong Shan Xuanji*, p. 681
37 Herrlee G. Creel, *Chinese Thought from Confucius to Mao Tse-tung* (Chicago, 1955), p. 56.
38 Cantlie and Jones, *Sun Yat-sen and the Awakening of China* (London, 1912), p. 152.
39 Charles Drage, *Two-Gun Cohen* (London, 1954), p. 126.
40 *Sun Zhong Shan Xuanji*, p. 684.
41 Drage, *op. cit.*, p. 131.
42 Ibid., p. 139.
43 Wong, *Origins*, p. 167.
44 Drage, *op. cit.*, p. 134.
45 *Sun Zhong Shan Xuanji*, p. 690.
46 *Sun Zhong Shan Xuanji*, p. 649. Sun Yat-sen, *San Min Chu-I*, trans Frank Price (Shanghai, 1927), p. 65.
47 Sun Yat-sen to Qu Fengzhi (Quoted in Wong, *Origins*), p. 197.
48 Treadgold, *op. cit.*, p. 93.

10 The Influence of Confucianism on Sun Yat-sen

1 T'ang Liang Li, *The Inner History of the Chinese Revolution* (London, 1930), p. 16.
2 Ying-shih Yu in *Sun Yat-sen's Doctrine in the Modern World* (ed.) Chu-yuan Cheng (Boulder, 1989), p. 80.

Notes 213

3 Winston Hsieh, *Chinese Historiography on the Revolution of 1911* (Stanford, 1975), p. 70 (for criticism of 1958 version in detail).
4 Chun-tu Hsüeh (ed.), *The Chinese Revolution of 1911: New Perspectives* (Hong Kong, 1986), p. 34.
5 H. Z. Schiffrin, *Sun Yat-sen: Reluctant Revolutionary* (Toronto, 1980), p. 26.
6 H. Z. Schiffrin, *Sun Yat-sen and the Origins of the Chinese Revolution* (Los Angeles, 1970), p. 148.
7 Philip C. Huang, *Liang Ch'i-ch'ao and Modern Chinese Liberalism* (Seattle, 1972), p. 120.
8 *The New York Times*, 23 March 1897, p. 6.
9 *Sun Zhong Shan Xuanji* (Beijing, 1981), p. 170.
10 *Ibid.*, p. 59.
11 Frederick Wakeman, *History and Will* (Berkeley, 1973), p. 99.
12 *Sun Zhong Shan Xuanji*, p. 844.
13 *Ibid.*, p. 674.
14 *Ibid.*, p. 675.
15 *Sun Zhong Shan Xuanji*, p. 684.
16 See A. C. Wells, *The Political Thought of Sun Yat-sen*, Phd thesis (London, 1994) chapter 10.54.
17 Gottfried-Karl Kindermann, *East/West Synthesis – Sun Yat-sen: Founder and Symbol of China's Revolutionary Nation-Building* (Munich, 1982), p. 89.
18 Jurgen Domes, *Ibid.*, p. 289.
19 Sun Yat-sen, *The Vital Problem of China* (Taipei, 1953), p. 167.
20 *Sun Zhong Shan Xuanji*, pp. 690–1. Sun Yat-sen, *San Min Chu-I*, pp. 146–7.
21 *Ibid.*, pp. 691, 148.
22 Richard Wilhelm's preface to Tai Chi-t'ao's *Die Geistigen Grundlagen des Sun Yat-senismus* (Berlin, 1931), p. 8.
23 *Sun Zhong Shan Xuanji*, p. 684. Sun Yat-sen, *San Min Chu-I*, p. 134.
24 *Times Higher Educational Supplement*, 13 December 1991, p. 9.
25 Herman Kahn, *World Economic Development 1979 and Beyond* (Boulder, 1979), p. 121.
26 Charles Drage, *Two-Gun Cohen* (London, 1934), p. 143.

11 The Development of Sun Yat-sen's Political Thought by Chiang Kai-shek

1 Chiang Kai-shek, *Soviet Russia in China* (London, 1957), p. 22.
2 *Ibid.*, p. 23.
3 C. Martin Wilbur in *The Cambridge History of China* Vol. 12. (ed.) John K. Fairbank (Cambridge, 1983), p. 607.
4 Chester Tan, *Chinese Political Thought in the Twentieth Century* (Newton Abbot, 1972), p. 176.
5 Chiang Kai-shek, *China's Destiny* (with commentary by Philip Jaffe) (London, 1947), p. 208.
6 *Ibid.*, p. 209.
7 *Ibid.*, p. 95.
8 *Ibid.*, p. 100.
9 Chiang Kai-shek, *China at the Crossroads* (London, 1937), p. 185.
10 *Ibid.*, p. 205.

11 Sun Youli, *China and the Origins of the Pacific War, 1931–1941* (New York, 1993), pp. 80–3.
12 Paul Linebarger, *The China of Chiang Kai-shek* (Boston, USA, 1941), p. 371.
13 Sun Fo, *China Looks Forward* (Aberdeen, 1944), p. 140.
14 *Ibid.*, p. 83.
15 Philip Jaffe in Chiang Kai-shek's *China's Destiny*, p. 314.
16 *Ibid.*, p. 313.
17 *Ibid.*, p. 311.
18 *Ibid.*, p. 311.
19 *Ibid.*, p. 311.
20 Chen Yuan-chyuan in G. K. Kindermann, *Sun Yat-sen: Founder and Symbol of China's Revolutionary Nation Building* (Munich, 1982), p. 153.

12 The Development of Sun Yat-sen's Ideas by Wang Ching-Wei, Hu Han-Min and Tai Chi-T'ao

1 Wang Ching-wei, *Problèmes Chinois et Leurs Solutions* (Shanghai, 1935), p. 58: 'Les conditions economiques en Chine sont telles que les buts visès par le Dr Sun Yat-sen dans son livre Principes de la Vie du Peuple, ne peuvent être atteints par des procédès modérés et pacifiques'.
2 *Ibid.*, p. 55: 'A son issue, on publiait une double déclaration specifiant que ni le communisme ni le système sovietique ne convenant au peuple Chinois, mais que le Russie aiderait la Chine a réaliser son unification et son indépendance nationales selon ses propres vues'.
3 *China's Own Critics* (Tientsin, 1931), p. 62.
4 *Ibid.*, p. 28.
5 *Ibid.*, p. 43.
6 Wang Ching-wei and others, *The National Chinese Revolution* (Shanghai, 1931), p. 21.
7 *Ibid.*, p. 17.
8 *Ibid.*, p. 23.
9 *Ibid.*, p. 24.
10 *Ibid.*, p. 31.
11 *Ibid.*, p. 31.
12 *Ibid.*, p. 40.
13 *Ibid.*, p. 82.
14 *Ibid.*, p. 24.
15 John Hunter Boyle, *China and Japan at War 1937–1945* (California, 1972), p. 229.
16 *Ibid.*, p. 246.
17 *Ibid.*, p. 16.
18 Tai Chi-t'ao, *Sun Wen chu-I chih che-hsüeh ti chi-chu* (Shanghai, 1927), p. 46 ('The Philosophical Foundation of Sun Yat-senism').
19 *Ibid.*, p. 34.
20 *Ibid.*, p. 43.
21 *Tai Chi-t'ao yen-hsiang-lu* (ed.) Shih Hsi-tseng (Shanghai, 1932), p. 2910 (Collected Speeches of Tai Chi-t'ao).
22 *Tai Chi-t'ao hsien-sheng wen tsan* (Taipei, 1939), p. 1462 (Collected Works of Tai Chi-t'ao).

23 *Ibid.*, p. 1463.
24 *Tai Chi-t'ao yen-hsiang-lu* (ed.) Shih Hsi-tseng, p. 2690.
25 *Ibid.*, p. 2750.
26 *Ibid.*, p. 2690.
27 Prayer offered to the Spirit of Chu Yuan-shang, founder of the Ming Dynasty, by Sun Yat-sen on 15 February 1912, quoted in Gangulee, *op. cit.*, p. 3.
28 Herman Mast III and William G. Saywell, *Journal of Asian Studies*, November 1974, 'Revolution and Tradition: The Political Ideology of Tai Chi-tao', p. 77.
29 *Ibid.*, p. 86.
30 Martin Bernal, *Chinese Socialism to 1907* (Ithaca, 1976), p. 150.
31 *Ibid.*, p. 150.
32 Edward J. M. Rhoads, *China's Republican Revolution* (The Case of Kwangtung 1895–1913), (Harvard, 1975), p. 259.
33 *Hu Han-min* (Hu Han-min hsüan chi, writings selected by Wu Man-chun) (Taipei, 1959), p. 204.
34 *Ibid.*, p. 215.

13 Sun Yat-sen's Three Principles and the Chinese Communist Party

1 Teng Hsiao-p'ing, 'The Present Situation and Tasks', 16 January 1980 in *Wen Hsuan 1975–1982* (Beijing, 1983), p. 231.
2 Sun Yat-sen, *San Min Chu I*, trans Frank Price (Shanghai, 1927), p. 192, *Sun Zhong Shan Xuanji* (Beijing, 1981), p. 172.
3 John C. Kuan, *The KMT–CCP Wartime Negotiations 1937–1945* (Taipei, 1982), p. 1.
4 Stuart Schram, *Mao Tse-tung* (Harmondsworth, 1967), p. 202.
5 Kuan, *op. cit.*, p. 13.
6 *Ibid.*, p. 18.
7 *Ibid.*, p. 22.
8 Schram, *op. cit.*, p. 201.
9 *Ibid.*, p. 201.
10 Liu Shao-chi, 'How to be a Good Communist', July 1939, in *Hsüan-chi*, Vol. 1 (Beijing, 1981), p. 110.
11 Mao Tse-tung, 'On New Democracy', January 1940, in *Hsüan-chi*, Vol. 2 (Beijing, 1960), p. 670.
12 *Ibid.*, p. 671.
13 Mao Tse-tung, 'The Chinese Revolution and the Chinese Communist Party', December 1939, in *op. cit.*, p. 642.
14 Liu Shao-chi, 'Prepare for the Counter Offensive, Build a New China', 20 July 1942, in *op. cit.*, p. 226.
15 *Ibid.*, p. 176, 'On Anti-Japanese Democratic Political Power', December 1940.
16 Mao Tse-tung, 'The Current Problems of Tactics in the Anti-Japanese United Front', 11 March 1940, in *op. cit.*, p. 764.
17 Mao Tse-tung, 'The Chinese People Have Stood Up', 21 September 1949, in *Hsüan-chi*, Vol. 5 (Beijing, 1961), p. 5.
18 Mao Tse-tung, 'On the People's Democratic Dictatorship', 30 June 1949, in *op. cit.* (Beijing, 1961) Vol. 4, p. 1492.
19 *Ibid.*, p. 1494.

20 *Ibid.*, p. 1479.
21 Jung Chang with Jon Holliday, *Mme Sun Yat-sen* (Harmondsworth, 1986), p. 113.
22 *Ibid.*, p. 124.
23 Teng Hsiao-p'ing, 'The United Front and the Tasks of the Chinese People's Consultative Conference in the New Period', 15 June 1979, in *op. cit.*, p. 172.
24 *Ibid.*, p. 231, 'The Present Situation and Tasks', 16 January 1980.
25 *Ibid.*, p. 346, 'Problems on the Ideological Front', 17 July 1981.
26 Michael Fathers and Andrew Higgins, *Tiananmen: The Rape of Peking* (London, 1989), p. 109.
27 *Ibid.*, p. 67.
28 *Ibid.*, p. 89.
29 Han Min Zhu, *Cries for Democracy: Writings and Speeches from the 1989 Chinese Democracy Movement* (Princeton, 1990), p. 51.
30 *Ibid.*, p. 51.
31 *Ibid.*, p. 159.
32 Jude Howell, 'A Silent Revolution', in *China Review* (Summer 2000), p. 11.

14 The Implementation of Sun Yat-sen's Three Principles in Taiwan

1 *The Economist*, 5 March 1988.
2 Quoted by Ching-yuan Lin, in *The Taiwan Experience 1950–1980* (ed.) James C. Hsiung (New York, 1981), p. 140.
3 Ching-yuan Lin, in *op. cit.*, p. 141.
4 *The Economist*, March 1988.
5 Sun Yat-sen, *San Min Chu-I*, trans Frank Price (Shanghai, 1927), p. 456. *Sun Zhong Shan Xuanji*, p. 850.
6 Robert G. Sutter, *Taiwan: Entering the 21st Century* (London, 1988), p. 23.
7 *The Economist*, 5 March 1988.
8 Ministry of Finance of the ROC, *Taxation in the Republic of China in 1991* (Taipei, 1991), p. 135.
9 Sun Yat-sen, *op. cit.*, p. 478. *Sun Zhong Shan, op. cit.*, p. 861.
10 *Ibid.*, p. 444. *Sun Zhong Shan, op. cit.*, p. 844.
11 *Ibid.*, p. 391. *Sun Zhong Shan op. cit.*, p. 816.
12 Chalmers Johnson, in *The Taiwan Experience 1950–1980* (ed.) James C. Hsiung (New York, 1981), p. 10.
13 *Ibid.*, p. 10.
14 Sun Yat-sen, *op. cit.*, p. 409. *Sun Zhong Shan, op. cit.*, p. 826.
15 *Ibid.*, p. 826.
16 *Ibid.*, pp. 442, 843.
17 *The Economist*, 5 March 1988.
18 James Schreiber, *US Corporate Investment in Taiwan* (New York, 1970), p. 11.
19 Robert G. Sutter, *Taiwan: Entering the 21st Century* (London, 1988), p. 24.
20 Joseph A. Yager, *Economic Transformation in Taiwan* (Taipei, 1986), p. 14.
21 H. S. Duller, *Technique in Taiwan: The Role of Technology in Taiwan: Past and Present Development* (Taipei, 1983), p. 8.
22 Sun Yat-sen, *op. cit.*, p. 496. *Sun Zhong Shan, op. cit.*, p. 870.
23 Schreiber, *op. cit.*, p. 18.

24 Sun Yat-sen, *op. cit.*, p. 465. *Sun Zhong Shan, op. cit.*, p. 854.
25 Duller, *op. cit.*, p. 18.
26 *Ibid.*, p. 18.
27 *Ibid.*, p. 18.
28 Yager, *op. cit.*, p. 14.
29 Duller, *op. cit.*, p. 40.
30 For a fuller discussion of this topic see my PhD thesis *The Political Thought of Sun Yat-sen* (London, 1994), p. 329.
31 See Chapter 9.
32 *The Economist*, 5 March 1988.
33 Sun Yat-sen, *op. cit.*, p. 453. *Sun Zhong Shan, op. cit.*, p. 848.
34 Sun Yat-sen, *op. cit.*, p. 473. *Sun Zhong Shan, op. cit.*, p. 858.
35 Sun Yat-sen, *op. cit.*, p. 475. *Sun Zhong Shan, op. cit.*, p. 859.
36 *The Economist*, 5 March 1988.
37 A. James Gregor, *Ideology and Development: Sun Yat-sen and the Economic History of Taiwan* (Berkeley, 1981), p. 43.
38 *Ibid.*, p. 101.
39 *Ibid.*, p. 93.
40 A. James Gregor and Maria Hsia Chang, *Essays on Sun Yat-sen and the Economic Development of Taiwan* (Baltimore, 1983), p. 26.
41 Chiang Kai-shek, *China's Destiny* (with commentary by Philip Jaffe) (London, 1947), p. 236.
42 *Ibid.*, p. 32.
43 *Ibid.*, p. 51.
44 John F. Copper, in *The Taiwan Experience 1950–1980* (ed.) James C. Hsiung (New York, 1981), p. 376.
45 For earlier history of constitutional redrafting see my thesis, *op. cit.*, p. 340.
46 John F. Copper (with George P. Chen), *Taiwan's Elections: Political Development and Democratization in the Republic of China* (USA, 1984), p. 53.
47 Hung Da Chu in *Hsiung, op. cit.*, p. 315.
48 Copper, *ibid.*, p. 378.
49 *The Economist*, 5 March 1988.
50 Steve Tsang, *In the Shadow of China: Political Development in Taiwan Since 1949* (London, 1993), p. 4.
51 Sun Yat-sen, *Fundamentals of National Reconstruction* (Taipei, 1953), p. 47.
52 *Time*, 23 August 1993.
53 *Taipei Times*, 26 April 2000.

15 Sun Yat-sen and Other Third World Countries

1 Sukarno, 'Pantja Sila', in *The Indonesian Revolution: Basic Documents* (Jakarta, 1960), p. 42.
2 Charles A. Coppel, in *The Chinese in Indonesia* (ed.) J. A. C. Mackie (Melbourne, Australia, 1976), p. 26.
3 Sukarno, *op. cit.*, p. 47.
4 Sukarno, *op. cit.*, p. 42.
5 Bernard Dahm, *Sukarno and the Struggle for Indonesian Independence* (New York, 1966), p. 34.
6 David Reeve, *Golkar of Indonesia* (Oxford, 1985), p. 33.

7 Sukarno, *op. cit.*, p. 37.
8 *Ibid.*, p. 39.
9 *Ibid.*, p. 41.
10 Dahm, *op. cit.*, p. 116.
11 Sukarno, *op. cit.*, p. 43.
12 *Ibid.*, p. 43.
13 *Ibid.*, p. 42.
14 Sun Yat-sen, *San Min Chu-I*, p. 147. *Sun Zhong Shan Xuanji* (Beijing, 1981), p. 691.
15 *Ibid.*, p. 89. *Sun Zhong Shan Xuanji* (Beijing, 1981), p. 662.
16 Sukarno, *op. cit.*, p. 46.
17 *Ibid.*, p. 47.
18 *Ibid.*, p. 45.
19 *Ibid.*, p. 50.
20 *Ibid.*, p. 50.
21 *Ibid.*, p. 51.
22 *Ibid.*, p. 90.
23 *Ibid.*, p. 91.
24 Reeve, *op. cit.*, p. 69.
25 *The Indonesian Revolution: Basic Documents*, p. 113.
26 Sukarno, *op. cit.*, p. 45.
27 Reeve, *op. cit.*, p. 28.
28 Dick Wilson, *Asia Awakes* (London, 1970), p. 280.
29 Jorgen Unselt, in Kindermann, *op. cit.*, p. 174.
30 *Ibid.*, p. 174.
31 The information on Phan-boi has been derived from the above work.
32 Hoai Thanh *et al.*, *Days with Ho Chi Minh* (Hanoi, 1963), p. 116.
33 *Ibid.*, p. 114.
34 Jules Archer, *Ho Chi Minh* (London, 1973), p. 5.
35 Hoai Thanh, *op. cit.*, p. 35.
36 Archer, *op. cit.*, p. 7.
37 Jean Lacouture, *Ho Chi Minh* (London, 1968), p. 211.
38 *China Forum*, p. 204.
39 *Ibid.*, p. 206.
40 *Ibid.*, p. 206.
41 *Ibid.*, p. 207.
42 *Ibid.*, p. 207.
43 Mariano Ponce, *Sun Yat-sen: The Founder of the Republic of China* (Manila, 1965), p. 1.
44 *Ibid.*, p. x.
45 *Ibid.*, p. xiii.
46 *Ibid.*, p. xvi.
47 *Ibid.*, p. 40.
48 *Ibid.*, p. 39.
49 *Ibid.*, p. 3.
50 *China Forum*, p. 224.
51 Antonio Tan, *The Chinese in the Philippines 1898–1935* (Quezon City, 1972), p. 31.
52 *Ibid.*, p. 93.
53 *Ibid.*, p. 116.

54 *Ibid.*, p. 116.
55 *Ibid.*, p. 320.

16 Sun Yat-sen's Influence on Muammar Gaddafi

1 Chou En-lai in *Dr Sun Yat-sen: Commemorative Articles and Speeches* (Peking, 1957), p. 23.
2 *Evening Standard*, 27 January 1989.
3 *The Times*, 4 August 1989, 2(a).
4 Ali A. Mazrui and Michael Tidy, *Nationalism and New States in Africa* (London, 1989), p. 267.
5 Richard Wilhelm's Preface to Tai Chi-t'ao, *Die Geistigen Grundlagen des Sun Yat-senismus*, trans Richard Wilhelm (Berlin, 1931), p. 8.
6 Sun Yat-sen, *San Min Chu-I*, trans Frank Price (Shanghai, 1927), p. 412. *Sun Zhong Shan Xuanji* (Beijing, 1981), p. 828.
7 Sun Yat-sen, *op. cit.*, p. 133. *Sun Zhong Shan, op. cit.*, p. 684.
8 Muammar Gaddafi, *The Green Book* (Tripoli, 1976), p. 35.
9 Mirella Bianco, *Gaddafi: Voice from the Desert* (London, 1975), p. 83.
10 Jonathan Bearman, *Qadhafi's Libya* (London, 1986), p. 164.
11 Bianco, *op. cit.*, p. 83 (see also Musa M. Kousa, *The Political Leader and His Social Background: Muamar Qadafi the Libyan Leader* (unpublished M.A. thesis Michigan State University, 1978), p. 135; 'I read about the life of Sun-Yat-sen').
12 Bianco, *op. cit.*, p. 85.
13 Donald W. Treadgold, *The West in Russia and China* Vol. 2 (London, 1973), p. 93.
14 Bianco, *op. cit.*, p. 84.
15 Sun Yat-sen, *op. cit.*, p. 289. *Sun Zhong Shan, op. cit.*, p. 763.
16 Sun Yat-sen, *op. cit.*, p. 331. *Sun Zhong Shan, op. cit.*, p. 785.
17 Gaddafi, *op. cit.*, p. 22.
18 *Ibid.*, pp. 9–10.
19 Sun Yat-sen, *op. cit.*, p. 289. *Sun Zhong Shan, op. cit.*, p. 795.
20 Gaddafi, *op. cit.*, p. 24.
21 For an interesting discussion of this see Sami G. Hajjar 'The Jamahiriya Experiment in Libya: Qadhafi and Rousseau', *The Journal of Modern African Studies* 18/2 (1980), pp. 181–200. An amusing informative first-hand account of direct democracy in practice has been provided by J. Davis, *Qaddafi's Theory and Practice of Non-Represenative Government* in N. S. Hopkins and S. E. Ibrahim (eds) 'Arab Society' (American University in Cairo, 1977), pp. 357–61. Musa M. Kousa (*op. cit.*) p. 135 quotes Gaddafi as stating 'I read almost everything that was written on the French Revolution'. It is therefore most unlikely that he was unaware of Rousseau's ideas.
22 Sun Yat-sen, *op. cit.*, p. 177.
23 Gaddafi, *op. cit.*, p. 27.
24 *The Independent*, 3 March 2000.
25 Gaddafi, *op. cit.*, p. 27.
26 Sun Yat-sen, *op. cit.*, p. 480. *Sun Zhong Shan, op. cit.*, p. 862.
27 Gaddafi, *op. cit.*, p. 64.
28 Sun Yat-sen, *op. cit.*, p. 391. *Sun Zhong Shan, op. cit.*, p. 817.

220 Notes

29 See Maurice William, *The Social Interpretation of History* (New York, 1921) from which Sun, in his Lectures on Livelihood, quotes extensively. See also Maurice Zolotow, *Maurice William and Sun Yat-sen*. (London, 1948).
30 Gaddafi, *op, cit.*, p. 50.
31 David Blundy and Andrew Lycett, *Qaddafi and the Libyan Revolution* (London, 1987), p. 97.
32 Gaddafi, *op. cit.*, p. 31.
33 Sun Yat-sen, *op. cit.*, p. 429.
34 Gaddafi, *op. cit.*, p. 47.
35 *Ibid.*, p. 63.
36 *Ibid.*, p. 55.
37 Sun Yat-sen, *op. cit.*, p. 456. *Sun Zhong Shan*, *op. cit.*, p. 850.
38 John K. Cooley, *Libyan Sandstorm* (New York, 1982), p. 149.
39 Gaddafi, *op. cit.*, p. 76.
40 *Ibid.*, p. 77.
41 Sun Yat-sen, *op. cit.*, p. 10. *Sun Zhong Shan*, *op. cit.*, p. 620.

Bibliography

Primary Sources

Chiang Kai-shek and Mei-Ling (1944) *The Voice of China* (London).
Chiang Kai-shek (1947) *China's Destiny* (with commentary by Philip Jaffe) (London).
Chiang Kai-shek (1937) *China at the Crossroads* (London).
Chiang Kai-shek (1957) *Soviet Russia in China* (London).
Chiang Kai-shek (n.d.) *Two Supplementary Chapters to San Min Chu-I* (Taipei).
Teng Hsiao-p'ing (1983) *Wen Hsuan 1975–1982* (Beijing).
Hu Han-min (1959) (Hu Han-min hsüan-chi). Writings selected by Wu Man-chun.
Hu Shih and Lin Yu-tang (1931) with commentary by Wang Ching–wei, *China's Own Critics* (Peiping).
Liu Shao-chi (1981) *Hsüan-chi* (Selected Works) Vol. 1 (Beijing).
Mao Tse-tung (1960) *Hsüan-chi* (Selected Works) Vol. 1 (Beijing).
Mao Tse-tung (1961) *Hsüan-chi* (Selected Works) Vol. 5 (Beijing).
Mao Tse-tung et al. (1957) *Dr. Sun Yat-sen Commemorative Articles and Speeches* (Peking).
Shih Hsi-tseng (ed.) (1932) *Tai Chi-t'ao yen-hsiang-lu* ('Collected Speeches of Tai Chi-t' ao') (Shanghai).
Sukarno (1960) 'Pantja Sila', in *The Indonesian Revolution: Basic Documents* (Jakarta).
Sun Chung-shan ch'üan-chi (1981) (Complete Collected Works of Sun Yat-sen) (Beijing).
Sun Fo (1944) *China Looks Forward* (Aberdeen).
Sun (Wen) Chung-Shan Ch'üanshu (1928) (Complete Works of the Founding Father of the Nation) (Shanghai).
Sun Wen, *Kuo-fu ch'üan-chi* (1957) (Complete Works of the Father of the Nation) (Taipei).
Sun Yat-sen (1897) *Kidnapped in London* (Bristol).
Sun Yat-sen (1927) *Memoirs of a Chinese Revolutionary* (London).
Sun Yat-sen (1927) *San Min Chu-1* (The Three Principles of the People) trans. Frank Price (Shanghai).
Sun Yat-sen (1953) *Fundamentals of National Reconstruction* (Taipei).
Sun Yat-sen (1922) *The International Development of China* (New York and London).
Sun Yat-sen (1953) *The Vital Problem of China* (Taipei).
Sun Zhong Shan Xuanji (1981) (Selected Works of Sun Yat-sen) (Beijing).
Tai Chi-t'ao (1927) *Sun Wen chu-I chih che-hsüeh ti chi-ch'u* ('The Philosophical Foundation of Sun Yat-senism') (Shanghai).
Wang Ching-wei (1937) *Wang Ching-wei hsien-sheng tsui chin yen lun chi (1932–37)* (Collection of Wang Ching-wei's recent lectures) (Shanghai).
Wang Ching-wei (1935) *Problèmes Chinois et Leurs Solutions* (Shanghai).
Wang Ching-wei and others (1931) *The Chinese National Revolution* (Shanghai).
Wei Yung (1931) *The Cult of Dr. Sun*, trans Wei Yung (Shanghai).

Wu Man-chun (1959) *Hu Han-min hsüan-chi* (Selected writings of Hu Han Min (Taipei).
Wu Yuzhang (1962) *Recollections of the Revolution of 1911* (Beijing).

Secondary Sources

Archer, J. (1973) *Ho Chi Minh* (London).
Barker, R. (1978) *Political Ideas in Modern Britain* (London).
Barlow, J. G. (1979) *Sun Yat-sen and the French 1900–1908* (California).
Bergère, M-C. (1998) *Sun Yat-sen* (Stanford).
Bearman, J. (1986) *Qadhafi's Libya* (London).
Bernal, M. (1976) *Chinese Socialism to 1907* (Ithaca).
Bianco, M. (1975) *Gaddafi: Voice from the Desert* (London).
Blundy, D. (1987) *Qaddafi and the Libya Revolution* (London).
Bluntschli, J. K. (1883) *The Theory of the State* (Oxford).
Boyle, J. H. (1972) *China and Japan at War 1937–1945* (California).
Cantlie, J. and Sheridan Jones, C. (1912) *Sun Yat-sen and the Awakening of China* (London).
Chang, J. with Halliday, J. (1986) *Mme Sun Yat-sen* (Harmondsworth, England).
Chang, M. H. (1983) *The Chinese Blue Shirt Society* (California).
Chang, S. H. and Gordon, L. H. D. (1991) *All Under Heaven: Sun Yat-sen and His Revolutionary Thought* (Stanford).
Chapman, H. O. (1928) *The Chinese Revolution 1926–27* (London).
Chatterji, K. (1958) *National Movement in Modern China* (Calcutta).
Chu-yuan Cheng (ed.) (1989) *Sun Yat-sen's Doctrine in the Modern World* (Boulder).
Chien Tuan-sheng (1950) *The Government and Politics of China* (Massachusetts).
Chiou, C. L. (1995) *Democratising Oriental Despotism* (New York).
Chun-tu Hsüeh (ed.) (1986) *The Chinese Revolution of 1911 New Perspectives* (Hong Kong).
Cole, G. D. H. (1941) *James Keir Hardie* (London).
Cooley, J. K. (1982) *Libyan Sandstorm* (New York).
Copper, J. F. (1984) *Taiwan's Elections: Political Development and Democratization in the Republic of China* (Baltimore).
Cordier, H. (1902) *Histoire des Relations de la Chine avec les Puissances Occidentales 1860–1902* (Paris).
Creel, H. G. (1953) *Chinese Thought from Confucius to Mao Tse-tung* (Chicago).
Crozier, R. C. (ed.) (1970) *China's Cultural Legacy and Communism* (London).
Cui, D. (1998) *The Cultural Contribution of British Protestant Missionaries and British American Cooperation to China's National Development During the 1920's* (Maryland).
Dahm, B. (1960) *Sukarno and the Struggle for Indonesian Independence* (Cornell).
Dawson, R. (1972) *Imperial China* (Harmondsworth).
Dawson, R. (1964) *The Legacy of China* (Oxford).
Dickson, B. J. (1997) *Democratization in China and Taiwan* (Oxford).
Diosy, A. (1900) *The New Far East* (London).
Douglas, R. K. (1899) *China Story of the Nation* (London).
Douglas, R. K. (1913) *Europe and the Far East* (London).
Douglas, R. K. (1895) *Li Hung Chang* (London).

Drage, C. (1934) *Two-Gun Cohen* (London).
Duller, H. S. (1983) *Technique in Taiwan: The Role of Technology in Taiwan: Past and Present Development* (Taipei).
Eastman, L. (1974) *The Abortive Revolution* (Massachusetts).
Esherick, J. W. (1976) *Reform and Revolution in China: The 1911 Revolution in Hunan and Hubei* (Berkeley).
Fairbank, J. K. (ed.) (1973) *The Cambridge History of China* (Cambridge).
Fathers, M. and Higgins, A. (1989) *Tiananmen: The Rape of Peking* (London).
Fenn, C. (1973) *Ho Chi Minh* (London).
Fitzgerald, C. P. (1952) *The Birth of Communist China* (London).
Franke, W. (1952) *A Century of Chinese Revolution* (London).
Friedman, W. (1951) *An Introduction to World Politics* (London).
Fukuyama, F. (1992) *The End of History and the Last Man* (London).
Fung Yu-lan, (1947) *The Spirit of Chinese Philosophy* (London).
Gangulee, N. (1945) *The Teachings of Sun Yat-sen* (London).
Gaaster, M. (1969) *Chinese Intellectuals and the Revolution of 1911* (Washington).
Gaddafi, M. (n.d.) *The Green Book* (Tripoli).
Glasier, C. J. B. (1919) *James Keir Hardie* (London).
Gray, J. (ed.) (1969) *Modern China's Search for a Political Form* (London).
Gregor, A. J. and Chang, M. H. (1987) *Essays on Sun Yat-sen* (Baltimore).
Hardie, J. K. (1907) *All About Keir Hardie* (London).
Hardie, J. K. (1915) *Memoir* (London).
Hayes, P. (1973) *Fascism* (London).
Hensman, C. R. (1971) *Sun Yat-sen* (London).
Holcombe, A. N. (1931) *The Chinese Revolution* (Harvard).
Horowitz, D. (1965) *From Yalta to Vietnam* (London).
Hsien, W. (1975) *Chinese Histography on the Revolution of 1911* (Stanford).
Hsiung, J. C. (1981) *The Taiwan Experience* (New York).
Hsu, L. (1933) *Sun Yat-sen, His Political and Social Ideals* (Los Angeles).
Sheng, H. (ed.) (1983) *The 1911 Revolution: a Retrospective after 70 years* (Beijing).
Huang, P. (1972) *Liang Ch'i-ch'ao and Modern Chinese Liberalism* (Seattle).
Hutt, A. (1975) *British Trade Unionism* (London).
Jansen, M. B. (1954) *The Japanese and Sun Yat-sen* (California).
Kahn, H. (1979) *World Economic Development 1979 and Beyond* (Boulder).
Kapp, Y. (1972) *Eleanor Marx*, Vols I & II (London).
Kindermann, G.-K. (1982) *East/West Synthesis – Sun Yat-sen: Founder and Symbol of China's Revolutionary Nation-Building* (Munich).
Kuan, J. C. (1982) *The KMT–CCP Wartime Negotiations 1937–1945* (Taipei).
Kwei, C.-Q. (1970) *The Kuomintang-Communist Struggle in China, 1922–1949* (The Hague).
Lacouture, J. (1968) *Ho Chi Minh* (London).
Lafargue, P. (1959) *Letters: Engels* (London).
Lafargue, P. (1895) *La Propriété* (London).
Leng, S. C. and Palmer, N. (1961) *Sun Yat-sen and Communism* (London).
Levenson, J. R. (1958) *Confucian China and its Modern Fate*, Vols I & II (London).
Levenson, J. R. (1953) *Liang Ch'i Ch'ao and the Mind of Modern China* (London).
Leys, S. (1977) *The Chairman's New Clothes* (London).
Yu-ning, L. (1971) *The Introduction of Socialism into China* (New York).
Linebarger, P. M. (1937) *The Political Doctrines of Sun Yat-sen* (Baltimore).

Linebarger, P. (1941) *The China of Chiang Kai-shek* (Boston, USA).
Linebarger, P. (1925) *Sun Yat-sen and the Republic of China* (London, New York).
Lo C.-L. (1969) *Kuo-fu nien-pu* (Chronological Biography of Sun Yat-sen) (Taipei).
Longuet, J. (1913) *Le Mouvement Socialiste International* (Paris).
Longuet, J. (1911) *Mémoire Présente* (Paris).
Longuet, J. (1918) *La Politique Internationale* (Paris).
Eve Armentraut, M. L. (1900) *Revolutionaries, Monarchists and China town: Chinese Politics in the Americas and the 1911 Revolution* (Honolulu).
Mackenzie, R. (1880) *Nineteenth Century* (London).
Maitron, J. (1975) *Dictionnaire Bibliographique du Movement Ouvrier Francais* (Paris).
Martin, B. (1944) *Strange Vigour* (London).
Maybon, A. (1908) *La Politique Chinoise* (Paris).
Maybon, A. (1904) *La Republique Chinoise* (Paris).
Mazrui, A. A. and Tidy, M. (1989) *Nationalism and New States in Africa* (London).
Michael, F. and Chung-li, C. (1966–71) *The Taiping Rebellion: History and Documents*, 3 vols (Seattle).
Mill, J. S. (1864) *On Liberty* (London).
Moise, E. (1980) *Modern China* (London, New York).
Oakeshott, M. (1962) *Rationalism in Politics* (London).
Pateman, C. (1970) *Participation and Democratic Theory* (Cambridge).
Sir Petrie, C. (1929) *The History of Government* (London).
Ponce, M. (1965) *Sun Yat-sen: The Founder of the Republic of China* (Manila, Philippines).
Radhakrishnan, S. (1957) *India and China* (Bombay).
Ransome, A. (1927) *The Chinese Puzzle* (London).
Reeve, D. (1985) *Golkar of Indonesia* (Oxford).
Restarick, H. B. (1931) *Sun Yat-sen* (London).
Rhoads, E. J. M. (1975) *China's Republican Revolution (The Case of Kwangtung 1895–1913)* (Harvard).
Richard, T. (1907) *Conversion by the Million* (Shanghai).
Richard, T. (1916) *Forty-Five Years in China* (New York).
Rodes, J. (1910) *La Chine Nouvelle* (Paris).
Rodes, J. (1913) *La Chine et le Mouvement Constitutionnel (1910–1911)* (Paris).
Schiffrin, H. Z. (1980) *Sun Yat-sen, Reluctant Revolutionary* (Boston).
Schiffrin, H. Z. (1970) *Sun Yat-sen and the Origins of the Chinese Revolution* (Los Angeles).
Schram, S. (1966) *Mao Tse-tung* (Harmondsworth).
Schreiber, J. (1920) *US Corporate Investment in Taiwan* (New York).
Schurmann, F. and Schell, O. (1967) *Communist China* (Harmondsworth).
Sharman, L. (1934) *Sun Yat-sen: His Life and Its Meaning* (New York).
Shieh, M. J. T. (1970) *The Kuomintang, Selected Historical Documents, 1894–1969* (New York).
Shinkichi, E. and Schiffrin, H. Z. (1984) *The 1911 Revolution in China: Interpretative Essays* (Tokyo).
Sih, P. (1959) *De Confucius au Christ* (Paris).
Smith, A. D. (1982) *Ethnic Identity of World Order* (5th Millennium Conference of LSE).
Spence, J. D. (1981) *The Gate of Heavenly Peace* (New York).
Sutter, R. G. (1988) *Taiwan: Entering the 21st Century* (London).

Sun, Y. (1993) *China and the Origins of the Pacific War, 1931–1941* (New York).
Tan, A. (1972) *The Chinese in the Philippines 1898–1935* (Quezon City).
Tan, C. (1972) *Chinese Political Thought in the Twentieth Century* (Newton Abbot).
Li, T. L. (1930) *The Inner History of the Chinese Revolution* (London).
Teng, S. Y. and Fairbank, J. K. (1975) *China's Response to the West* (New York).
Thanh, H. et al., (1963) *Days with Hi Chi Minh* (Hanoi).
Townsend, J. R. (1967) *Political Participation in Communist China* (Berkley).
Treadgold, D. W. (1973) *The West in Russia and China* Vol. 2 (Cambridge).
Trotsky, L. (1932) *Problems of the Chinese Revolution* (New York).
Trevelyan, M. (1900) *Britain's Greatness Foretold* (London).
Tsang, S. (1993) *In the Shadow of China: Political Development in Taiwan Since 1949* (London).
Tsang, S. and Tien, H. (1999) *Democratization in Taiwan* (London).
Wakeman, F. (1973) *History and Will* (Berkeley).
Wilbur, C. M. (1976) *Sun Yat-sen, Frustrated Patriot* (New York).
Wilbur, C. M. and Lien-ling How, J. (1956) *Documents on Communism, Nationalism and Soviet Advisers, Papers Seized in the 1927 Peking Raid* (New York).
Wilhelm, R. (trans.) Tai Chi-t'ao (1931) *Die Geistigen Grundlagen des Sun Yat-senismus* (Berlin).
Wilcox, D. (1912) *Government by All the People* (New York).
William, M. (1921) *The Social Interpretation of History* (New York).
Yager, J. A. (1986) *Economic Transformation in Taiwan* (Taipei).
Wong, J. Y. (1986) *The Origins of a Heroic Image* (Hong Kong).
Wong, J. Y. (1987) *Sun Yat-sen. His International Ideas and International Connections* (Sydney).
Yang, C. K. (1970) *Religion in Society* (London).
Zhou Xun (2001) *Chinese Perceptions of the 'Jews' and Judaism* (Richmond, Surrey).
Zolotow, M. (1948) *Maurice William and Sun Yat-sen* (London).

Newspapers

Charing Cross Hospital Gazette
The Clarion
Evening Standard
Gazette de France
The Globe
The Glasgow Herald
The Herald (Montreal)
Hong Kong Telegraph
L'Humanité
Justice
The Labour Leader
The London and China Express
Montreal Daily Star
The New York Times

Oxford City and County Chronicle (1897)
Oxford Review (1897)
Oxfordshire Weekly News (1897)
Oxford Times (1897)
Pall Mall Gazette
The Province (Vancouver)
Peking and Tientsin Times
Le Peuple
Le Temps
The Times
The Times Higher Education Supplement
La Vie Ouvrière
Vooruit
Westminster Gazette
Westminster and Pimlico News

Periodicals

Archiv Orientalni
The American Political Science Review
Blackwoods Magazine
China Forum
China Quarterly
East Asia
Far Eastern Economic Review
Fortnightly Review
Free Russia
History Today
The Independent
International Socialist Review
Journal of Asian Studies
Modern Asian Studies
Taipei Times

Ph.D theses consulted

Barrett, D. P. (1978) *Socialism, Marxism and Communism in the Thought of Hu Hanmin* (London University).
Hsien, C. S. (1962) *The T'ung Meng Hui Its Organisation, Leadership and Finances, 1905–12* (Washington University).
Liu Yeou-hwa (1983) *A Comparative Study of Dr. Sun Yat-sen's and Montesquieu's Theory of Separation of Powers* (Claremont College, USA).

M.A. thesis consulted

Kousa Musa, M. (1978) *The Political Leader and His Social Background: Muamar Qadafi the Libyan Leader* (Michigan State University).

Archives

Foreign Office Records
I.L.P. Archives

Index

Africa, 36, 37, 189
Agency for International Development, 159
agricultural skills, 3
Agricultural Studies Society, 8
agriculture, 4, 5, 15, 93, 145, 149, 155
Aguinaldo, Emilio, 184
American missionary, 3, 29, 106, 107
Annam, 39, 67, 119
Armenians, 12

benevolence, 120, 136, 186
benevolent neutrality, 19, 20, 22, 200
Bergère, Marie-Claire, xiv, 6, 208 note 12
Bernal, Martin, 34
Bismarck, Otto, 78, 79
Bluntschli, Johan, 31–3, 37, 200
Boers, 36, 37
Bolshevik Revolution, 43, 54, 68, 72, 94
Borodin, Michael, 124, 133, 138, 181
Boxer Rebellion, 35, 105, 106, 109
Burgess, John, 87
Burma, 119, 175, 180

Cantlie, Dr James, 9–18, 23, 26, 27, 37, 39, 110
Canton: uprising in 1895, 8; military government, 43, 44, 54, 55
Cecil, Lord Hugh, 87
Chang Hsi-jo, 127, 128
Chang Hsüeh-liang, 126
Ch'en Ch'eng, 154
Ch'en Ch'iung-ming, 55, 61, 74
Chen Shui-bian, 169, 170
Ch'en Tu-hsiu, 135
Cheng Kuan-ying, 3, 4
Chiang Kai-shek: anti-Communism, 101, 122–6; neglects peasants, 94, 101; suppression of opposition, 52, 59, 126–129; two supplementary chapters to The Three Principles, 93; United Front, 125, 126
Chiang Ching-kuo, 166, 167
Chicherin, Georgi V., 123
Chien-she, 42, 43, 85
'China's Present and Future', 14, 16, 19, 20, 22, 24
Chinese Communist Party: United Front, 142; support for The Three Principles, 142–6; Sun criticised for relying on 'bourgeoisie', 147; Sun and democracy, 150–2 *passim*
Chinese New Party, 168
Chinese Revolutionary Party, 68
Chou En-lai, 179, 202
Christianity, 6, 95, 101–9, 112, 118, 202
Chu Chih-hsin, 43, 94
Ch'ü Feng-ch'ih, 3, 106, 114
Clans in China, 20–3, 63, 67, 69, 71, 117, 197
Cleveland, USA, 40–2, 85
Cohen, Morris, 61, 110, 111, 121
Cole, George, 10, 12, 13, 27, 111
Collins, Edwin, 14, 19, 21, 22, 24
Comintern, 124, 141, 181
Confucianism: Sun read Confucian classics, 113, 114; Sun's Confucian values, 117–21; *see also* Kang Yu-wei
Constitutional Club, 23
Control Election Committee, 168
Control Yuan, 57, 80, 81, 86, 88, 150, 165, 166, 168, 176; relevance today, 88, 200
Creel, Herrlee G., 110
Cult of Sun Wen, 49
Cultural Revolution, 149, 150, 152

Damon, Rev. Francis, 106
Darwin, Charles, 3, 51, 109

Democracy: influence of England on Sun, 23–6; Sun's Principle of (1906), 35, 36; Sun's theory of direct participation, 40–3; Sun's Principle of (1924), 73–90; CCP and, xiii, 150–2 *passim*; in Taiwan, 164–70; Sun's Principle of, relevance today, 85, 86, 200–2
Democratic Progressive Party, 167, 169
Denver, Colorado, 39
Dewey, John, 49, 52
direct democracy, 42, 43, 53, 50, 80–5, 193, 194, 201
Douglas, Professor R. K., 14, 15

Eddy, George Sherwood, 107
Eighth Miners' International Congress, 27
Electoral College, 85
d'Elia, Paschal, 33
Ely, Richard, 29
Engineering Lock-out, 27
England, 2, 3, 9, 10, 35, 36, 64, 65, 73, 74, 82, 87, 106, 159, 175, 191; Sun's stay in, ((1896–97), 10–28; Sun fails to win support of, (1912), 39; (1921), 54, 55
equalisation of land rights, 30, 92, 139, 155–7, 197
Examination Yuan, 5, 57, 80, 81, 86–8, 120, 165, 168, 200; relevance today, 86, 87, 200, 201
Executive Yuan, 134, 139, 160

Fabians, 99, 100, 202
famine, 19, 96
Fascism, 47, 124, 163, 194, 198
federalism, 57, 77, 208 note 12
Feng Tzu-yu, 6
Feng Yulan, 71
Five-Power Constitution, 36, 56, 80–8, 127, 129, 143, 145, 168, 169, 200
flood, 19, 93, 96, 133, 161
Ford factories, 92, 98
Formosa Magazine, 165
Formosa Plastics, 157
Fortnightly Review, 14, 16, 19, 20, 23, 24, 28, 33

France, 12, 35, 39, 55, 59, 64, 65, 67, 119, 134; defeats China (1885), 3, 22, 70; civil service examination, 87; agriculture, 93;
Free Russia, 13, 23
French Revolution, 32, 34, 74, 75, 77, 81, 145, 171; Sun aware of mob tyranny, 82, 84
Fundamentals of National Reconstruction, 55, 59, 60, 82, 85, 86
Furen Literary Society, 8
future unearned increment, 27

Gaddafi, Muammar, x, xi, xv, 187–198, 203; expressed admiration for Sun Yat-sen, 188; studied Sun's revolution, 190; read life of Sun, 219 note 11; Sun's influence on his socialism, 196, democracy, 193, nationalism, 197
Gandhi, 67, 69, 176, 203
George, Henry, 15, 27–30, 94, 96, 139
George, Lloyd, 36
Germany, 28, 35, 43, 50, 54, 74, 78, 79, 82, 87
Giles, Herbert, 3
golkar, 177, 178, 195
Goodnow, Dr. Frank, 41
Gregor, A. James, 162–4
Guided Democracy, 177, 178

Hager, Charles, 3, 106, 109
Hana, Corinna, 42, 43
Hardie, Keir, 12
Ho Chi Minh, 180–2
Ho Kai, 32
Hoai Thanh, 181
Holland, 58
Hong Kong, 2–9, 32, 37, 54, 67, 100, 106, 110, 114, 134, 140, 159, 167, 183, 184, 200, 202
Honolulu, 5, 183
Houses of Parliament, 23
Hsing Chung Hui, 2, 5–8, 30, 183, 200
Hsu, Leonard, 7
Hu Han-min, 138–40
Hu Shih, 52, 53, 131
hua ch'iao, 9, 186

230 *Index*

Hung Hsiu-ch'üan, 1, 2, 108, 109
Hung Jen-kan, 109
hypo-colony, 64

Independent Labour Party, 12, 13
India, 67, 87, 154, 180, 201
Indonesia, xiv, 171–9, 202
International Development of China, 39, 44, 45, 162, 163
international law, 15
Inukai Ki, 185
Islam, 172, 173, 176, 189, 190, 198

J. G. White Engineering Corporation, 158
Jansen, Marius B., 166, 167
Japan: war with China (1894–95), 4, 5, 8, 19; Sun's ideas refined in, 29–38; and Versailles Peace Conference, 43, 63; Sun fears, 65; Sun believes Japan example for China, 68, 70; Sun suggests pact with, 101, 119; invasion of China (1937), 126, 142, 143; investment in Taiwan, 159, 160
Jaurès, Jean, 13, 176
Java, 36, 174
Jen, Timothy, 99
Jews, 65, 72, 123, 198
'Judicial Reform in China', 21, 22

K'ang Yu-wei, 176–179, 281, 305
Kahn, Herman, 120
Kalaw, Teodoro N., 184, 186
Kaohsiung, 160, 165, 166
Kedourie, Elie, 70, 71
Kerr, John, 3
Kiaochow, 28, 35
Kidnapped in London, 10, 13, 16, 23, 26
'ko-ming', 9, 118
Korea, 119, 157, 161, 167, 180, 184
Kuomintang: formed, 40; illegalised by Yüan Shih-k'ai, 40; Sun-Joffe agreement, 55, 94; tutelage of, 59, 83; under Chiang Kai-shek, 83, 84, 101, 122–9; factions in, 130–40; United Front, 141–3; in Taiwan, 153–70; corruption, 88, 168, 169
Kwangtung, 1, 139, 186

'L', 14, 20–4, 28, 33, 56
Labour Union Law, 162
Labour Party, 26, 78, 95, 99, 100
Labour Standards Law (Taiwan), 162
Lafargue, Paul, 12, 13
land ownership, 30, 92, 128, 154, 157, 197
land reform, 94–6, 144, 148, 153–5, 157, 164, 197, 201
Land Tax Law (Taiwan), 155
land-to-the-tiller programme, 93, 154
Lee Teng-hui, 167
Legge, James, 109
Legislative Yuan, 57, 139, 165–9
Lenin, Vladimir, 43, 65, 66, 68, 97
Li Hung-chang, 4, 5, 7, 8, 34
Liang Ch'i-ch'ao, 29–31, 56, 115, 116, 139, 186, 202
Liao Chung-k'ai, 43, 85
Libya, 187, 189, 194, 195, 197, 203
likin tax, 4, 93
Lincoln, Abraham, 34, 182
Lincolnism, 182
Linebarger, Paul, 33, 104, 126, 186
Liu Ch'eng Yü, 109, 116
Liu Shao-chi, 143–5
Liu Yeou-hwa, 31, 207 note 16
Livelihood, Principle of: early influences on Sun, 26–8; (1906), 35, 36; (1924), 91–101; Chiang Kai-shek and, 124; in Taiwan, 153–164; relevance today, 201
Lockhart, Sir J. S., 110
London Missionary Society, 3, 106, 107, 114
Longuet, Charles, 12
Longuet, Jean, 12
Lu Hao-tung, 2, 4, 9, 106

Macao, 1, 3, 9, 108
Macartney, Sir Halliday, 10, 11
Madame Sun Yat-sen, *see* Soong Ching-ling
Manchus: Sun's oppostion to, 2, 3, 5, 7, 8, 19, 20, 35; anti-Manchu uprising (1895), 8, 9; overthrow of, 39

Mao Tse-tung: xv, 96; Report on
  Hunan Peasant Movement, 101;
  and Sun's Three Principles, 142–6;
  in power, 147–9
Marhaen, 179
Maritime Customs, 93
Marx, Karl: 12, 15, 29 139, 181, 195,
  197; Sun's Principle of Livelihood
  and, 91–8
May Fourth Movement, 43, 45, 54,
  68, 70
Memoirs of a Chinese Revolutionary, 49
Mencius, 74, 113, 115
Merchant Volunteer Corps, 100
Mill, John Stuart, 27, 33, 58
min-ch'üan, *see* Democracy, Principle of
Min Pao, 30, 34, 138
Minakata Kumagusu, 14
min-sheng, 5, 7, 30, 34, 91, 93, 97,
  155, 156, 178; *see also* Livelihood,
  Principle of
min-tsu, 34, 68, 71, 178; *see also*
  Nationalism, Principle of
missionaries, 21, 29, 96, 104–7,
  109, 112
Miyazaki Torazo, 33, 34, 185
Mo Tzu, 103, 110
Mongolia, 42, 45
Mongols, 63
Montesquieu, 15, 31, 87
Morrison, G. E., 39
Mulkern, Rowland J., 14

Nakamura Haizu, 185
Nakamura Tadashi, 16
Nanking, 39, 124, 131, 134, 139,
  165, 203
National Assembly, 42, 57, 82–5, 126,
  129; in Taiwan, 165–9
Nationalism, Sun's Principle of: early
  influences, 22, 23, 30; (1905),
  35–7; (1924), 62–72; Sun wants
  China's political machinery to
  be superior to West's, 86; Sun's
  Nationalism and Confucianism,
  117, 121; *see also* Clans in China
New Culture, 46, 66
New Democracy, 143–6
New Life Movement, 125, 172

New Party, 169
New Zealand, 24, 96

Oahu College, 2
Oakeshott, Michael, 46, 48
Oath of Hsing Chung Hui, 6, 7, 30

Pan-Asianism, 14, 119, 134, 135, 175
Pantja Sila, 171–4, 177, 179
Paris Peace Conference (1919), 65,
  66, 69
Peking: 19, 40, 43, 46; Britain supports
  government of (1921), 54, 55;
  Sun meets warlords in and dies,
  101, 138; Western Hills Group in,
  133, 135, 136
People's Congress, *see* National
  Assembly
Phan-boi Chau, 180, 181
Philippines, 9, 35, 154, 166, 171, 203;
  Sun's influence on, 182–6
*Philosophical Foundation of Sun
  Yat-senism*, 135, 136
Plato, 53, 78, 86, 201
Poland, 148
Poles, 65
Ponce, Mariano, 183–6
Protect the Emperor Society, 64,
  116, 186
Psychological Reconstruction of China,
  39, 46, 47, 49, 53, 60

recall, right of: Sun and (1916), 41, 42;
  Sun and (1924), 56–8, 78, 80, 82,
  83; Chiang Kai-shek and, 126, 129;
  CCP and, 151; in Taiwan, 168, 169
referendum, right of: Sun and (1916),
  42; Sun and (1924), 56, 57, 59, 82,
  83; Chiang Kai-shek and, 126,
  129; in Taiwan, 169
Reminiscences, My, 12, 107
republicanism, 36, 74
Revive China Society, 5, 70
Revolution of 1911, 64, 66, 68, 102,
  105, 146, 186
Revolutionary Alliance, 34
Revolutionary Association, 28
Revolutionary League, 7
Richard, Timothy, 14, 21

232 Index

Rizal, Dr. Jose, 182–4
ROC, see Taiwan
ROC-USA Economic Council, 158
Rousseau, Jean-Jacques, 15, 31–3, 74, 81, 183, 193, 198
Russia: threat to China, 17, 18, 20; see also Sun-Joffe agreement
Russian Revolution, 30, 65, 66, 69, 72; see also Bolshevik Revolution
Russo-Japanese War, 63, 94
Russophobia, 63

San Min Chu-I, 124, 126, 142, 173, 177, 178; see also Three People's Principles
San Min Chu I Monthly, 140
San-ho-hui, 64
Schiffrin, H. Z., 6, 7, 16, 27, 29, 33, 99, 107–9, 111, 114
secret societies, 64, 65, 69, 205 note 24
self-government, 40–2, 56, 131, 170
sericulture, 4, 93
Shanghai: land value increasing in, 28; Sun in (1916), 40; Sun returns to (1918–20), 44–6, 52; mills collapse in, 64; Communists massacred (1927), 101, 124
Shimonoseki, 94
Siam, 39, 119
Sian, 125, 126
Singapore, 159, 169
single tax, 30, 36, 94
Sino-Japanese war, 7
Sino-Soviet split, 149
Slater's Detective Agency, 10, 23
social revolutionaries, 30
Socialism: Sun's socialist sympathies, in London (1896–97), 25–8 ; Japanese socialism, 29, 30; German socialism, 78; democracy and socialism, 89, 90; Principle of Livelihood and socialism, 91–101; Chiang Kai-shek and, 124; Sukarno and, 178–9; Ho Chi Minh and, 182; Sun's influence on Gaddafi's socialism, 196
Socialist International, 22

Soong Ching-ling, 44, 105, 148
Soong, Charles, 105
Spaann, Othmar, 163
Ssu-pu pei-ya, 114
Strand Magazine, 12, 107
Sukarno, xiv, xv, 171–9
Sun Fo, 43, 126, 127
Sun-Joffe agreement (1923), 55, 94
Sun Mei, 5, 12
Sun Yat-sen: early life and evolution of thought, 1–4; writes petition to Li Hung-chang (1894), 4, 5; Hsing Chung Hui (1894), 7–9; uprising in Canton (1895), 8, 9; Sun in Japan (1895), 9; in England (1896–7), 10–28; kidnapped 10–11; returns to Japan, 29–38; 1911 Revolution, Sun provisional President, 39; Sun yields to Yüan Shih-k'ai, flees to Japan, 40; returns to China (1916), speech on self-government and direct democracy, 40–3; International Development of China, 44–6; Psychological Reconstruction of China, 46–53; Sun in Canton (1920), 54; is refused support by USA and Britain, 54–5; Sun-Joffe agreement, 55; Fundamentals of National Reconstruction, 55–60; Three Principles of the People, 61–101; see also Principles of Nationalism, Democracy and Livelihood; Sun and environment, 93, 96, 101; Sun's death, 101; Sun's Christianity, 101–12; Sun's Confucianism, 113–21
Sung Chiao-jen, 40
Sunshine law, 169
Switzerland, 31, 43, 85, 193

T'ang Liang-li, 94, 95, 108, 113
t'ien-hsia, 71, 121
Tai Chi-t'ao, 135–139
Taiping Rebellion, 1, 2, 65, 66, 74, 103, 105–9, 125, 186
Taiwan, 22, 42, 45, 84, 87, 88, 120, 149, 151, 153–70, 197, 202
tang-wai, 164, 166, 167

Tan, Chester, 89, 124
Tao, Hsi-sheng, 124, 163
Tartars, 6, 7, 17, 18
Ta-t'ung, 30, 115, 117
Teng Hsiao-p'ing, 44, 141, 149–51, 167
Thanh Nien, 181
Three Gorges dam project, 45
Three Principles of the People: early formulation, 11, 12, 15, 22–8; in 1905, 34; influence of Abraham Lincoln, 34; influence of French Revolution, 34, 74; in 1906, 34–7, in 1924, 61–101; aim of (people's 'full happiness'), 11, 22, 26, 28, 38, 80, 81, 202; *see also* Principles of Nationalism, Democracy and Livelihood
Tibet, 42, 45, 73, 137, 170,
Tokyo, 34, 138, 180, 184, 185
Transvaal, 35, 36
Treadgold, Donald W., 49, 89, 107–109
Trevelyan, Marie, 14
Triads, 9
Trotsky, Leon, 123
True Solution to the Chinese Question, 33
Ts'ai Yüan-pei, 71
Tseng Kuo-fan, 125
T'ung Meng Hui, 30, 34, 39, 40, 138
tutelage, 20, 21, 24, 33, 55, 56, 59, 83, 127, 128, 140, 148, 166, 177, 195
Twenty-One Demands (Japan 1915), 46
Two-Gun Cohen, 61, 121

unearned increment, 27, 28, 56, 92
United Front, 125, 126, 141–8
USA, 10, 34, 58, 66, 77, 85–7, 92, 99, 150, 153; Sun criticises demagogues in, 36; fundraising in, 39; Sun praises local direct democracy in, 40–2; does not support Sun (1921), 54–6; and Taiwan, 157–65
USA Agency for International Development (AID), 158

Versailles Peace Conference, 63
Vietnam, 170, 180–2
village committee, 42
Village Committee Law, 151
Vital Problem of China, 43
Volkhovsky, Felix, 13, 23

Waichow campaign, 14
Wang Ching-wei, 130–5, 138, 140
Wang Yang-ming, 48
Washington Conference, 55
Webb, Sidney and Beatrice, 99, 100
Whampoa Military Academy, 114, 123
Wilbur, C. Martin, xiv
Wilcox, Delos F., 43, 85
Wilhelm, Richard, xiii
William, Maurice, 72, 95, 97–100, 140, 196
Wong, J. Y., xiv, 16, 23
Wu Chih-hui, 15, 16, 105, 140
Wu Xiangxiang, 21
Wu Yü-chang, 6, 30, 105
Wuhan, 150

Yang Ch'ü-yün, 7, 8
Yu Ying-shih, 113, 114
Yüan Shih-k'ai, 39–41, 74, 103, 189, 202
yüeh-fa, 33

Zinoviev, 123
Zionism, 72